The

By

Graham Temby

Woodbridge Publishers

1200 Century Way, Thorpe Park,
Leeds, LS158ZA

First Edition

ISBN (Paperback): 978-1-916849-28-0

If applicable
Cover Design by Woodbridge Publishers.

WOODBRIDGE
PUBLISHERS

For my wonderful family, for all the love and support they have given me.

Prologue

You wish to know my story? Then I shall tell you about the many tales I have heard and the things I have seen in my long life. I was but a boy when the Terror began, and already I had seen and done many things that a young man of 11 or 12 should not have seen, nor should ever see. The fates had decreed that due to the turmoil in our kingdom and the battles fought to protect it from invasion, my father had been taken from us, and I was now the man of the family and chief protector of my mother, aunt, grandfather and four siblings, following the untimely and violent death of my father.

Let me tell you how this came about. I am an old man now, so you will need to be patient with me as I relay this tale. I must begin by telling you what went on before if you are to make any sense of what I have to tell you. It is a bloody tale of death and destruction.

My name is John Aelricson. As I grew up, I lived with my family in the small village of Brockford in Northumbria. My father, Aelric, was a churl. He farmed the family's land, along with the other churls in the village. We rented our land from our thegn (thane), Cerdic. As I recall, he lived in his own compound, a little way from the village, and he was a good and kindly thegn. He was not a big man, but wiry and strong. He had a grey beard, I remember, that made him seem older than he really was.

Our Earl of Northumbria, at the time, was Tostig Godwinson, brother of Harold, soon to be King of England. Oh, but he was an evil man, Tostig. I spit upon his memory. He made our lives a misery. But every evil man must, in the end, suffer for his wickedness. And so it happened. I marched with my father and many men from our village and many other villages and towns of Northumbria, to York, where we sacked his headquarters and killed his Danish house carls —the men who had carried out his vile deeds. Sadly, we couldn't bring about the demise of Tostig himself at that time, as he was away from York, hunting with the king.

But it was in York that I became a warrior —a sword-Saxon— when I was first responsible for the death of a man! I shall never forget it. I still dream about it to this day. Dream or nightmare? I don't know.

But that was not the end of the affair. We then went with the fyrd to support Harold Godwinson at Stamford Bridge, where we took part in the defeat of the Norseman, Harald Hardrada, and where the treacherous Tostig finally met his doom as he fought against us. The fyrd, in those days, I should tell you, was a reserve army that could be called upon by local nobles to fight for them. We were a backup, I suppose, to the professional armies of the day.

But still, we could not find peace. From there, we tramped south to Hastings, where, at a place called Senlac Hill, we battled the invading Normans under William of Normandy. Oh, but it was a terrible battle. I can still hear the cries of the wounded and dying, the stink of blood and soiled leggings invading my nostrils. It was there that my father lost his life to a Norman spearman. Broken-hearted, I gave him as good a burial as I could and left him there. I was then alone, a young boy, left to make my own way home by sea. I reached home just before Christmas 1066, when William was crowned king of our land in Westminster Abbey.

Did I tell you that I was now home and taking on the role of my father at an earlier age than I had expected? Now, surely, I would find peace to farm the land, care for my family, perhaps, and have a family of my own someday. But it was not to be. How cruel the fates can be.

(Read about John's exploits and his rise to a warrior in 'Conflict' by the same author.)

Chapter 1

A Messenger

Christmas had come and gone. The days were brittle cold in the deep winter, and the ploughed and fallow land was hard as iron. It needed to be broken if we were to set seed for the spring.

I recall the whole family: my mother, aunt, elderly grandfather and my younger siblings, Edmund, Arthur, Aelfled and Cathryn, joined in with hammers and hoes to break the surface. Oh, how numb our fingers were at the end of a hard day's toil in the sharp frosts of winter.

As I hammered and prodded at the hard Earth, my mind would slip back to my father and the terrible things I had seen. Oftentimes, I awoke from my thoughts and glanced at my mother to see her staring at me. I am certain that she knew the thoughts passing through my mind. A mother seems to sense what her children are thinking.

Then, it was the turn of the ox and harrow to break up the ground further. The harrow was dragged behind the ox and had sharp metal teeth to break up the clods into fine Earth. That was my job, as it called for strength. Though, in truth, I struggled as an eleven-year-old boy would.

Before midday, my mother would leave the field, and we all knew why she went. Our mouths would begin to water at the thought of her pies, cheese and soft bread. As we finished a furlong (one furrow long), we, too, would down our tools and wander back to the village.

In summer, we would eat in the fields, but in winter, if we were close enough, we returned home for some warmth to eat our midday meal. It was always hard to return to the cold.

Once the field was soft and smooth, we would sow the wheat. Slowly, we would follow the scratch-plough and make our way up and down the strips, sowing the seed into the Earth and hoping that it would provide us with a good harvest in the months to come.

Little by little, the seed we had held back from last year was cast into the furrows made by the plough. Edmund and Arthur followed the plough with a bag of stones to scare off the birds from the seeds. The village dogs would also run up and down the furrows, barking and snapping at the thieving crows.

Once sown, the harrow was pulled again over the field to cover the seed with rich Earth. Now, there was little we could do. We simply had to leave it to the land to feed us next year.

During the worst of the winter weather, in the coldest part of the year, when the Sun rises so slowly and sets so quickly, there was little other work that could be done outdoors. The animals left after the autumn slaughter were in their byres, away from the cold. Some we kept in the house with us to provide a little more warmth.

We were snug in those bitter days. We spent our time beside the fire, mending tools and clothes, making and mending baskets and carving wooden platters. The home was lit by rush lights and by the fire in the centre of the room.

As my mother sat sewing and spinning, she would glance up at our stores of food, and I knew that she was pondering whether they would last us until the better weather. Would there be enough salt pork in the barrel? Was there enough smoked fish? Would the corn last out? My own thoughts were with the wood supply and the hay for the animals. In the byres, the animals would grow thin over the winter as supplies ran low. I hoped that they would last and that we would not need to slaughter more animals than we needed to. Dead animals cannot breed next year.

It was on such a winter's day that a visitor came to our village.

We knew nothing of his arrival until Cerdic rode into the village and called to us, "Good people of Brockford. Come out."

We emerged to see the thegn astride his horse with the visitor. They dismounted and entered Benjamin the Smith's house, and we all followed — at least the men did, and I was pleased, these days, to be counted among them. How my chest swelled with pride as I entered with the other churls.

We sat around the edges of the house whilst Cerdic and the messenger settled themselves by the fire.

The thegn swept his gaze around the assembled throng and then spoke, "The man before you is Abeodan. He comes north with news of how things fare in the south of the county since the Normans took over this land. Hear what he has to say."

Abeodan, a small, wiry man with a short, fair beard, nodded to Cerdic and began to tell us his message.

"My brothers," he began, "I must tell you how things are. Since William the Bastard became king of this noble land, life for people in the south has been very different. William and his followers have embarked on a cruel campaign to subdue the English people. It seems he is keeping his promises to his barons who fought at his side, and is giving them land taken from the Saxon nobles."

I glanced at Cerdic's face at that moment and saw a look of deep concern etched across it. That look was mirrored by many of the other faces within the room. Cerdic was a good thegn and had always treated us well. We had no desire for a Norman master.

Abeodan continued, "William is nothing if not a shrewd man. So far, he has distributed land in different parts of the country as he subdues it, making it much more difficult to raise an army in secret against him. He quickly throws up a wooden castle wherever he thinks it will help to subdue the locals and keep the peace. In exchange for this generous distribution of land amongst his followers, the barons must be loyal to him and provide knights and troops to fight his cause whenever he might need them."

We nodded our understanding of this policy. Saxon kings had always been careful to keep the nobles loyal to them, so this was understandable.

"In their turn, the barons can grant land to their followers. The knights given land must also be loyal to the barons and provide forces as a fyrd."

Further nods of understanding followed.

"Peasants, such as yourselves, will be required to work the land, and also at the knight's land, and pay your new lords in produce so they are always provided with food. Ordinary people will rarely be allowed to leave their villages."

Most of this, again, was hardly a surprise. We already farmed at Cerdic's land and paid him in produce. We used his mill to grind our corn and fished and hunted wildfowl on his riverbanks. Though not being allowed to leave the village was difficult for us to understand. In truth, we had never ventured far from our own land, as travel was difficult (though I had already seen more of this country than most people would see in a lifetime, as I followed the fyrd in battle). But Cerdic had never, to my recollection, ever stopped a man from travelling, should he want to. But then, I could not remember any man wanting to.

"But the main news of the day is that William has left our shores and returned to Normandy, leaving this land of ours to his troops and administrators. He has taken Edgar Atheling as his captive."

'*This land of ours*.' It sounded so strange now. It *had* been our land, but no longer, and it rankled with the people. But this was news. Did the Conqueror, as people called him, intend to rule us or simply leave us to his followers and cream off the riches of the land from afar? What would be the fate of the people of the north? We had, in truth, always tended toward Danish custom and tradition, and this was still largely true. Life must change for us, I'm sure we all felt in our gut. But how it would change, we couldn't know.

Chapter 2

Bloodshed at Dover

And so, we worried daily about what might happen to us in the future, and what would happen when William's grasp tightened around us here in the north. But we simply had to continue to live our lives as we had done for many generations, still untouched by the invasion of William and his Normans. But things were not so settled in other parts of the realm. There was much bloodshed ahead.

William had begun to dismantle many Saxon buildings and was beginning to replace them with new structures in the Norman style. He seemed particularly bent upon replacing churches. His men destroyed many, and I know not why.

But all was not going William's way. We heard the tale from a passing tinker, who was always a reliable source of news. As the year turned, rebels in Kent plotted and planned. I will tell the tale as I heard it around the fire.

***

At a small village not far from the Saxon port of Dover —now, of course, in Norman hands— a small group of Saxon thegns met one cold and misty night at the compound of one of their numbers. They sat around a blazing log fire and supped sweet ale as they waited.

"Do you think the Norman Count will come, or is it but a cunning trap laid for us by a weasel?"

"I cannot say, but we will, by no doubt, know our fate within the hour; whether it will be to defeat William or to meet our maker."

The assembled men looked from one to another. The tension could almost be touched in the air. Men stared into the fire. Their very lives and those of their families were at stake here.

"Why would William's Count of Boulogne wish to join with us in rebellion? Is he not a Norman noble himself?"

"He is, but I hear that he is greatly troubled. He grows dissatisfied with his lot in life, and a dissatisfied man is a very dangerous man."

"As the Saxon people are dissatisfied with their lot. But tell us, what do you know of him?"

"It is said that back a number of years, there was a rebellion in Normandy by William of Talou. It seems that Count Eustace might have been involved in that treachery, though no man could bring evidence against him."

"A weasel to watch, then."

"Aye. The following years were a little better for Eustace as he watched many of his rivals flourish in William's eyes. He has a great dislike for Baldwin of Flanders, I hear. Eustace also lost his stepson to William after he had tried to claim the County of Maine."

"And yet I thought Eustace fought with William at Hastings?"

"Aye, it is so. Though, I hear that his conduct on the battlefield was less than what might be expected from a nobleman. It is said by those who were there, that at one point, Eustace was preparing a cowardly retreat from the field with his fifty followers and advised William to do the same. I heard that, at the moment he spoke the words to William, he was struck between the shoulders by a Saxon axe. The blow, they say, was so hard that blood gushed from his mouth and nose, and he appeared to those around him, a dead man. But his followers lifted him and carried him from the field, and he survived to see William victorious."

"And William still tolerates him at court?"

At that moment, the door to the hall creaked open and a Saxon soldier entered.

He bowed briskly to the assembled thegns and announced, "My Lords, riders approach from the direction of Dover."

The thegns looked at one another. This would be the moment they would find out whether or not they could trust Eustace or if their plans were discovered, and a terrible death would be the only ending. The men-at-arms and thegns alike fingered the hilts of their swords and eased them in their fleece-lined scabbards.

A few minutes later, the doors were opened again by a guard and a Norman noble and his followers swept into the hall. The nobleman was tall, with a tightly-cut shock of dark hair. His face was pinched, and his eyes and mouth cruel.

Men-at-arms held out their hands to take weapons from the visitors, but they were ignored. (It was the accepted good manners that weapons should be discarded when entering another man's house, but Eustace obviously had other ideas). The thegns and guards frowned, and more looks were exchanged. Tension hung in the air like a morning fog.

"I am Eustace II, Count of Boulogne," the nobleman announced as if any of the assembled needed to be told.

He approached the circle and seated himself in a proffered chair.

"I hear that you have a plan which you think will 'make life better' for the Saxon people and we Normans alike."

The thegns looked from one to another. Improving the life of the Saxon people was the aim, but they cared little as to whether it improved the lot of the Norman invaders. One of the leading thegns, Bawdewyn, stood and spoke.

“You are well instructed, Sir. We do have a plan to begin the process of ‘improving life’, but will it be a plan that you will support?”

“You will not know unless you lay it before me.”

Bawdewyn nodded. He swallowed and drew a large breath.

“We would drive out William and restore this land to Saxon rule, with a high position for yourself, of course.” An uneasy silence followed.

“And why do you think that I, a Norman, would support you in this cause?”

“You are not as happy with your lot as it would seem, we are told,” replied Bawdewyn.

Eustace gazed at him.

“Perhaps not,” he allowed.

Daegal, another thegn, spoke, “You are dissatisfied with your share of the spoils of war and your position, I hear.”

Eustace smiled.

“You are well informed,” he conceded, “I will listen to your plan.”

That night, Saxons and Norman sat and ate and drank ale and laid their plans. As the dawn was beginning to streak the eastern sky, Norman horses and men cantered away from the hall.

Now, at this time, William had entrusted Dover to his half-brother, Bishop Odo. On the day of the planned insurrection, under cover of darkness, Eustace's men, along with the assembled fyrd of the men of Kent, approached Dover Castle from differing directions; the better to surround and attack the fortification. They had chosen that day as their intelligence had told them that Odo and most of the garrison would not be present. Indeed, men had watched as, at dawn, Odo and his personal forces rode out of the great gates and headed north to the Thames. The rebels shivered in the cold of dawn but smiled to each other at the thought of the much smaller garrison inside that was left to defend the fort —Normans feasting, with Bishop Odo saying grace. (From the Bayeux Tapestry)

Slowly and stealthily, the attacking forces stalked toward the castle. Once all were in place, a signal was given, and a rickety covered cart appeared on the road and was driven toward the great gates.

Soldiers on the ramparts watched as the cart, which seemed to be driven by an old tinker, slowly approached. It drew to a halt at the gates, and the old man looked up through rheumy eyes to the soldiers.

"Will you let an old tinker in to ply his trade?" the old man's cracked voice asked.

The soldiers looked from one to another, and one called to his comrades below.

"Open the gate for an old tinker! Take care not to get too close, or the smell of him might kill you."

Other men-at-arms laughed. Slowly, the wooden gates creaked and yawned open to allow the old man's entry to the bailey.

As the cart entered, the covers were suddenly thrown off onto the trampled Earth of the bailey, and armed men leapt to the ground. The stunned Norman soldiers on the wooden ramparts stared, open-mouthed, as the attackers drew swords and began to murder the guards at the gate.

Immediately, more hidden Saxons and Norman troops loyal to Eustace appeared like ghosts from the shadow of the surrounding undergrowth and flooded in through the open jaws of the gates. Swords were drawn from scabbards, and a great battle commenced.

Swords and axes whirled and crashed into shields. Men screamed, their eyes wide, as fatal wounds were opened. Blood erupted from mouths, and men fell to the ground, writhing in agony. The stench of fear was everywhere.

Back and forth the battle went as Norman troops emerged from the keep, bleary-eyed and unprepared for battle to bolster the remaining garrison forces, and more men poured in at the gates to support the attackers.

A Norman sword flashed in the rising Sun, and a Saxon head flew into the air and rolled to a halt between the two armies —its eyes now sightless. Blood slicked the floor, and men slipped on the greasy flow from the dead and dying.

Bawdewyn had, by now, assembled a shield wall to try to force the Normans back, but Odo's soldiers held firm with their own wall. Saxon axes were hooked over Norman shields to pull them down and allow the spearmen behind to thrust their weapons at the enemy's faces and throats. Many a Norman eye widened as a sharp metal spearhead found its way into the man's gullet. Others ducked low and thrust their swords at the legs of their adversaries in an attempt to cut and cripple and maim.

Daegal, who was fighting the battle of his life in the line a little way from Bawdewyn, thrust his shield boss into the face of a Norman soldier and watched as the man's nose-guard bent and his nose and jaw were crushed. A hail of blood and teeth rained onto the floor before him.

The battle raged and screams rent the air as more men died. The two shield walls pushed back and forward. But soon, it became apparent to all that the defenders were beginning to take a great toll on the attackers and that the attacking army was being forced back toward the gates. Had the attackers made a grave error in their estimation of the defensive force? Now, the Normans were heartened and began a vigorous attack. Loud battle cries erupted in the air, now in Norman French.

Eustace, the Norman traitor, looked around him, now anxious that the plan was not working and that he and his men might meet their doom in Dover.

He yelled at one of his commanders, "Give the signal to retreat to the ships. We must away from this place or perish."

The commander passed the order down the line, and Eustace's men gradually began the retreat. The Normans pushed even harder now, sensing a victory was theirs.

Someone shouted above the noise of battle, "Odo returns! They are too strong for us!"

That now caused the terrified Saxon army to panic, and Saxon's and Eustace's men alike fled the field of battle. (In fact, Odo was not returning).

Eustace sprinted from the castle as quickly as his heavy mail coat would allow and grabbed the reins of a mount that was being held there by a young Saxon lad. He clambered into the saddle and spurred the horse toward the shore where his ships were anchored, around a headland and out of sight of the castle. He looked back as he rode away, just in time to see his nephew taken prisoner and being bundled away by the Norman soldiers. He shrugged.

"He must care for himself," he said.

The men of Kent now also saw the folly of further attack, and they, too, retreated through the gates, step by step, and fled in all directions. The Norman commander signalled his men to return to the fort and let them flee.

"We cannot catch them all. What point in capturing a few Saxon peasants? We have a prize. We have the castle, and we also have Eustace's nephew. The Count of Boulogne was among the attackers. I saw him there. What will William do now to our treacherous Count?"

"Surely, he must surrender his English fiefs at the very least," said a senior man-at-arms.

"Were it up to me, he would surrender his head!" his commander replied, his face grim.

Chapter 3

Eadric the Wild

But was that the only rebellion against William and his Norman horde in 1067? No. The Saxon people, like myself, were unhappy about their country being taken over by a foreign force, and were determined to resist and drive William from the land.

I shall tell you of another story I heard about a ferocious man from Mercia and the Welsh borders. His name was Eadric the Wild.

***

Now, Eadric was a land-owner, a thegn who held lands in Shropshire and Herefordshire, and also in the Welsh Marcherland. (The Marcherland is the borderland between England and Wales).

He was a huge man with arms like the trunks of trees, a fair beard and wild fair hair that blew around his head in the wind.

The story goes that Eadric had not been at the Battle of Hastings, or his lands would have been forfeited immediately to a Norman lord. I did hear the tale, though, that he was a 'shipman' and so was at sea at the time, trying to blockade the Norman beachheads. Whatever the truth of the matter, it seems that Eadric had not delayed the bending of the knee to William after his coronation, and many Saxons did just that to save themselves and their families.

All might have been well, but for two Norman earls who saw an opportunity to enrich themselves at the cost of the enormous Saxon.

One cold and windy morning, as white clouds scudded across the sky and people pulled their cloaks tightly about them, a troop of Norman cavalry rode up to Eadric's enclosure. It was led by Richard Fitz Scrob, a Norman who had settled in this land of ours during the reign of old Edward the Confessor, and built for himself a fortress known as "Richard's Castle" in the north of Herefordshire.

As the column of troops entered the compound, Eadric and two of his men emerged from his hall to 'greet' the guests. (Though 'greet' seems, perhaps, an inappropriate word, given the bad blood that already existed between Eadric and his Norman neighbours).

"Eadric, greetings to you. May we enter your hall? We have things to discuss," announced Richard Fitz Scrob.

His captain sniggered, which was not lost on the Saxon thegn. Eadric's men looked at one another with anxious glances.

Eadric looked for a long moment at the Norman seated before him on a large stallion.

"My lord, Richard, you are welcome to my humble abode. Pray, leave your horse and come for refreshments at my table. My men will provide ale for your troops."

The men dismounted, and Eadric led the leaders to his hall, where a table was quickly set with cold meats, bread, honey-cakes and ale. Normans and Saxons sat down together to enjoy the light repast.

After a short while of small talk about the weather and crops and whether the hunting was good or bad this year, Eadric sat back in his chair at the head of the table and broached the subject that had been niggling at the back of his mind since the arrival.

"My lord, Richard," he said courteously, "Tell me, what errand brings you to my lands this day?"

"It is a matter of your lands that I would speak to you," Richard said rather carefully.

"It seems that two of the new local earls have placed a claim upon the lands that you occupy. They say that the over-lordship of the land should be theirs, though, of course, they would be willing to allow you to farm the land in their names and pay them tithes."

Eadric stiffened, and his face changed. A purple flush spread across his features.

"Under what right do they claim my land?" he asked, "I have lived here and worked this land along with my churls all my life. I will not give it up to a Norman interloper who dreams up a 'right' to the title."

Hands on both sides went to sword hilts, and men eyed each other warily. (Neither side had been comfortable enough to give up their weapons on entering the hall, as was the custom).

"My lord, Eadric," Richard said, "The title to the land is, I am afraid, now beyond question. A ruling has been made. There must be a fair redistribution of land now that the country has a new ruler and a new regime. Surely, you must see that."

"I see nothing but Norman aggression and theft of land and possessions of the Saxon people of this country. I will not allow these men to trespass on my lands! And I will not pay tithes to them for the produce of my own land and my own hard work!"

At this, Eadric's men began slowly to draw the swords from their scabbards.

"Stand down!" Eadric snapped, "Sir Richard and his men are leaving."

The Norman and his troops paused for a heartbeat and then rose and strode from the hall and remounted their horses.

"The re-distribution of lands will happen, Eadric. You and your Saxon thegns and churls will be made to accept the changes to your land under your new and rightful king," and, with a scowl for Eadric, Richard Fitz Scrob led them through the gates to canter away toward the forest road.

Eadric knew in his heart, of course, that this was not the end of the matter and he began to make plans for what he knew must surely come.

***

Two days later, a young boy, his clothes ragged and his flesh torn by thorns, stumbled into Eadric's compound. He collapsed in a heap before the doors to the hall. Two of Eadric's churls ran to him and raised him to his feet. His knees buckled again, and one of the churls —a huge man whose muscles strained at the seams of his woollen shirt— lifted him into his arms and carried him into his master's hall.

The boy was gently laid upon a rough wooden table, and Eadric was sent for. The churls helped the boy to sit up when the thegn arrived, though the poor child seemed not to have a pinch of strength in his body to support himself.

"What ails you, boy?" Eadric said, looking at the boy's pale face and studying the cuts and bruises on his body.

"They have raided our village, my Lord," he replied.

A pot of ale was brought, and the boy sipped it.

"They came yesterday, in the dawn. They murdered many people in the village, took what they could and then burned it to the ground. I ran. I know not what has happened to my family."

"Who did this?" Eadric questioned.

"My Lord, the Normans. It was the Normans."

Eadric stood back, and a look of anger darkened his face. He had known that something would happen, but to murder peasants and burn a village? That was beneath even the Normans, he had thought.

"Ready the horses and men. We ride as soon as we are able."

Eadric's men ran to do his bidding, and soon, the compound was a hive of activity. Men ran hither and thither, saddling horses, collecting arms, and pulling on leather and mail. Women scuttled around, loading supplies into bags for the troops to carry with them on their mission. No one was in any doubt that Eadric would already be planning to take revenge for what had happened.

"I must come with you, my Lord," the boy said.

"You will stay here and rest. You have seen enough for one so young. See that the boy has everything he needs. Take good care of him," he said to his servants.

Eadric and his men cantered out into the countryside. For a while, they trotted their horses, until one man pointed to a low hill before them.

"There, my Lord!" he exclaimed.

All eyes turned to see a few dying wisps of black, greasy smoke rising into the still air of late morning. No doubt, what was left of the village behind the hill was still smouldering. But that was not all they could see. Their gaze fell upon the horizon, and heads turned. More smoke could be seen. More smoke than would be normal for a Saxon village arising and lighting cooking fires.

"They have laid waste," Eadric said in a low whisper as he thought of what had happened.

The troops, their hearts now deep in their boots, rode quickly over the hill to where the boy's village lay. Could they provide help for the remaining villagers? Eadric threw up a gloved hand, and the troops halted to stare down into the valley. Devastation! The huts and out-buildings of the people lay in piles of grey ash. Animals lay scattered where they had been slaughtered, their carcasses beginning to bloat. But worst of all, people lay where they, too, had been slain. Not just the men, but also the women and children.

The Saxons rode slowly down the slope, through the lightly wooded hillside to the village. They stared around them. Never since the Viking raids had they seen such carnage. Death stalked the land all about them. Men had been killed as they resisted the Norman troops. Some were run through with spears. Others were beheaded.

Women lay, cut down from behind as they had tried to flee with their children. Blood stains had spread across woollen clothing. Brown stains of dried blood could still be seen on the ground. Crows and ravens retreated at the sight of the Saxons, and sat watching, waiting for the men to leave so that they could go back to their grisly feast. Eadric stopped his horse and stared around him at the horror.

Men behind him —hard men, used to fighting and bloodshed— wiped tears from their eyes. One man pulled his horse to the side and splashed vomit over the ground at the sight.

The huge Saxon and his men dismounted, tied their horses, and slowly gathered the pathetic bodies together. There was little talk as they dug a wide but shallow hole in the Earth with the farming tools they found there that had not been destroyed in the attack, and laid the villagers quietly to rest. A rough wooden cross, fashioned by one of the soldiers, was pushed into the disturbed ground to mark their burial place.

Once finished, the men stood for a while, taking in the scene, a prayer was said, and they mounted their horses and sadly moved on. Their heads were low, but a fire raged in their chests at the horrific toll that had been taken on their people by the monstrous men who now ruled their fair land.

But the day got no better for the Saxons. By the time the Sun began to squeeze down beneath the western horizon, the troops had stumbled on five more villages. Some were less ravaged than the first, and the people who had escaped or had been spared for one reason or another were burying the dead and trying to scrape together whatever was useful. Men were grim-faced. Women and children wept as they told their terrible stories to Eadric. Other villages, like the first, had been destroyed completely.

The troop camped overnight in one of the villages before setting off for home at dawn. What would he tell the boy, Eadric thought. His family was no more; at least no survivors from his village had been found.

It was a weary group of men who walked their horses into Eadric's compound the following day. Anxious eyes scanned their faces for clues as to what had happened. They were left in no doubt as to what the troops had found. The young boy burst from

Eadric's hall and ran to meet the men. A woman tried to grab him, but he twisted and avoided her grip.

"Is anyone left alive? Did you find my family?" he asked, his face hopeful for a happy answer.

Eadric gazed down upon his young face and shook his head. The boy collapsed in a heap and sobbed into the Earth, though he must have known in his heart that the news from his village would not be good.

"I have no family left!" he wailed.

Eadric dismounted and picked the boy up from the cold Earth.

"You will stay here," he said, "I will raise you to serve me. You will be well-treated."

The woman approached and laid an arm around his shoulders, shepherding him away. At that, the grim-faced Saxon thegn strode to his hall, accompanied by his leading men. He had plans to lay.

***

Three days later, Eadric and his troops, rested now from their ordeal, rode from the compound again. Local churls and servants watched as the troop passed through the gates. What would happen now? This time, the troop turned their steeds toward the wild border lands with Wales.

After a day in the saddle, the Saxon troops crossed the border and made their way into Powys, toward Gwynedd, the seat of two brothers, Bleddyn ap Cynfyn, and his younger brother, Riwallon. It was a hard journey across wild lands, by all accounts, and Eadric's men were worn and weary by the time they made Bleddyn's stronghold at Mathrafal Castle.

Of course, Bleddyn —whose name meant 'wolf' in Welsh— and Riwallon had known for some time that Eadric was approaching and had posted men to either side of the column to flank it on their journey. The Saxons knew they were there as the Welsh warriors rode along the ridges above the valleys above them.

The two brothers watched from a wooden rampart. Mathrafal Castle was a roughly 100-yard square, rectangular compound defended by earthworks. Wattle and daub thatched buildings stood within the stockade, smoke rising lazily from their roof vents. A long wooden hall stood on a small mound at one end, and a deep ditch ran around the perimeter.

The lion of Bleddyn hung from the rampart and flew from pennants on the walls. Eadric's men looked around them at the surroundings and the soldiers placed around the castle. As they arrived in the compound, the two Welsh noblemen descended the steps to the rampart and approached to meet the guests.

"Eadric, I heard you were heading towards us," said Bleddyn.

"What brings you to Wales? Not trouble with your Norman masters, surely?" he added.

Of course, both Bleddyn and Riwallon knew in their own minds exactly why Eadric was there. Their spies had been out and about, and they knew of the horror of the Norman raids on the Saxon lands.

Eadric and his leading men dismounted and handed their horses to servants, who whisked them away to be rubbed down and fed. The thegn greeted the Welshmen with a curt bow, and they entered the great hall of the castle.

Over a meal and ale, Eadric told of the horrors that had befallen his lands. The Welsh princes listened intently to every word. Their faces showed shock, and they murmured their sorrow for what had happened.

In fact, Bleddyn and his brother were little interested in the suffering of their Saxon neighbours. Bleddyn knew that he owed his position to the goodwill of the late Harold, king of England, but that he had not been a subject of Edward, and so he cared little for the fortunes of the 'Lloegyr' —meaning anything that was not Welsh. Everything east of

Offa's great dyke could be wiped from the map as far as he and his kin were concerned, and they would lose not a night of sleep over it.

The Britons, as the Welsh once were, had been on the island of Britannia from time immemorial. On the other hand, the Saxons, Angles and Jutes were as foreign to them as the Normans. They had sailed to Britannia from their godforsaken pagan lands to the east, and had driven the British to the very edges of the land in Wales, Cornwall and Brittany.

Legend had it that the great King Arthur and his knights of the Round Table and the great magician Merlin, had defeated a Saxon army at Mynydd Baddon. But Arthur had died many, many decades ago and now lay in his grave at Avalon. The old stories said that one day, Arthur would rise again and take back the lands that were once those of the British. Bleddyn and Riwallon longed for that day. When he arose, they would follow Arthur to the ends of the Earth.

(**Defeat of the Saxons by Arthur:** King Arthur was a legendary British leader of the late 5th and early 6th centuries, who, according to medieval histories and romances, led the defence of Romano-Celtic Britain against Saxon invaders in the early 6th century. The details of Arthur's story are mainly composed of folklore and literary invention, and his historical existence is debated and disputed by modern historians [Wikipedia])

No, Bleddyn and Riwallon were not interested in the suffering of their guest and his people, but in what could benefit them in the situation. Bleddyn had ambitions, you see, to rule all of Wales and to become Brenin y Brythoniaid —King of the Britons. How might Eadric benefit their cause?

"And what would you propose we do?" asked Bleddyn.

"I propose," said Eadric, "That we work together to drive the Normans from the land. If we rise up, many more will follow. Left alone, this canker amongst us will only spread, and that could threaten your own lands," he added.

"Do you think that the Norman aggressor will be satisfied to end his invasion at the Marcherland?"

The two brothers looked at each other. Each man knew that what Eadric said was true. They were comfortable in their Welsh domain for now, but could the Normans be trusted not to push into Wales and do exactly the same to them?

Eadric then dropped in the bait that he hoped would tempt the two Welsh lords.

"Of course, we would all benefit from whatever plunder we could find as we destroy the Norman threat to our lands and people."

"Outline your plans, Eadric," said Riwallon.

The three men talked late into the night over sweet-meats and ale.

***

On a bright dawn with a soft sea breeze blowing across the land, Welsh warriors busied themselves in preparation for the journey to Herefordshire. The weapons were already sharpened, and leather and mail tunics strapped on. Boys brought forth the horses they had worked on since before the Sun had risen above the horizon. The horses, it always seemed, knew what was afoot and what was to be asked of them. They buried their noses into feed bags and enjoyed a meal of grain before the hard toil of the day.

As the Sun began to rise into a crystal-clear blue sky, the men mounted and rode from the castle of Bleddyn and Riwallon. The journey would be almost 60 miles, and most of the journey would need to be covered in one day so that the troops would be fresh for what was to happen the following day. The two Welsh princes knew that troops would also be moving up from Shropshire, where Eadric would be marshalling his own forces. The journey for them would be much less —a mere 25 miles. The target: Herefordshire and Hereford Castle.

(It has been said —though I have no proof of this— that Godwine Haroldson and his brothers — the sons of King Harold— with men from the east also provided men to Eadric's cause.)

The wooden castle of Hereford had been built before 1052. It was one of the first castles in our land. It had already been sacked by the Welsh in 1055 but had been rebuilt. Its Norman earl was now one William Fitz Osborn. He was a shrewd man, and he had built new fortresses at Clifford, Wigmore, Kilpeck, Long-town, and other such spots that would help him stamp out local resistance. The men of Herefordshire were as unhappy with the new state of things as many others of the Saxon race, and opposition to William's rule simmered here as much it did in the east and north.

***

On the following morning, the Welsh warriors crossed the border into Herefordshire. Their leaders began to separate them into smaller troops under the command of captains. Each troop moved off in different directions —they were hunting. But not hunting for food or for furs. They were hunting for Normans (and if Saxons also suffered, then so be it).

The troop under Riwallon turned their horses north and moved slowly and quietly through the countryside. They passed through woodland where they could, keeping their silhouettes below the horizon where possible, watching, searching for any opportunity.

At midday, the troop pushed on around the edge of a small hill. Directly before them sat a small troop of Norman men-at-arms, enjoying a break from the saddle. Helmets lay on the grass as men chewed on what provisions they had managed to scavenge and steal, and drank from skins of ale they had taken from a nearby village. Two young Saxon girls sat nearby, their wrists bound, eyes red-rimmed and faces miserable.

As the Welshmen hove into view, the Normans looked up, surprised. They had not thought to find any other warriors on their patrol. As the realisation dawned, cries rang out, and the Normans leapt to their feet, grabbing for helmets, shields and weapons. But it was too late. The moment the Welsh warriors had sighted the resting troops, swords and axes were drawn, and now they charged down upon them. Weapons flashed in the Sun as muscled arms whirled and stabbed them at their quarry. Many swords were soon slicked with red.

Riwallon rode down the commander of the Norman troops, and his sword came down upon the man's still-unprotected head. Blood and grey matter flew and the man dropped to the floor, dead before he hit the ground.

When the fighting had ended, the troop of Normans lay upon the Earth. A Welsh warrior brought a Norman, still alive, to his master. The Norman was roughly flung to his knees before Riwallon.

"One survives," the warrior said.

Riwallon gazed down upon the man, whose face betrayed the fear behind his eyes. This, surely, would be his end. But the Welsh prince looked thoughtful. He turned to the young girls.

"From where were you taken?" he asked.

"From a small village up the valley," one replied.

"Then we must return you to your homes," he announced, "Tie him tightly and put him on a horse. He will return them to their families."

The Norman looked alarmed by this turn of affairs. It would be one thing to die at the hands of the fierce Welsh warriors, but another to die at the hands of the villagers they had just pillaged.

Shortly afterwards, the Welsh troop rode into the village of the kidnapped girls. Villagers looked alarmed at the heavily armed men but knew they were not Normans. Were they Saxons, then? If so, who led them, and why were they here?

Women herded children into huts, and men casually picked up farming tools in case the situation turned violent. They would, at least, try to protect their families from this new threat.

One of the women, who had been sitting by a hut, sobbing, saw the two Saxon girls and shrieked. She dashed toward them, and strong Welsh arms lifted them down to their mother, who flung her arms around her offspring. Tears of joy ran down her cheeks, and she turned to the ferocious-looking men.

"Thank you, my lords," she cried, "Thank you."

A middle-aged churl strode toward the troop.

"My lords, you are welcome in our village. I thank you for returning our daughters. We thought we would never see them again. But who are you, sirs? And how do you come to be in our lands?" he eyed the weapons.

Riwallon looked down at him.

"We found the girls with a troop of Norman soldiers," he said.

"Soldiers who are now in a better place," he added.

"They have gone to their maker."

The men of the village muttered to one another happily.

"Except this one," Riwallon added, drawing the horse of the bound and tied Norman prisoner.

"We thought you might like to 'entertain' him."

The churl grinned a toothless grin.

"He will be most welcome, my Lord. We will show him some Saxon hospitality. Then he can join his friends."

A look of horror crossed the Norman's face.

"Will you take refreshment from us, my Lord? We are poor people and have little, but you are welcome to what we have."

Riwallon smiled down at him.

"No, we must be on our way. But thank you."

He turned to the Norman.

"Enjoy your stay with these good people," he grinned, "I am sure they will show you true Saxon hospitality."

Then, he turned his horse and led the troops away. Shouts from the village followed the Welshmen as they rode off. Riwallon grinned again.

Chapter 4

Death and Elves Come To Hereford

It was around the time of the Assumption of St. Mary that death came to Hereford. Bleddyn ap Cynfyn and his brother Riwallon had been making steady progress through Herefordshire, killing unwary Normans where they found them (and not always restricting the murder and mayhem to Normans). Many Saxon villages and burghs were robbed of their possessions —particularly any gold or silver that the Welshmen might find.

Eadric, it has to be said, was more protective of the Saxons he encountered, but was not averse to filling his treasure chests with loot whenever he found it.

As the Saxon lord made his way across the land, he tried as he could to recruit more men behind him as a fyrd. Eadric approached a village in the middle of a warm, breezy morning. The people, at first, made their way to a patch of woodland, hoping not to be seen slinking away. After all, these poor people had no way of knowing whether the fearsome visitors meant them harm or not.

The Saxons trotted into the centre of the village. The village seemed empty and deserted. A number of thatched huts surrounded a central area. Some looked old and in poor repair, whilst others had new thatch that had not yet grown moss upon them. Eadric stopped his mount and looked about him.

"Come out, villagers," he called, "I am Eadric, a Saxon, and I mean you no harm."

Nothing stirred. The village remained still and quiet. The Saxons turned in their creaking saddles to try to catch a glimpse of the population of the village. At length, a man appeared from the woodland. In his hand, he carried a sickle. Slowly, he approached the Saxon troops.

As the man stopped in front of Eadric's horse, the Saxon leader looked down upon him.

"What is your name?" he asked.

"I am Hereric," the man replied.

"I am a churl of this village. The others will not come out. They are afraid of you," he said.

"Tell them they have nothing to fear," said Eadric.

The churl looked at him and the weapons he and his troops carried.

"Then why are you here, Lord?" he asked.

Eadric hesitated.

"We make our way to Hereford," he said, "We would drive the Normans from the lands of Herefordshire."

The man smiled.

"And I will be King of the Fairies," he muttered.

Then, he turned and called the villagers. Slowly, men, women and children began to emerge from the thick woodland. Warily, they approached.

Once assembled, Eadric addressed them.

"Good people of this village," he began, "My name is Eadric. I possess lands in Herefordshire and Shropshire. Like you, I groan under the Norman yoke that is now upon all of our people. I would lift that yoke from your shoulders. I go to Hereford with Welsh allies to kill the Normans occupying that place and to begin the drive to evict the Normans from our land forever. I ask if any man will join me in this task, as every man who comes with us strengthens our cause."

The people looked from one to another, but none spoke. Eventually, the churl, Hereric, spoke up.

"My Lord, our people are under the Norman yoke, as you say. But our land is not under threat at this time. If we follow you and we fail, then we risk what little goods we have and could even be dragged into slavery by the very Welsh you ally yourself with. We have no trust of the Welsh."

Eadric was disappointed but nodded his head to the churl.

"You speak boldly for your people," he said, impressed that the churl had dared to speak to him in this manner.

But he knew that what Hereric had said was true. The Saxons he had managed to recruit would find themselves confronting a very new and very efficient fighting machine in the Normans. The relatively new idea of lines of castles was proving to be a strong point for the invaders. Few castles had been seen in our country before the Conquest. Oh, we had our burghs, but though they proved strong defence against Viking invaders, they were not as efficient as the Norman castles. Indeed, these new structures were to prove the best weapon in the Norman armour against the English and Welsh rebels.

Castles were a strong defence against attack and were also a powerful base from which to mount offensives against raiders and locals alike. Both troops and weapons could be safely housed there. Men could rest there in safety.

Eadric looked around at the poor villagers.

"I wish you peace," he said, and then turned his horse and left the village for Hereford and whatever fate awaited them.

Each of the armies gradually made their way toward Hereford. The city, you will recall, was in the hands of one of William's ablest and most trusted lieutenants, William Fitz Osbern, Lord of Breteuil. Fitz Osbern was William's second cousin and hereditary steward of Normandy.

One day, at dusk, as Mother Earth unrolled her cloak of darkness, the commanders met in a woodland clearing. As the two Welsh princes approached, Eadric rose from the fire he had been sitting by to greet them.

"My Lords, I trust your journey was a 'pleasant' one."

"Oh, very pleasant," Bleddyn replied with a grin.

"And profitable, too," added Riwallon and he let out a chuckle.

Eadric winced. He hoped that the Welshmen had not afflicted too much pain and anguish upon his fellow Saxons of the land, but he knew that without the two Welshmen, his cause was lost. And, of course, he, too, had gathered loot along the road to Hereford wherever he could find it, he reflected.

"The local people have been very generous in providing us with funds for our cause," continued Riwallon.

He swept a hand to indicate a number of wagons being hauled up by their drivers into the camp.

“And I have a special gift for the people of Hereford tonight,” said Riwallon.

He called one of the cart drivers. The man and a helper carried sacks to the seated nobles.

“I took them today,” Riwallon grinned.

He opened one of the sacks to reveal a grisly plunder. For there, in the rough sack, was a collection of fresh Norman heads. Eadric reared backwards from the sight, and the two Welshmen laughed.

“I will send out troops tonight, under the cover of darkness,” said Bleddyn, “And they can mount them on branches for the people of Hereford to see come the dawn.”

And so it was. A small band of Welsh troops rode out in the night, their horses’ hooves muffled so that they might approach the city without detection to plant their gruesome gift to the people of Hereford.

On the following morning, the troops were up and about long before the Sun peeped over the eastern horizon. They busied themselves about, preparing for what, they knew, would be a ghastly day’s work. They knew, to a man, that this dawn might be the last one they ever saw.

Horses were fed and rubbed down. Tack was fitted to them. Leather over-shirts were donned and topped with mail and helmets. Weapons had been sharpened beside campfires the night before and now lay ready for bloody action.

Once all was prepared and the men had eaten and supped, the armies mounted if they had horses or fell in behind if they were infantry, and all moved out of their camp.

In Hereford, in the meantime, the people had arisen and discovered the macabre gift that the Welsh troops had left for them. People came to stare at the grisly sight. All was panic in the city. They had known about the rampage of the Welsh and Saxon armies in the countryside, but now the horror was upon their own doors.

Norman men-at-arms trooped out of the castle stockade to remove the heads of their fallen comrades and to set guard upon the place. Men stood, heads turned this way and that. Anxious eyes scanned the countryside for signs of the marauders. Guts tightened at the thought of what might be about to befall them. Tension in the air bore down upon them like a heavy cloak.

But soon, the armies were visible to both the Normans and locals alike. A huge band of heavily armed men was slowly surrounding Hereford like a noose. The attackers stood stock-still for a while. Then, one after another, different sections began to advance. People fled to find shelter from the coming storm of terror. They hid where they could, in homes and outbuildings. Mothers grabbed screaming children around them and shepherded them to any corner, nook or cranny where they might find safety.

Norman troops lined up to repulse the attack. The two sides eyed each other as the gap between them closed like a trap.

All at once, a cry went up from one section of the army.

"Ymosodiad!" the voice cried (attack!).

From another quarter, "Nid arbedant dyn sengl!" (Spare not a single man!)

Now, the warriors picked up the pace and charged toward Hereford. With a great clash, they met the Norman resistance. Swords flashed. Axes whirled in the air. Shields shook with the force of weapons striking them. The air was filled with blood-curdling screams and shrieks as men fell in pools of their own blood.

Onward, the Welsh and Saxon forces pressed. The Norman garrison was no match for such ferocious warriors, who seemed to care nothing for their own safety but attacked like madmen.

The Normans fell like autumn leaves on the lanes of Hereford. As the raiders marched on, men behind them looted houses and shops and took every bit of plunder they could carry away. Men, women and children fell to Welsh swords, whilst Eadric and his

Saxons looked the other way. Death and destruction roamed the city's streets. Houses were pulled down or set alight. Whole lives were destroyed in the madness that always follows when men take up arms against each other.

Soon, the Norman soldiers who were still in the city began to retreat to the wooden castle that had been built upon a mound, as was the custom of the Normans. The Saxons and Welsh now scented victory and surged after their prey.

The Normans, who made it back to their fortress, crowded to cross the narrow bridge across the earthworks that surrounded the bailey walls. But it was a flight in vain as their assailants followed and entered the courtyard of the bailey. Fighting was now even more ferocious as the garrison within the castle joined in the struggle.

Slowly, slowly, the aggressors fought their way to the keep —the inner sanctum— and surrounded it. Now, all was lost for the Normans. The floor of the bailey was littered with bodies gazing up from sightless eyes. Blood seeped into the dust. Not a single Norman outside the keep remained alive. But arrows now flew from slits in the wooden walls and began to take their toll on the Welsh and Saxons too. Shields were held above heads, and soon, the massed ranks of warriors looked like hedgehogs, bristled as they were with arrows.

"We shall never take the tower and Fitz-Osbern," yelled Eadric.

The Welsh princes looked longingly toward the keep, thinking greedily of the treasures that would lie inside. But they were also realistic.

"What you say is true," agreed Bleddyn, looking around him at his men who were beginning to fall under the Norman archers' onslaught.

"Aye, we must away," agreed his brother.

"Encilio, gadewch i ni fynd yn ôl at ein bryniau annwyl," he called to his men. (Retreat, let us go back to our beloved hills).

Slowly, slowly, the attackers retreated from the bailey under the protection of their shields. Once upon the streets of Hereford again, the withdrawing armies took what little plunder there was left and made haste to depart the area back to the safety of their wild Welsh hills. Eadric, too, withdrew his troops and marched away. He had made his point to the hated Norman rulers, even if he had not yet driven them from his lands.

***

But is that the last we shall hear of Eadric? No, my tale is not yet all told, for a strange thing happened on the long road home. I cannot say if this is true or false, but it is what I heard of the matter.

It seems that Eadric and his men were making their way south again, back to his lands, when they passed through a woodland glade in which there was a small cottage. Here, they stopped and dismounted their horses to eat and drink. The glade, at first, appeared to be deserted, which was no surprise to the men, who knew that their appearance was terrifying to ordinary men and women. But, as they sat upon the woodland mounds and took out from their packs the food and drink they had stolen from the people of Hereford, a strange thing happened.

A mysterious young lady suddenly appeared at the edge of the glade and stood, looking at the Saxon warriors. As they noticed her, the troopers stopped in mid-bite of their meal. Men blinked and shook their heads to rid themselves of what must be a vision. But the vision remained. It was a slight girl, her yellow hair cascading down her back and over her shoulders. She was dressed in a pink over-shirt and blue breeches. But most amazing of all were the two gossamer wings that protruded at her back.

Now, I know you disbelieve me, but this is the story I was told. I swear it. Eadric stood, his mouth open and a pie poised to be bitten into, and stared in wonder at the creature. Without fear, the apparition entered the clearing and walked to the centre.

"Welcome to my humble home," she said simply.

She turned to Eadric, who had by now dropped the pie to the Earth.

"I know who you are," she said, "You are Eadric. I have heard of your exploits to protect the Saxon people and drive out the conquerors."

Eadric was almost speechless. His men stared in wonder.

"I…I am Eadric," he stammered, "But who are you?"

"I am Coventina," she replied.

The Saxon thought he had never seen such a beautiful woman in his entire life. He slowly sat again at the fire, and Coventina sat beside him on a small tussock of grass.

"You must tell me about yourself. How did you come to be here. How did you come to be a…" he broke off.

"How I came to be an elf," she said, "I was born an elf. I have always been an elf. I live here alone. I am quite safe. No one in the outside world would wish me harm."

"No," replied Eadric, "Or they will answer to me."

It was all he could think of to say to the vision of beauty before him.

Well, legend has it that they two talked well into the night, and the next dawn, Coventina was seated upon a mare for the journey to Eadric's home, having consented to be his wife. The elf had promised to endow Eadric with wealth and good health, provided that he never said a bad word about her home or her fairy sisters.

Eadric, it seems, agreed, and the two lived happily for a while. But, one day, after returning from hunting across his lands, he could not find his elfin wife. He searched high and low, but she was nowhere to be seen. When Coventina did return, Eadric was in a foul temper and accused her of going off to see her sisters. At that, the beautiful bride vanished, and Eadric never saw her again. They say that, when he died, he was still heartbroken over his loss.

Surely, my tale of Eadric the Wild must end there. But no! There is a little more. For legend has it, after Eadric shed this mortal life, he was reunited with this fairy wife, and the two now lead the 'Wild Hunt' across Shropshire. The Wild Hunt is a pack of ghostly hounds that rampage across the night skies —sometimes seen, sometimes only heard. But what is certain, they say, is that Eadric's Wild Hunt is a portent of doom! It is always seen or heard before great death and destruction befall the land.

You might scoff at my tale, but it is firmly believed by the good people of that part of England.

Chapter 5

Outlaws!

Time passed in our little village of Brockford in Northumbria. We saw little of the terrors that were happening in other parts of the country, though we heard the news from passing tinkers, who carried the stories from village to village. Heaven knows how the stories became twisted and exaggerated with the telling, but it was the only way we could hear what was happening —other than from the brothers at the monastery, who often received news from the Shire Reeves and passed it on to Cerdic the thegn.

One day, around the time for the midday meal, an old tinker rode his ageing horse and rickety wagon into our village. The tinker called his wares, and the women, though busily preparing the midday meal, came from the houses to see what the old man might have to sell. All would be interested in bags of salt and, of course, any other items that might catch their eyes. The children swarmed around him, asking for a story. Many of the tinkers would tell the children tales of the legends they had heard on their travels or the things they had seen, and the children devoured them greedily.

Once the women had finished their haggling with the old man, the men gathered around and asked for news.

"Tell us what happens in the land," said the smith, wiping his sweaty brow on a huge forearm.

The old man sat down upon one of his packs and cocked his head on one side to get a better look at us from his good eye. He opened his cavernous mouth and gave a huge yawn.

"Tis a thirsty business, this story-telling," he said.

A chuckle ran around the assembled throng, and one of the churls called for a jug of ale for the old man, from which he drank deeply before he began his tale.

"Well," he began, "You will have heard of the goings-on in Hereford by Eadric the Wild and the Welsh princes."

We nodded assent at this.

"Well now," he continued, "I have heard that another uprising took place when Eadric and Bleddyn joined forces with Edwin of Mercia and his brother, Earl Morcar. They do say that great preparations were underway for a new challenge to the Normans in Mercia, but it seems Edwin was not the man that people thought he was. He proved to be weak, and scarcely had the struggle begun when

Edwin laid down his arms, stood down his troops and bent his knee to William. Much good he was to the cause!"

There was much muttering amongst the men.

"But what of Eadric and the Welsh?" someone called out.

"Oh, they fled back to the Welsh Marcherlands. They are bowed but not yet broken, by all accounts. I don't think we have heard the last of them yet."

"And what of the people further south?" I asked.

"Oh, most have surrendered to the Norman yoke. A few still resist. Many men who resisted are beginning to move north, to where they feel safer."

He spread his arms wide.

"You might have seen them here."

We shook our heads. We had seen no one who was not local moving through the landscape.

"But I have heard tales of rebellions past…and some still to come," he whispered as if the Normans might be listening at the door.

"One not too far from where we now sit."

The men looked from one to another.

"We *should* resist!" called a churl from the back. "The people of Northumbria have always favoured the Danish rule, even over that of Wessex. Why should we now bend the knee to the Normans?"

There was much agreement, and the tinker watched carefully. No doubt, this would enhance his story at the next village he visited.

As the old man finished telling the news as he knew it, villagers began to return to their tasks. The land waits for no lazy man, and the work must be done if we are to eat. There was a good deal of muttering amongst the men as we left, and small groups huddled together, discussing the tinker's news and what might be the fate of our people.

The children, however, crowded around the old man and begged again for a story. Parents nodded their consent that their children might tarry a little longer. It was not often that they heard new stories, and all looked forward to it.

"I shall tell you about old St. Cuthbert," the tinker announced, "I am certain the monks have told you a little about him before, but I shall tell his story as I heard it."

"Well now, the story I shall tell you is from as long ago as 878AD. It was Easter, and at that time, old King Alfred the Great and all his followers were hidden amongst the swampland and marshes in the Isle of Athelney, in the Somerset levels. It was the last Anglo-Saxon stronghold in the battle with the Vikings.

Alfred looked around him at his dwindling band of men, and he knew that his position seemed hopeless. Men were leaving day by day, back to their homes and families, giving up on what looked to everyone like a lost cause.

Now, one evening, as Alfred sat upon a low stool and looked around his camp in despair, there appeared a mysterious traveller. He came into Alfred's camp begging for scraps of food. Alfred was astonished by this, as he didn't think that anyone could find him there.

Alfred had very little for himself, but he offered to share his meagre meal with the traveller. Just as he did this kind deed, the traveller disappeared into nothing! Vanished!"

The children gasped at the tale. How could a man just appear or disappear into thin air? Where did he go? Was he magical? Was he a sorcerer?

The tinker continued.

"Later that night, as all were wrapped in their robes against the chill of the night air, the visitor returned in a vision to Alfred. Now, he was dressed in his Bishop's robes, with a tall mitre and a crook in his hand. He told Alfred that he must love God, be a just ruler and a merciful one to those beneath him. Cuthbert promised Alfred that he would win a great victory and that England would be ruled by him and his sons.

A few short days later, Alfred and his troops rode out from Athelney and won a great victory over the Vikings. Old St Cuthbert's prophecy had come true."

The children were astonished by the tale, though I had heard the same story from the monks at the monastery. I think old brother Samuel told it to me. I forget.

The tinker packed his cart, and with a wave, he left the village and headed out over the wooded hill to the next village where he might sell more of his wares.

We worked until the Sun began to sink below the horizon and then headed home to a hot meal of pottage and ale. That night, I pondered on what the tinker had told us. A rebellion? Near to here? Had we not had enough of that trouble in our land with the rebellion against Tostig and the battles we had fought for Harold?

***

We rose the following morning to a dawn as grey as a trout's belly. We stretched and yawned as we took tools from the byres and trudged into the fields for another day of toil. The morning wore on and we all looked forward to the midday meal. Suddenly, from the tree line on the hill above the fields, one of the boys of the village burst forth and ran towards us, his arms flailing, and he was shrieking in horror. We all stopped working and gazed at him. His own father dropped a hoe and ran towards him. When he brought the lad safely down to the field, he was shaking, and his eyes were wild.

The boy had been in the woodland, caring for the swine that rooted there for food. As he sat upon the ground, still shivering, he told us what he had discovered.

"I…I was walking th…through the forest, following the pigs. They began to snort and root beneath a bush. I wondered what they had found and went to look. It is…the tinker. I think he is dead!"

A gasp rose from every mouth.

"What do you mean?" the boy's father asked, "How do you know he is dead? Might he not just be sleeping beneath the bush, out of the wind?"

The boy looked up into his father's face.

"His throat is cut!" he cried.

Now, we all gasped again. Who would murder the tinker? Why? He was a harmless old man. I could almost feel the blood draining from my face as I struggled to take in what I had just heard. A young churl had run towards Cerdic's compound to tell the thegn the news that the boy had just brought us, and it was not long before Cerdic and a trooper in his service rode out to us. They spoke to the lad, and he told them what he had seen.

When Cerdic had heard the story, he looked thoughtful. For what seemed forever, he mused. He turned to the boy.

"Mount my horse with me, and then you must lead us to where you found the tinker."

The boy looked terrified at the thought of returning to the forest and to the horrific scene he had discovered. His face was a mask of terror. But Cerdic mounted, and I lifted the boy onto the horse in front of him, and they set off for the forest. We returned to our work but with little appetite for the job. Our thoughts were with the old tinker who, only the day before, had told us his news and regaled the children with a story.

It was later in the afternoon when the horses emerged again from the woodland edge. This time, they were being led, and across one of the saddles was the body of the tinker. We stood and stared at the sad sight until they met us in the fields. Men stood aghast and shook their heads in disbelief.

***

As dawn broke the following morn, we arose and collected what few weapons we had. I belted on the sword and seax I had taken from the battles I had been involved in. We collected in the centre of the village and awaited Cerdic's arrival. Very shortly, our thegn arrived, along with five mounted men. After brief orders, we set out for the forest. There was a cool dampness in the wind as we approached the tree line. Once within the wood, we were split into groups, and each group moved through the woodland with one of Cerdic's men to lead us.

Slowly and quietly, we trudged through the sodden woodland, the overnight rain dripping from the leaves and soaking our leggings and woollen shirts.

I was passing by a large bramble patch, looking around me and listening for any unusual noise, when a shout went up.

"John!" I turned in the direction of the call from my friend and then felt a large arm circle my neck and a sharp point jabbed into my ribs. I gasped in astonishment and stiffened, unsure what to do. The world seemed to stand still, and the men of my group stood and stared at me.

"Move, and the boy dies," a gruff voice said.

My nose was filled with the stink of the man's dirty shirt, but I was unable to move a muscle. The knife was removed from my ribs but appeared in front of my face. Then the man shifted his grip on me and the flat of the knife blade ran along my throat. I swallowed hard and began to tremble. Two more heavily armed men now emerged from the bramble patch. They were filthy and unkempt. Their hair hung in rat-tails over their shoulders, and bushy beards sprouted from their chins.

"Leave the woodland the way you came," demanded one of the men.

"If you leave quietly and let us be on our way, the boy lives. Follow us, and he dies."

I shuddered uncontrollably.

"How do we know that you would honour what you say?" asked Cerdic's house carl.

"You don't, but what choice do you have?" the man replied, "If you value the boy's life, you will do as we say."

The men of the village looked from one to another, unsure as to what to do. They couldn't call for help from other groups, as that might lead to my demise. But how could they desert me? Would the rough men really let me go or simply slit my throat and escape, leaving me to be found dead like the tinker?

After all I had gone through in battles, this was the most terrified I had been. At least, in the shield wall, you are fighting beside friends and colleagues. I knew now that death might only be a whisker away. Cerdic's man nodded his head at the villagers, and the men turned and slowly made their way back the way they had come. We stood awhile and watched their backs retreat into the leafy distance. They looked around from time to time, obviously concerned for my fate as they left me.

The man who held me gradually slackened his grip and took the knife from my throat. He spun me around and leered into my face.

"Now you will come with us for a while. Just until we know your friends are not following our tracks. If you try to escape from us, you will not see another dawn."

I swallowed again and nodded my head. I could say not a word.

One of the men unbelted my sword and seax and admired them.

"Now here's a nice little prize," he laughed and belted them on himself.

I was bundled through the forest to a clearing, which, given a few more minutes, we would have stumbled upon. That was undoubtedly why the men decided to make the first move. In the clearing was the tinker's old horse and cart. The poor beast just stood there, with its head hung low. Its ribs showed under a scabbed pelt. I would barely make one good meal for a dog. The men had obviously gone through the tinker's goods and stored anything that might be useful to them on the cart. The rest was strewn around the site.

"We must move on," said the man who had first taken hold of me.

He appeared to be the leader. The others nodded and loaded what little else they valued onto the cart. The other two men then grasped me whilst the leader —I never did find out their names— bound me tightly, hand and foot and threw me onto the cart, amongst the goods.

"Cry out, and I'll slit your young throat!" the leader exclaimed.

The cart began to move off along a forest track, and I wondered what the outcome of my plight might be.

For what seemed like hours, we trundled along a track through the woodland, always going north. I knew the direction of travel as I followed the path of the Sun, even though it was through the leafy canopy of the trees.

Eventually, we came to a halt within another clearing. In truth, it was little more than a day-bed that had been used by deer, but it provided excellent cover. The men unloaded me from the back of the cart and dumped me beneath the boughs of a large oak tree. I was still bound with lengths of jute string. My muscles ached to shift position, but I couldn't move against my bonds. The men set to making a meal from the food within the tinker's cart. The leader looked across at me.

"Untie his hands. He can have some food and drink," he said to 'Long Beard' as I had named him.

He sat close to me, cleaning and admiring the sword and seax he had taken from me. He pushed me forward and untied my hands. I was brought a lump of dried meat and a little dry bread. I was hungry now and devoured it quickly. A small pot of ale was brought for me to wash it all down.

When I had finished the meagre meal, I sat and watched the men and listened as they talked between them. It didn't seem to occur to them to re-tie my hands, or perhaps they thought I was in no danger of escaping or doing them harm.

As I sat there, to my right, I noticed a number of bird alarm calls. The men didn't seem to notice it or simply disregarded it. A deer barked a little way away. I pricked up my ears, but still, there was no reaction from the men. Perhaps, I thought, they were not countrymen but from a burgh. Their accents told me they were not local men but from south of here. To my left, there was a call of 'Ke-wick, ke-wick.' And from the right again, the reply of 'Whooooo.' Now, the men looked up.

"Owls," I said to no one in particular.

"Letting each other know where they are."

The men looked around but then fell back into their conversation.

A thump made us all sit up and take notice. The man closest to me was sitting with his back against a tree, staring at the arrow that had suddenly grown from his chest. His eyes were wide and wild, and a red rose was spreading across his chest. The other two men were stunned and sat with jaws open. I took advantage of the pause in time and, with a great heave, hauled myself to my bound feet. I hopped and grabbed the sword from the now-dead man's hands. I immediately swung it and pointed it at the throat of the leader.

From the thick bushes came four men; all of them were Cerdic's household men. They quickly pointed weapons at the remaining murderers. The men raised their hands into the air and stared at the certain death before them if they tried to make a break for freedom.

Cerdic pushed his way through the underbrush and stood before the men.

"You will be taken into my custody for the murder of the old tinker. From there, you will be taken to the Shire Reeve, where you will be tried. I have no doubt as to what your fate will be."

"It will not matter to this man," said one of the men-at-arms.

He pushed the body of the dead outlaw with his foot, and it fell over and collapsed in a heap beneath the tree. Quickly, the outlaws were tightly bound, and I was freed from the last of my bonds.

Cerdic turned to me.

"Did you think we would leave you to these ruffians, John?"

"No," I said, "I had no doubt you would come for me."

He slapped me on the back and urged me to mount up for the journey home.

We travelled slowly back to the village and arrived well after darkness had fallen. The dead body was thrown into a small room in Cerdic's hall, and the other outlaws locked away, with guards on the door. I returned to my family home, where my mother threw her arms around me and wept. My brothers and sisters milled around me. They thought me quite the hero.

Two days later, armed men arrived from the Shire Reeve. They stopped awhile to eat and then loaded the bound men onto horses to take them to their demise. We all knew what that meant. The men were already found guilty in reality, and there could be only one result.

As we watched the miserable men's backs as they rode away, Cerdic stood with us.

"They were victims of the Normans," he said, "They had resisted the Norman invasion of their lands and had to escape north."

"There, but for the grace of God, go I," one of the churls breathed.

We all looked at him, the same thoughts going through our own minds.

"Aye," said Cerdic, "Who knows what the future holds for any of us."

Chapter 6

Copsi

The culture of our northern lands before William ravaged the countryside, killing and burning all those who would not bend the knee to him and a good number of others who would have always been Anglo-Scandinavian, as I have told you. I suppose it was a mixture of the old Viking and Anglo-Saxon traditions that had held sway here for many generations. Indeed, I had found, in my travels fighting for Harold, that the language we spoke here in the north was difficult for the people of the south to understand, and the reverse was also true.

The leading families here were mostly of Danish descent, and even the Anglo-Saxon kings from Wessex held only limited power in the northern shires.

Now, after the conquest of our country, we in the north found ourselves unguarded by any king's shield, for William, even after all his successes in the south, had still not secured his victory in the outer regions of his realm. Indeed, William saw us, I am sure, as wild northern rebels of old King Edward and his descendants who might well disrupt his kingdom.

Our Earl of Northumbria at the time of the conquest had been Morcar. It was he who had replaced the hated Earl Tostig —the rat whom we evicted from York and finally exterminated as you would such a rodent at Stamford Bridge. Morcar had ruled us since 1065, and we were happy under his jurisdiction. But William had other plans.

Once his foothold in the south was secure —or as secure as he could make it— he turned his attention to the outer fringes. His first act here was to request the presence of one Copsi. A strange name, I hear you say. Copsi was a Northumbrian aristocrat in the times leading up to our conquest. He was yet another rodent and had been a great supporter of the hated Tostig, brother of Harold. He had, to his shame, been Tostig's former deputy, and we had successfully exiled him along with Tostig in 1065. He fled to Orkney, with his tail between his spindly legs, back to the protection of the Norsemen who ruled there.

He had rejoined Tostig and Harald Hardrada and survived —more's the pity— the battle at Stamford Bridge, where Tostig met his doom.

But now, in March 1067, he headed to Barking with a patrol of men-at-arms to bend the knee and pay homage to our new Norman king.

Copsi and his men duly arrived at Barking, where William resided whilst what we now know as his

‘White Tower’ was being planned beside the Thames in London. Copsi swept into the hall where William was holding court, but was curtly stopped in his tracks by a cohort of William’s troops, who quickly relieved him and his men of their weapons. Copsi then strutted through the assembled courtiers to where William was seated and fell to his knee.

Hanging his head, he said, “My Lord King, I bend the knee and pay homage to the rightful ruler of our land. Though I have fought alongside the Norsemen and West Saxons, I have always been of the opinion that you were the true heir to Edward.”

William raised his eyebrows and stared down at the man kneeling before him. He glanced around him at his court and was well aware of the smirks on a goodly number of faces. Though his face was straight, his eyes betrayed his thoughts to those near him.

“My Lord Copsi,” he began, “pray, raise yourself and approach.”

Copsi did as he was bid and reached out to William’s proffered hand and kissed his ring.

“So, you are a happy man at the outcome of this affair. It is good to know that men of stature in our outer regions have come to terms with the situation and welcome us with open arms, as brothers.”

More smirks from the assembled court and, indeed, some had to turn away and stifle their laughter.

William sat for a while, considering the Saxon before him. Deep in the pit of his stomach, he felt a loathing for the man. How could a man change sides and betray his sacred oath so many times in an attempt to back the winning side and advance his own fortunes? But this man could be useful to him. For had Morcar and his brother, Edwin, not thrown their support behind Edgar the Aetheling after Hastings?

Though the two men had now submitted to his rule, and Edwin was governing for him in Mercia, William knew he could never entirely trust them. But could he trust the snivelling apology from a man before him? Yes, he decided. He could trust this man, as he would be out for nothing noble but for his own advancement. That, William decided, would ensure that he did not rise up against him.

"My Lord Copsi," William mused, "I feel that you are a very worthy man and that you would protect our interests in the northern reaches of our kingdom."

Further smirks and stifled chuckles. William looked sharply around him, and the chuckles died as quickly as they were born.

"I have it in mind to invest you as my Earl of Northumbria in place of Morcar, whom I fear I cannot entrust with such an important part of the kingdom. What say you to that?"

"Oh, oh, my Lord. I…I would be greatly honoured to serve as your Earl of Northumbria. I can assure you that I will run that part of your kingdom fairly and for the benefit of my new king."

"Then it shall be so," replied William, "Now, if you would join us yourself in food and wine, I am sure your troops will be catered for by my servants."

Copsi rose to his full height and puffed out his chest. He was the Earl of Northumbria. He was to dine with the king. Now, how would the others regard him when he returned to York and his new northern earldom?

And so it was that Copsi became our earl…for a while.

***

Now, there was another nobleman in Northumbria at that time. His name was Osulf II of Bamburgh. He was no less than the son of Eadulf III, Earl of Bamburgh, and the grandson of Uchtred the Bold, Earl of Northumbria, who was killed in 1016. What violent times we lived in! Osulf's family had ruled as High Reeves of Bamburgh for many years until 1041, when Siward killed Eadulf and reunited Northumbria under his rule.

When Morcar had succeeded Tostig, he appointed Osulf to rule the area north of the River Tyne.

In February —at least I think it was— Copsi rode north with his attendant troops and took charge in York. He called Osulf to him, and when the aristocrat attended, Copsi made it very plain to all in attendance that Osulf had no future in Northumbria and should leave the area and go into exile.

Osulf stormed from the meeting and returned to his home. Here, the Saxon nobleman brooded over his meal of venison pie, cheese, cakes and ale. After a while, he called his family and leading supporters. He began to tell the tale of what Copsi had told him, but it soon became apparent that the story had already come to the ears of the local people.

"What is to be done, my Lord?" one man asked.

Osulf turned to his family.

"We must gather together all of our goods that can be transported and leave the area by sunset tomorrow. Set the servants to the task immediately. You, my faithful followers, must gather together your arms and armour. We leave for the hills. There we shall gather as many followers as we can and depose this weasel that the Norman has imposed upon us."

His men nodded their heads in agreement and left immediately to organise the resistance.

The following dawn, Osulf and his family departed their home — the women and younger members of the family with tears streaming down their faces. What fate awaited them? None could know. The men were grim-faced. The local people stood and watched as the sad procession passed by.

***

The Saxon lord and his retinue now sat sadly around their camp fires, deep in the hills to the west of Northumbria. Here, they would be safe for now and could gather an army around them.

A rider approached and was challenged by the guard, "Halt and declare yourself!"

"It is Acwellen," the rider replied, "I bring news."

The guard stood aside and allowed the Saxon warrior to pass into the camp. Acwellen dismounted and handed his horse's bridle to a young lad. He approached the fire and stood before Osulf.

"What news, Acwellen?" Osulf asked.

"My lord, men approach from all parts of Northumbria. Copsi is regarded by the people as nothing more than an invader and a griping tax collector for William. He is deeply unpopular amongst our own people, both north and south of the Tees. I am sure that, before the days lengthen to their full, we will have a mighty fighting force to tackle both him and his master."

"I have further news of Copsi, Lord," the man added, and Osulf and his leading retainers leaned forward to hear the news.

***

It was on the 12th day of March, I recall, that Osulf marched his now considerable force to try to take his revenge upon the hated Copsi.

A bright day had dawned, and Osulf's men had risen early. They had breakfasted and gathered together their weapons and tack. Horses were readied, men mounted their saddles and settled down for a long ride out of their hilly stronghold. Each man knew where he was headed. Their destination was the royal vill of Neuburna, which lay on the banks of the River Tyne. In those days, it was the most easterly fordable place on the Tyne.

Roman remains still lay there, but now in disuse and decay. Indeed, the Romans had marked the ford with large stones and had built a fort there to guard the crossing and dissuade outlaws from attacking supplies en route to the great Roman wall that stretched for miles across our country, from coast to coast.

But why, you might ask, were Osulf and his men making their way there? I will tell you. It was all to do with the news that the messenger, Acwellen, had brought to his master. The word was that Copsi and his men were to attend a banquet there, no doubt feasting upon the best Northumbria could provide. Oh, yes. He would be there.

As the force rode eastward, Osulf paused and gathered his commanders together. He gave orders to each, and all heads nodded in understanding of the role they were to play.

The troops split so that some travelled south and some would remain to the south of Neuburna. Others would continue east and then return north until they were stationed west of the vill. That would give Copsi little room for manoeuvre when they were attacked.

Slowly, the troops moved toward their prey. Slowly, the noose tightened around them until Osulf and his men lay only a short distance away from where they could see the buildings. Copsi had obviously thought that he was in little danger in the middle of his fiefdom and had posted no sentries to guard his position.

"That was very obliging of him," said Osulf, and his men chortled.

Slowly, Osulf and his men trotted forward and were a little distance from the compound at

Neuburna when they were finally spotted in the haze by a lazy soldier who had been asleep but had roused himself to pee. The man rapidly forgot his purpose and dashed back into the hall where the banquet was in full swing.

"My Lord," he gasped, urine running down his leg, "troops approach from the west."

Food and drink were left unattended as Copsi and his followers rushed outside and gazed out across the country. Not only were troops approaching from the west, but also the south and east. Copsi shuddered and tried to control his terror.

"Ehm, take to weapons. Marshall the troops and set defences at all sides."

"What about the land to the north, my Lord?" one commander asked, "Should we make haste to cross the river and make a stand there?"

It would have been an idea, as that side was not threatened, but Copsi dithered. What, he thought, if the enemy had troops stationed to the north? He would be no better off but would give up his position to the south side.

"No! Make defences here. We shall leave the north side. They can only cross there in small numbers."

That much was true.

Slowly, slowly, the forces of Osulf approached. Now, a little distance from the compound of Neuburna, they dismounted and formed themselves into an attacking shield wall. Copsi, likewise, lined up his troops.

"Who can it be that leads this force, my Lord?" a retainer asked.

"Who else?" Copsi spat out, "It is the wolf, Osulf! He shall not defeat me this day!"

Slowly, slowly, the shield wall advanced until the men could almost smell the rancid breath of their opponents. At a call from Osulf, his men charged at Copsi's wall, and the two sides collided in a melee of noise and action. Shield-boss met shield-boss, and axes were hooked over the top of shields, the better to pull them down and expose the man behind it. Swords crashed into lime wood planks, splintering and shattering them. Now swords and spears found their first human targets, and screams and oaths rent the air. Blood spouted and sprayed over men and weapons. Men fell, with unseeing eyes, to the dirt below.

The two shield-walls heaved and throbbed, first surging this way and then that. What mayhem was loosed on that day!

Now, Osulf could finally see the man who had caused his misery. The same man who had caused his family to flee in the night. There he stood, well behind the line of his shield wall, of course, bawling instructions at the men who *had* the stomach to fight. Osulf spat upon the ground in his disgust. This man was a canker on the face of Northumbria and would not see another dawn if Osulf could arrange it.

Osulf's troops now closed the trap more tightly around Copsi and his men. From three sides, they pushed and heaved, and Copsi's men began to fall back. Now, Copsi thought, it might have been better to retreat across the ford, but it was too late. His men, and more to the point, he himself, would be slaughtered before they reached the opposite bank if he retreated now.

Copsi knew, and his troops knew, that the end was near. They could never out-fight the massive force that Osulf had put into the field against them. Men began to lay down their arms and surrender to the attackers. Copsi looked around him madly, trying to work out an escape route, for he knew that if he was captured, his days on this Earth would be numbered.

His eyes lit upon a small church at one corner of the settlement.

"To the church! To the church!" he urged his personal bodyguard around him.

"We will defend from inside."

Of course, it was obvious to all that few of his troops could fit within the confines of the small Saxon church and that many of his men would be left outside, at the mercy of Osulf's troops. But such small considerations were of no matter to Copsi.

The Earl and his hand-picked men entered the church and barred the doors behind them. Now, Copsi sat on a bench and stared at the ground before him.

"What are we to do, Lord?" a commander asked.

Copsi shook his head. He had no orders, as he knew in his heart that there was to be no escape.

A little while later, the noise outside subsided. Copsi and his men lifted their heads and sniffed the air around them. Smoke! Their heads flopped onto chests. Osulf was burning the church.

Wisps of grey smoke now rose from the base of the wattle and daub walls. The crackle of fire could be heard all around them. What was to be done? Could they break out and run? They certainly couldn't break out and fight. Still, the smoke rose to the ceiling and began to fill the air. The air became hotter as the flames rose from every direction. Men began to sweat and claw at their clothes. They began to cough and choke on the fumes.

"My Lord, we must open the doors and surrender to our attackers. We have no choice, other than to roast alive in this house of God."

Copsi nodded, and the doors were unbarred. He and his men emerged and stumbled into the sunshine, coughing, retching, and blinking in the light. They stood there, a beaten rabble, before Osulf and his men.

"Copsi, how good it is to see you again!" cried Osulf.

His men laughed. Copsi didn't. Copsi just stared at his opponent with a malevolent frown.

"What would you do with me now?" he snarled, "I am the rightful Earl of Northumbria, appointed by the king, and your army is but a rabble, roused to fight against their proper rulers."

The remainder of Copsi's armed force stood, surrounded by Osulf's men, their heads hung low.

Osulf sat his horse for a while.

"Your men may leave, without their weapons, of course. We have no quarrel with them. They are men of Northumbria, in the main, and were only following your orders. The Normans under your command, however, will remain. As will you…for now."

The Saxon troops of Copsi gathered what they could and slowly made their way south toward York.

In truth, there were few of them to make the journey. Most of their comrades lay upon the cold Earth and would make no further journeys except for a final one, six feet below the soil.

"Now, what is to be done with you?" Osulf pondered, staring again at Copsi and his Norman followers.

"My thoughts are that your weasely plotting and dire deeds originate in your head, Copsi. There, you plot and plan how to do down your fellow men to your own advantage. I think that is your problem, and so, I shall relieve you of it."

Strong arms grabbed Copsi, and he was led before Osulf. There, he was forced to his knees. A huge Northumbrian stepped forward, bearing a large sword whose edges were honed to sharpness. Osulf nodded, and the sword fell upon Copsi's neck, severing it from his body. The head rolled to the side and stared up, sightless, at Osulf, mounted upon his horse. Blood spurted from the body and spilt its slipperiness onto the ground. Northumbrians cheered and waved their weapons whilst Normans stared in terror at the fate of their leader.

I never did hear what happened to the Normans, captured there on that fateful day of March. It is left for us to speculate.

Just days later, Osulf crossed the Tyne and led his men to the north and east, where he seized control of Bamburgh, and no expeditionary force either removed or threatened him.

Chapter 7

Death and Opportunity

It was in the autumn of 1067. Osulf sat within his hall at Bamburgh. He stared into the fire and mused on the happenings that had led him to his position. Surely, this was his rightful position. No man could argue otherwise. Osulf was, after all, the son of Eadulf III, Earl of Bamburgh, and grandson of Uchtred the Bold, Earl of Northumbria. Had not Osulf's family ruled as "High-Reeves" or ealdormen of Bamburgh from 954 until 1041, when Siward had killed Eadulf and usurped his position in Northumbria?

He had seized back his heritage from the hated Copsi and his Norman leeches, who were slowly bleeding the Saxon country to death. And no man had come to try to take his part of Northumbria away from him. He had been left alone. Did they accept his position, or did they not dare to attack him now that he had a formidable fighting force at his disposal? He enjoyed the thought.

He was jolted from his reverie by an urgent call from without. A man-at-arms entered and announced a message. Osulf nodded at the guard, and one of his retainers swept into the hall.

"My lord, I bring sad news."

Osulf sat up in his chair and listened to the man.

"My lord, there has been a murder in the burgh. Old Tom, the carter, has been found foully murdered in his hovel. He was stabbed, and his throat was cut from side to side. His possessions have been taken, along with a quantity of food. Tom had been helping with the wood-cutting, carrying it back to the burgh in his cart."

Osulf sat and took in the news. He knew old Tom and liked the man. His wife had died some years ago, and they had no offspring. Tom was alone in the world, other than for those who appreciated him in Bamburgh.

"I have heard news that a number of outlaws have been raiding barns and storehouses in the area. I sent out a patrol yesterday to ride the area and report back to me. Now, it seems, the outlaws might be closer to home than we thought. I will ride immediately with a troop to search the immediate area. Give the order to my commander."

The messenger bowed to his lord and left to do his bidding. Soon, a troop of mounted men-at-arms, under the command of one of Osulf's most trusted men, were sitting their horses, waiting for their lord to join them.

Osulf emerged from his hall, equipped for a search, and mounted the black palfrey that had been saddled for him. It was a magnificent specimen of the most expensive and highly-bred kinds of horse of our time.

The earl waved a gloved hand, and the troop left the compound. The soldiers trotted out into the Northumbrian countryside. The leaves on the trees were gradually turning to colours of red, orange and yellow. A mist rose from the river and spread over the treetops like a blanket.

Osulf gazed around him in appreciation of the landscape that he now ruled over. Truly, he was home and in the position that was rightfully his by birth. He loved this land of Northumbria, and in particular, the land north of the River Tyne. He could gaze out over the sea to the Holy Island of Lindisfarne and the Farne Islands, covered by seabirds and seals, when they bore their pups on the shoreline. He loved to walk along the golden sandy beach in the evenings, breathing in the bracing sea air. He always felt so invigorated by the smell of the sea and the seaweed that lay along the strandline. He knew that the churls of the area collected the dead stands of seaweed to fertilize their land. Men said that it made the fruit sweeter.

The troop turned sharp left, following their leader into a woodland trail. Osulf looked up into the canopy and saw the acorns ripening there. Soon, the jays would eat their fill, and badgers would snout them from the soil surface to fill their bellies for winter.

The soldiers rode on for almost an hour until a sound reached their ears. It was the beat of a hammer on metal. Osulf was sure there was not a smithy this deep into the woodland. He held up his hand,, and the troop hauled on their reins behind him and sat their horses. They knew better than to speak to ask the reason for the halt. Osulf's commander walked his horse slowly forward until he sat level with the earl. The two men listened and looked at one another when the faint sound of hammering came again.

Gently, to avoid rattling the tack and weapons, the troop dismounted and began to make their way along the woodland track, toward the sound. As they got closer, another sound came to them on the breeze. It was the sound of voices.

"There, that spearhead be as good as new."

"Had you not bent it running the old man through, you wouldn't have needed to mend it."

"Well, it can't be helped now. At least the old crow won't be able to tell anyone what happened to him."

"I think the good people of Bamburgh might just be able to guess what happened to him."

"But they don't know who done it," came the reply.

"Humph!"

Osulf and his men crept forward until they could see into the small campsite. There were two men. They had one old nag between them, and the soldiers could see baskets and bags that had once belonged to the old carter. Osulf waved his gloved hand, and his men began to encircle the camp. When he knew they were all in position, he stepped forward into the clearing, his sword hissing from the fleece-lined scabbard.

The two outlaws looked up in surprise and leapt to their feet, glancing wildly about them. One man hung his head, and his shoulders slumped. He knew that the game was up and there was no escape for them. He knew that he would shortly end his days on the gallows at Bamburgh. The other snatched up the spear and pointed it at the men-at-arms around him. They just stood their ground, knowing that they had their quarry.

Osulf stepped forward.

"Put down the spear. We have heard your conversation and now know for certain that you killed old Tom, the carter, in Bamburgh. We will escort you back to your trial, where your fate is surely sealed. Drop all of your weapons and kneel on the Earth."

He stepped forward again at exactly the same time as the spearman leapt toward him. The man thrust the spear into Osulf's stomach, unguarded as it was by a mail coat, and ran the weapon through the earl until it appeared from his back.

Osulf's eyes widened, and a gout of blood erupted from his mouth. He slowly sank to his knees, dragging the spear down with him.

In an instant, a soldier had run forward, and his sword came down heavily upon the skull of the spearman, cleaving it in two and showering his body in blood and grey matter. He was a dead man before his body touched the ground.

The second man dropped to his knees and held his head in his hands, weeping. He was quickly overcome and tied to the saddle of his thin horse for the journey back to Bamburgh. His companion was tied over a horse behind him.

Osulf was wrapped in a length of cloth from what was stolen from the carter and also strapped over his palfrey.

It was a sad and disconsolate troop who walked their horses back into Bamburgh that night. As they approached, Osulf's wife and children ran from the hall, screams and wails ringing out across the compound. They could see what had happened to the earl, and their lives were in tatters. What now? How would they live without the care and protection of the earl? How could they go on?

Earl Osulf was buried the following day at Bamburgh, the place he loved with all his heart. The atmosphere in the burgh was grim, and many tears were shed that day.

***

It is in the nature of men to look for an advantage in any sorry situation, and it was but the blinking of an eye from Osulf being buried at his beloved Bamburgh that his cousin, Gospatric, headed south to speak with the king.

Now, let me recall. Gospatric, I am sure, was a great-grandson of Ethelred II through the side of his mother, Eadglyth. His mother's grandmother, Aelfgifu, had married Uchtred the Bold. I think that is the way of it. No matter. Gospatric had a realistic claim to the Earldom, being related to both Osulf and Uchtred.

And so it was that, some days later, Gospatric and a group of followers rode into the king's compound and announced their arrival to a man-at-arms. Very soon, one of William's advisers was called and emerged into the sunlight of a crisp autumn day.

“What cause brings you here, Gospatric?” he asked.

“I have grave news for the king regarding my beloved cousin, Osulf,” he replied.

The adviser looked both intrigued and wary but led Gospatric and his retinue into the hall, where the king was meeting with a group of his earls from the south. The king was in the process of making plans for raising heavy taxes to swell his coffers again. The adviser coughed, and William and his party looked up at the doorway which framed the men.

“What is it, Walter?” he asked, a little irritated at being disturbed.

“My Lord, It is Gospatric of Northumbria. He says he brings grim news from that part of the kingdom.”

At this, William straightened and sat back. He had been concerned that all might not go well with the wild people of the north. What now disturbs the peace of the land?

“Enter, Gospatric,” he said, “What is it you have to tell me?”

Gospatric bowed low to the king and then straightened, a look of great sorrow upon his face.

“My Lord, I must bring to you evil news. My beloved cousin, Osulf, has been brutally killed. He was chasing outlaws, as is the duty of any earl, and, once upon them, was speared so that he died. Naturally, we are all desolate at his loss."

"Hm," mused William, "I seem to recall that it was no other but Osulf who had the head off my own earl, Copsi."

Gospatric shuffled, and a nervous look spread across his face.

"But then I was never fond of Copsi myself," William continued, "He was an obsequious little man. And Osulf seemed to be keeping that part of the country calm. That is why I didn't pursue him after Copsi's death."

"Indeed, Lord," Gospatric agreed.

"Now, my lords," he addressed his earls and advisors, "What am I to do with Northumbria?"

Gospatric again shuffled and cleared his throat.

"My lord," he ventured, "It is, of course, the decision of the king in such matters, but if I might put myself forward to help in this sad situation until my lord decides what must be done, I would be honoured to serve as Earl of Northumbria in place of my sadly-missed cousin."

William looked around the faces of his assembled advisers.

"My lords, Gospatric offers us a solution, at least in the short-term," he said, "What think you?"

A Norman of the name Goubert spoke, "My Lord, it might be one solution to the problem, at least for the time being," he paused, "Perhaps Gospatric would like to join us to consider the raising of funds that we must commence soon."

Gospatric looked from man to man, and each looked back at him with expectant smiles.

"Why, my Lord, I would be happy to donate a sum to the king's fund if that would be of any help."

William nodded his head as if in thought.

"A considerable contribution to funds would most certainly be greatly beneficial to the treasury. Pray join us, Gospatric, and we will come to terms."

And so, Gospatric joined the assembly and pledged a great sum to the king. We never did hear the size of it, but men said it was a colossal amount. And, of course, Gospatric rode home as the new Earl of Northumbria.

And did it all end happily, I hear you ask? Read on.

Chapter 8

Treasure and the Bishop

Another tale of our time? One bright and warm Sunday morning, we ambled out for Matins at our little church. The bell was pealing merrily, and villagers were all answering its call.

"A good morrow to you," we called to friends as they appeared from their houses and joined the procession toward the church.

As we entered the church, we became aware of the Abbot standing at the Nave, speaking solemnly to Cerdic. This was unusual, as it was generally one of the ordinary members of the monastery who led the services. It was only at Christmas and Easter that we were treated to a visit by the Abbot.

"What do you think is afoot?" Benjamin, the smith, asked me as we took our places to stand through the ceremony. We always stood. Seats were only kept there for the elderly and frail.

"I don't know," I replied, "I haven't heard anything of importance."

After a few minutes, Cerdic and the Abbot ceased their conversation, and the thegn took his place at the front of the church. The Abbot began the ceremony, and all seemed well. It was at the point of the sermon that the mood changed. The Abbot climbed into the pulpit to be better seen by the assembled congregation. He coughed a couple of times to clear his throat, gazed around him and then began.

"What I am about to tell you concerns the church and the good people of this land under our new masters, the Normans. I must tell you of deceit and wrong-doing in our church and about our submission to William at York."

We all knew that Cerdic had travelled to York recently after all the local thegns were commanded to York to see the Conqueror himself.

Now, you might think that life in the church would be a peaceful one, even in such terrible times as we lived through, but it was not always so.

The Abbot continued, "As you are all aware, in 1041, Aethelric was consecrated as Bishop of Durham and was later to resign his post after…an unfortunate incident."

We all knew he had boot-licked Earl Siward of Northumbria. Oh, but he was a poor excuse for a Bishop! Even amongst his own monks, he was about as popular as a hard frost! We also knew that he had resigned in 1056 but had never been told the whole story. There had been plenty of rumours, but then there always are when something is kept quiet by those in authority. Now, we were to finally be enlightened!

I shall tell it as I heard it from the Abbot on that late summer morning.

Well, now, the monks and a goodly number of lay workers were in the process of taking down the old church at Chester-le-Street, which had fallen into disrepair. It had been decided to build a new one at the same site. For many days, the monks, stone masons, and their labourers took down the walls of the old church stone by stone, being careful to retain anything that might be of use in building the new house of God.

A monk straightened himself and leaned back with his hands upon his hips to try to ease the pains from cramped muscles. He had lifted many stones that day and looked forward to the end of the labours and a meal and his mattress of straw in the monastery. He gazed around him at the busy site, where men toiled at their tasks, and he hoped that God would approve of the new church when it was finally built to His greater glory. But, oh, how his back ached.

The monk sighed and bent again to his labours and grasped the large stone before him. With great effort, he heaved at the monster and rolled it over onto its side to gain a better grip. But then he stopped dead. His eyes widened as he stared into the pit that had opened before him. For there, before his very eyes, was a treasure trove such as he had never seen before. There were coins with the heads of Roman emperors upon them. There were ornaments of solid gold! As he stood there, a shiver went down his spine.

After a moment, he stood straight and called out, “Treasure! I have found treasure! Come look!”

Heads turned, and men began to make their way through the mud to see what the monk had found, hidden deep beneath the foundations of the church. Sure enough, there it lay. Treasure! There were gasps and murmurings.

“It is a miracle!” called one elderly monk, who had been busy recording the site as he could no longer endure hard labour.

Now, as it happened, upon that day, none other than Bishop Aethelric was visiting the site to review its progress. A messenger was quickly dispatched to fetch him, and his eyes opened wide when he beheld the riches at his feet.

“Fetch a cart,” he ordered, “And load this hoard upon it. I shall take it back to the monastery with me. It is better that it is locked away as soon as possible. There are many men in these parts who would steal it from us.”

Monks now hurried about the business of drawing up a horse and cart and lifting the new-found riches from the ground. Soon, it was all loaded, and the Bishop and his party quickly hurried on their way to Durham.

I hear you cry, 'What a miracle for the church.' Oh, but you are so trusting of the men of God. For, believe it or not, the treasure seemed to disappear after a few weeks. Where had it gone? None knew. There was great muttering within the monastery, but Aethelric brushed aside any questions, saying the treasure was safely hidden away for fear of outlaws and cutthroats breaking in and stealing the hoard.

Unfortunately for Aethelric, there were those who *did* know. One of his lay servants was making merry in an inn a short while after. He had supped many a jug of ale and was becoming talkative. Indeed, he was becoming something of a nuisance in the inn (not least to one of the young serving wenches as she tried to go about her business).

"Sit upon my knee, fair maid," he said, "And I will tell a tale of treasure. But you must swear an oath that you will tell no other soul."

The maid stood and considered the man. Treasure? This was more interesting than the other foul rubbish he had spouted at her that evening. The maid sat down beside the man and listened. But hers were not the only ears to have pricked up at the sound of the word 'treasure.' Others now leaned in to listen to the tale.

Well, the man now told how he was a carter in the employ of the Bishop. He told the tale of how he and a group of men-at-arms had been sent, with a loaded cart, to the abbey of Peterborough. They had instructions that they were not to look into the boxes loaded onto the cart, which, of course, only served to make them more curious as to the nature of their cargo. And so, one evening, whilst making the cart secure at a local monastery, the old carter had opened the boxes. What do you suppose was in the boxes? Why, of course! It was the treasure of Chester-le-Street.

The carter and the troops had duly delivered *most* of their precious cargo and returned home. I am sure that you understand my meaning.

Of course, now that the tale was well known, all Hell broke loose in the monastery of Durham. Why, the monks would know, was their miraculous hoard destined to be spent upon the Lord's work in Durham, now in the clutches of the Abbot of Peterborough? It seems our wonderful Bishop would rather the riches were spent on building work in the south, from whence he had originally come.

Now Earl Siward, Aelthelric's protector, died shortly after, and Aethelric resigned his post and retired to Peterborough.

And so, it came to pass that we were sent another Bishop in 1056. Believe it or not, it was Aethelric's own brother, Athelwine! Hard to believe, I know, but that was the way of it. Aethelwine was to be the last Anglo-Saxon Bishop of Durham (he was also the only English Bishop at the time of our conquest who did not remain loyal to our new king.)

Aethelwine was consecrated Bishop by the hated Earl Tostig, of whom we finally rid ourselves at the Battle of Stamford Bridge some years later. Like his brother before him, Aethlewine was not a popular Bishop amongst the clergy of the cathedral. I fear that this was because he was Aethelric's brother, an 'outsider', and had been foisted upon the monastery without any consultation or discussion.

(If you have heard my tale of our lives leading up to the invasion of this kingdom, you will know that the monks of the cathedral were amongst the leaders of the revolt against the hated Tostig, where we sacked his palace at York, and finally slew the rat at Stamford Bridge.)

Aethelwine continued as Bishop after the sack of York and initially declared his loyalty to William after the Conquest.

Now, the Abbot told us of the recent happenings in York, where he and Cerdic were called to meet William.

In 1068, William's men were busily planning and building a great castle at York and had invited the local thegns of York and dignitaries to attend him there.

The Abbot now told us the tale of what had recently happened. This was the real news of the day. The previous part of the Abbot's sermon had only served to enlighten us as to the bad character of our former Bishop! I am pleased to say, though, that he did not escape from his crimes. For William had the loathsome man arrested, and he died in captivity in Westminster in 1070. No more than he deserved, I say!

The Abbot now told us that, as the thegns and clergymen arrived in York, each man and a selected group of followers were commanded to attend William. They were led to a great chamber within the castle, attended by the new king's men-at-arms. More troops lined the corridors and even the chamber itself. It seems that William was taking no chances on the loyalty of any Anglo-Saxon. All arms were removed from the visitors long before they reached the great hall.

Men tugged at their shirt collars as they were led into the hall to the presence of the Conqueror. And there William sat, upon a throne. There was no smile on the cruel face. His eyes seemed to bore into the very soul of any man who came before him. Guards stood at his back, spears in their hands. I am not sure what William expected the cowed Saxons to do against the overwhelming force arrayed against them.

Upon the day when the Abbot was in attendance, Athelwine arrived in York with a company of monks along with many more clergymen. He swept into the confines of William's still unfinished castle and announced himself to the guard.

"Out of my way!" he bawled, "Do you not know that I am Aethelwine, the Bishop of Durham?"

The commander of the Norman guard stood in his path.

"I care not if you are His Holiness the Pope himself," he rasped, "You will remain here until I tell you to enter the chamber."

Aethelwine swallowed hard and looked around him at the heavily armed soldiers.

"Of c-course…" he stammered.

His face flushed with the embarrassment of his situation. Here he was, an important Saxon Bishop, and he had been belittled by little more than a man-at-arms. Oh, how he squirmed.

At length, and with a scowl from the commander of the guard, Aethelwine was allowed to enter the chamber. He entered slowly, and with a false dignity he didn't really feel. He progressed through the already packed hall, followed by this entourage of clerics. The party approached the dais upon which William had his throne, and all bent their knees before the great man.

William stared at his Bishop as the man rose and knelt again before him. William offered his hand, and the Bishop took it and kissed the king's ring.

"My lord, I pledge myself and all of the see of Durham to your majesty."

William grunted and withdrew his hand.

"I understand that you have news for me from King Malcolm of Scotland. Is it so?"

"My lord king, it is so. Malcolm wishes nothing less than to live in peace with Your Majesty. It is well that our two countries will live together, side by side, without rancour and violence."

"Hm," the king replied, "Then I must send the Scottish king my terms for settlement and peace, which I hope he will accept. In that way, peace between us will become a reality. Should Malcolm not accept my terms…Now, attend me tomorrow at mid-morning. I will give you my terms in writing. You will take them to Malcolm and explain to him the situation that now exists in this country."

Athelwine nodded and bowed to the king, retreating backwards from the royal presence. Not until he was outside the room did he regain his composure and sweep again from the royal castle.

It was at this point that the Abbot gave us the next news. And it came as a shock to all of us. He hesitated.

"I must now give you further news. Next year, we are to have a new Earl of Northumbria. It will be Robert de Comines, a Norman whom William has appointed to rule over us."

"No!" cried Benjamin, "It cannot be so. A Norman to rule us?"

Many more churls muttered and grumbled between them until Cerdic stood and called for silence.

"We have no choice but to accept our situation and our fate. What can we do against a Norman army?"

"Rebel!" cried Luke the churl.

Chapter 9

Rebellion!

And so, the years 1067 to 1069 would be some of the most bloodthirsty in the history of this land. Oh, how we suffered. Oh, how many died needless and cruel deaths at the hands of our new masters!

Even before our rebellions, here in the north, there was a revolt in Exeter, in the southwest, which I shall tell you about. For here lived Gytha, the mother of our King Harold. She had born a bitter grudge after William refused to hand back to her the body of her son, the Saxon king.

But now, it seems, the outrageous taxes demanded by our new Norman landlords were also lighting the kindling of revolution. The people of the city of Exeter rebelled against these taxes and insisted that the tribute they paid to the sheriff and the queen should remain at £18. William, of course, was furious, and he marched his troops to the city in the spring of 1068.

As William approached Exeter upon the road, his commander held his hand high to halt his troops in their tracks. For, coming toward them was a large delegation of the citizens of Exeter, wishing to reach terms of compromise that would satisfy all.

William rode to the front of the procession and sat his horse, watching the arrival.

"What think you of this?" he asked of his commander.

"I know not, my Lord," the man replied, "They do not seem to carry enough arms to make them dangerous, but we must see. I will ensure that our troops are ready for all eventualities."

William nodded, and the commander retreated down the line to give the orders. He returned just as the delegation of citizens was nearing the king.

"My Lord King," one of the citizens called, "We come in peace to discuss with you the 'situation' between us. We are not heavily armed and mean no harm to your person."

William knew that they were amongst Exeter's leading men by the sumptuous clothes they wore. 'It seems there is money in Exeter,' he thought to himself.

"Then approach, but without arms," William replied.

The leading men disarmed and handed their weapons to their followers. Then, they approached William and his entourage on foot.

The men bent their knee, and their leader spoke, "My Lord, we must speak to you concerning the taxes you exact upon our people. We have always paid £18 to the sheriff and our queen, and we can badly afford further taxes upon our people if we are to prosper. Surely, you do not want the citizens under your rule to live in poverty. It is a yoke we cannot bear!"

At this, William's face clouded, and a red flush rose from his neck to cover his furious face.

"The 'yoke' of taxes you refer to are my rightful tithe upon your community. I will have it, and I care little if the people of Exeter live in silks or in rags! From what I see now, I think there is enough money in Exeter to pay my taxes! Seize them!"

And so the men of Exeter were quickly surrounded and seized by the Norman troops and led back to the city in bounds.

But, as William approached the walls of Exeter, he found the gates to the city firmly shut in his face. Armed men crowded the ramparts, and it was immediately obvious that they intended a resistance to his rule.

William sat his horse and gazed at the city before him. A cold March breeze ruffled the pennants of his troops and whistled through the branches of the trees. He pondered the situation for what must have seemed an eternity for those watching.

At length, he called back to his men, "Bring forward the spokesman of Exeter."

This done, William spoke quietly to a large man-at-arms. The man strode back and led up the leader of the citizens, now in William's custody. They all moved forward to where William knew they could be seen by the people on the walls.

Two men-at-arms now dragged the spokesman forward and held tightly onto his arms. The huge soldier drew a dagger from his belt and approached the terrified man. Time seemed to stand still. The tension in the air could be cut with a knife. The spokesman whimpered at the sight of the soldier and his knife. Was this to be his end? Would he see another dawn, or was a cold grave his only home now?

The man-at-arms stood before him and grinned. The spokesman could smell his stale breath and the stale stink of his body. But that was quickly replaced by another foul smell as his own bowels broke and his leggings were soiled beneath him. The Norman soldiers laughed.

Now, the knife was drawn up to his face, and the spokesman quickly muttered a prayer that he thought would be his last. The soldier stabbed quickly at the man's left eye, and his eyeball was ripped from its socket. The man let loose a piercing wail, and shocked muttering was heard all around, both from

William's force and from the walls of Exeter. Then the knife came again and relieved him of this right eye. Another great wail left his lips, and he was allowed to sink to the floor, with blood pouring from the empty sockets where his eyes had been.

William gestured to his men, and they lifted the citizen to his feet.

"Let the people see what I do to people who would defy me."

He wafted his hand in the direction of the walls, and the soldiers bundled the blinded man toward the gates of Exeter. The appalled citizens gave up a great roar, and arrows sailed out toward the Normans. The soldiers dropped their captive and retreated to their force. The man writhed on the ground, obviously in terrible pain, but the gates of Exeter remained firmly closed.

William mused again upon the subject of Exeter, watching the now-blind man raise himself and call for help from his fellows who didn't come. The man staggered around with no idea of where safety lay. After a while, he collapsed again into a heap and didn't stir.

Now William gave an order, "Surround the city with troops. No one shall enter or leave without my permission. We shall see how long these dogs can survive before they run out to lick my boots!"

And so it was. For eighteen days, the Norman troops held a noose around the neck of the city of Exeter, denying food or water from the river to its inhabitants. But did they meekly give in to the Norman? No! The good people of that city fought a brave battle against the daily onslaughts from the Norman soldiers, and William's troops suffered losses that he had not expected.

One morn, as William sat within his tent, chewing at his nails to the very quick and considering his options against the city, relief came. A guard entered the tent, and William looked up, startled by the man's arrival.

"My Lord, king," the man reported, "A delegation of the people of Exeter would speak peace with you."

"Would they, now?" William replied, smiling, "Then we must see what the good citizens would have to say."

At that, he rose and belted on his arms. He strode from the tent and approached the city walls with a bodyguard around him. He stood there, staring at the people gathered on the wall but saying nothing. Let them speak first, he thought to himself.

After a brief delay, when nought but silence and birdcall filled the spring air, someone on the walls rose up and spoke, "My lord, we would come to terms with you. Should we open our gates to you, we would seek your word that the city will not be razed and our citizens massacred."

"And why would I massacre the people who will be paying tax to me?" William replied.

Mutterings could be heard from the city walls.

"We would also ask that Queen Gytha be allowed to sail down the River Exe to exile without being harmed."

William pondered. Why not agree to the terms? He was heartily sick of this waste of time, particularly when there were other areas of the country that required his early attention. He was also impressed, though he would never admit it, by the resolve of the people of Exeter. And what was Gytha to him? She was but a woman and only the mother of the last king.

William approached a little closer. His guards huddled around him, with shields at the ready, should the citizens mount an archery assault.

"I will swear," he began, "Upon my honour, that no further harm shall come to the citizens of Exeter, should they peacefully submit to me and open their gates. I further swear that your old witch of a queen will be allowed to make her escape without harassment from my troops or anyone in my entourage."

Slowly, the creaking gates of Exeter swung open, and William and his bodyguard, accompanied by advisers and a small troop of men-at-arms, entered the city. The citizens stood upon the walls and grimly watched the procession. Others ran to their houses and closed doors and window shutters behind them. Tension hung in the air. But William was as good as his word. No citizen was harmed, and Gytha sailed off to safety.

***

On the following morning, William held talks with the leading citizens and agreed terms. *His* terms, of course. When the citizens left his presence, another entered it. He was one Baldwin de Redvers and was one of William's most trusted henchmen. Baldwin was one of William's Flemish allies.

The Fleming bowed low as he entered the king's presence.

"You wished to see me, Lord King," he said.

William ushered him to a chair beside the large table of the hall in which he now resided.

"Yes, Baldwin, I have a task for you."

The Fleming nodded his head respectfully.

"In this area of the city," and he pointed to a rough plan of the area he had his men draw up, "Is a large mound of the red Earth hereabouts. There stand 48 houses at the moment. You will take a force of men and demolish the homes, and there you will build a castle. The people of this city must be contained, and only a castle will suffice."

"And what of the people whose homes are destroyed, Lord?" asked Baldwin.

"What of them? They will need to build new ones. I care not where."

Baldwin nodded.

"There will be a gatehouse and a defensive ditch with a drawbridge."

Baldwin again nodded his understanding.

"And you, Baldwin, will be, henceforth, known as Sheriff of Devon."

"My Lord, it will be my honour," Baldwin replied.

And, after further discussion, the Fleming went about the business that had been entrusted to him.

And what of our king? Surely now, he must find some peace in his new kingdom? No. Now, he turned his attention to the north!

Chapter 10

Trouble in the North

I shall continue my tales of our times with stories of more trouble for William. For, although Southern England was now largely under Norman control, the people of the Midlands and the North were a very different matter for the Conqueror. My tale is one of thwarted love and the plotting and scheming that men do to get what they want. Pour me a pot of ale from the jug and gather around the fire. I am an old man, and the cold gets into my very bones these days.

As I have told you, at the time of the conquest, the north of our country was very much an Anglo-Scandinavian area. We had lived under the Danelaw for many years, and many of us had Scandinavian blood coursing through our veins. I don't think we were the worse for it. Most of our aristocracy was Danish in its origins.

We were a proud people, and we didn't suffer fools —or tyrannical West Saxon earls— lightly! And, although we did travel around —no one further than myself when I fought for Harold at Stamford Bridge and Hastings— communications between the

Saxon south and the Anglo-Scandinavian north had never been easy. Indeed, many people, such as merchants, found it easier to travel south from York by boat than by land (Something I had also tasted at a young and tender age!).

But in 1068, trouble was brewing in the north and Mercia. Our Saxon leaders were stirring insurrection like hot potage. Plots were laid, and weapons sharpened.

When William had returned to Normandy in 1067, he had taken Edgar the Aetheling with him as a hostage. I hear that the journey across the sea was a wild one, with the boats tossed and rolled by huge waves, whipped up by fierce gales. I heard that Edgar had a very poor time, vomiting everything he ate and drank over the side of the boat, and even over his own feet. They do say that his face turned as green as the spring grass. I have been to sea, and it is not an experience I would like to repeat.

When they returned, Edgar, it would seem, had given William the slip and fled like a startled deer to Scotland with his mother and sisters to seek protection in the Scottish court of Malcolm III. Malcolm married the sister of the Aetheling and agreed readily to help in the attempt to regain the throne of England from William. I am sure Malcolm would have been much happier to have the Aetheling as the ruler of England than the threatening William.

I am not so certain about what the Aetheling's sister thought of this deal, as I have heard that Malcolm had a mouth full of rotten teeth. But the marriage suited both sides and so the deed was done.

William, at this time, after marching to Cornwall and ruthlessly putting down all restlessness and disturbance, finally led his weary army back to Winchester, where he intended to celebrate Easter. A little while later, these shores played host to his wife, Lady Matilda, and she was pronounced queen at Westminster on Whit Sunday of 1068. Men say she was a small woman but as ferocious as a cornered bear. She had not been happy when her marriage to William was arranged. I hear she declared that she would never marry 'William the Bastard' (He was named thus, in Normandy, as his mother had not been the wife of his father). However, once married, the couple grew close, and she was now devoted to our new king. How happy our new sovereigns were. England seemed more peaceful, and they were free to spend a little time together.

But in Mercia, a plot was being hatched. I shall tell you the gossip of the matter, as it was related to me by a passing tinker. I was always wary of tinkers' tales, but I later heard much the same story from a monk at the abbey, so I am sure that most of it was true.

Edwin and his younger brother, Morcar, the sons of Earl Aelfgar of Mercia, had made their peace with the king after the conquest, and Edwin had been granted Mercia and superior authority over his brother, who had lost Northumbria. In fact, Edwin had authority over no less than one-third of England. What could make such a man revolt against his king? Had he not been given enough to keep any man happy? Ah, no. There was one more simple thing that irked Edwin. It was the single thing that raises many a man's unrest and will probably go on doing so until the world ends!

At his hall, one sunny morning, Edwin sat pondering his future. After the turmoil of the conquest, at last, all seemed to be going well. A roaring fire blazed within the room, and a table had been set with jugs of ale and eatables such as sheep's cheese, pies and sweet cakes. Two large dogs of the wolfhound strain lay beside the fire on the floor rushes. Their tongues lolled from their great jaws as they lay, occasionally opening one eye to see if Edwin would give them a titbit of pie.

A guard opened the great door to the chamber, and a familiar figure entered. It was Morcar, Edwin's brother. Edwin looked up from his musings.

"Good day, brother," he called cheerily, "It is a good day to be alive, is it not?"

"Indeed so, Edwin. I would sup with you and ask the question that I know fills your mind each waking hour."

"You mean, 'When does the lady arrive?' I cannot be certain, but I await news this very day. I know that she arrived on our shores with Lady Matilda. It cannot be long now before we are together."

"I hear that she is a pretty little filly and would please any man's heart. I am sure your excitement grows."

Despite his disappointments in life, he still wished well for his brother.

Edwin smiled at his brother's words and nodded his head in agreement. The two brothers sat at the great table and enjoyed a tasty meal and a jug of ale. They chatted about this and that. What was to be done in the lands under their control? What was happening in other parts? What did William plan to do next?

From time to time, the two men would throw a few tasty morsels to the floor, and the dogs, seemingly dozing, quickly leapt to their feet to retrieve them. One of the dogs nuzzled up to Morcar and licked his hand. The young man rubbed it against his breeches and scowled at the animal.

"Dog, you have worse breath than a boar of the forest," he declared.

The dog stared up at him with baleful eyes, unaware of the insult that had just been thrown at him.

Edwin chuckled.

"Smell they might, but both are good dogs at the hunt."

He rubbed the shaggy head of the other dog standing before him in anticipation. He cut off a lump of pie and tossed it into the air for the dog to catch. In an instant, the morsel was gone.

***

But in the court of the king, others had also been discussing the situation in the country and considering how they might enrich themselves, even at the cost of the Saxon aristocracy. Many Normans were still unhappy at their lot. They had expected more from their king after they had given him so much and put him on the throne of England.

In the great hall, flaming torches guttered in their holders upon the walls. Courtiers fussed hither and thither, exchanging greetings and gossip. Servants hovered with great platters of food. There was venison, cooked over a great spit, in the kitchen. A great goose lay upon a table, its skin brown and fat leaking from the carcase to pool in the bottom of the wooden platter. Cheeses, their rinds mottled brown and green, stood, along with apples to accompany them. Jugs of ale and pitchers of French wine sat there, tempting the courtiers with their deep, fruity flavours.

A great door swung open, and the king swept into the hall, glancing from side to side to see who was present. He nodded to a few of the assembled throng, but snubbed others who were not wholly in his favour. He could be a hard man to please, and his followers went out of their way to keep within his favour. A man's life could depend upon it. William seated himself upon a great chair at the back of the room, near the fire. He grasped the wooden arms of the chair and glowered at the assembly.

"What news then?" he growled, "I can see that some of you have something to say by your fussing and fawning."

A courtier —Bernard— approached the chair.

"My Lord King, we, your loyal followers, are…a little…concerned at the position in the north of the country. Most of the south is now under control and relatively peaceful, as is much of the rest of the country. However, the north is still under the authority of Saxon earls. We are uneasy that the king's peace might not be maintained there as easily without more of a Norman presence. Can we really trust Edwin and his weasely brother, Morcar, to do our bidding, keep the people under control, and raise the taxes we need?"

William pondered the words of the Norman aristocrat and rubbed his chin in thought. He was not fond of Bernard. He found him a toadying little man, though he was, undoubtedly, a fine commander in battle, and William appreciated him at such times.

"What brings you to think that they will not honour their words in the matter of administering the lands for which I have appointed them overseers?"

"Why, Sire, when Harold was struck down on Senlac Hill, did Edwin and Morcar not throw their full support behind Edgar the Aetheling and proclaim him king?"

"It is true, my Lord," said another by the name of Conrad, "Were it not for the fact that they failed to muster enough of a force to defy us, we might be fighting a bloody war with the Saxons to this day."

"The earls promised upon their knees to support me as king when they saw that the alternative was an impossible dream. I took their word, and I must trust that they will keep it."

"The alternative might be impossible in reality, Sire," said Bernard, and heads nodded in agreement, "But in men's hearts, impossible dreams can burn for many years, still not extinguished by the waters of their reality."

William pondered again.

"What *evidence* do you have that the northern earls *are* planning anything against the crown?"

"Why, nought but rumour at the moment, Sire," admitted Conrad, "But, as the old saying goes, 'There is no smoke without fire'."

"Tell me of these rumours."

And so the conversation carried on long into the night in William's court.

***

A week later, as the shadows were lengthening outside Edwin's hall, he sat with his brother, talking of hawks and falcons they had known. A loud report sounded at the door of the chamber. A man-at-arms entered and announced an arrival. Edwin nodded, and a messenger entered the room. He was a tall, lean young man and his face was flushed, whether by exertion or by what he had to relate, Edwin didn't know. Edwin looked at the messenger's face, studying it to see if he could assess the sort of message the man had brought for him.

The young man bowed curtly to the two earls — Edwin and his brother— and delivered into Edwin's hand a scroll containing a message.

"It is from the king, my lord," he briefly explained and then bowed low as if to keep favour with the Saxon nobles.

Edwin broke the seal and stared at the parchment before him. As he read the words, his face changed from the pleasant smile that had been etched there as he had chatted with his brother to the grimace of a betrayed man.

"The young lady does not come!" he cried, "He keeps her from me!"

The dogs by the fire lifted their heads at the sudden noise and looked toward the earls.

Morcar stared at his brother in disbelief.

"But he knows that you desire her and that you have waited long to be united in marriage with her. He gave a solemn promise to that when we bent the knee to him."

"Aye, it is true enough, but it seems that he no longer finds me fit to marry his daughter. It seems that he no longer trusts me. I can imagine who has been whispering in his ear to that effect. It is a conspiracy to take what is ours and give it to the Normans, who have always desired this land of ours."

"What will you do, brother? Will you go to him?"

"Oh, aye, I will go to him, but at the head of a force that will bring his demise. We must rouse our fellow countrymen again and rid ourselves of these oppressors. We will never be a free people under their yoke. But I *will* have his daughter. That much, I swear."

"And I shall be by your side, my brother. I will have my revenge also," replied Morcar.

The two Saxon aristocrats immediately began to plan for insurrection again. This time, they determined, they would not lose.

And so it happened that a goodly number of men reacted to the numerous envoys that were sent into all parts of the country to incite good men to become the comrades-in-arms of Earls Edwin and Morcar. All, it seems, were more than a little unhappy with their lot in life, and were more than happy to conspire against the man they still saw as their enemy. They all made firm oaths to fight to the very last man against the Normans.

Chapter 11

To York

It was the time when I became involved in the first outbreak in the lands north of the Humber. It was upon an unusually warm afternoon for the time of year, just after the sun had climbed to its highest point in the sky, and we worked with the sheep in the fields, that Cerdic rode toward us. We stopped in our labours, stretched our aching backs, and watched as he approached. He drew his horse to a stop and addressed us.

"My villagers, I have news."

He dismounted from his horse, and a young lad took the reins from him. We then sat upon the Earth and waited for what our thegn had to say. We all liked Cerdic. We would listen to anything he had to tell us, and most of us would have followed him to the ends of the world. Sadly, now, he is long dead, but I shall never forget his kindness to us.

We drew our jugs of ale from the field bank and took a drink. We always kept them near to quench the terrible thirst that a man can work up in the fields. I offered mine to Cerdic, but he politely declined.

"There is insurrection in the land."

At that, we all started, though I know not why. It was nothing more than we had expected. How could a proud people like ourselves live happily under foreign invaders?

Cerdic continued, “Edwin and Morcar are rousing men to rebel against William. Many men are arming and coming together. We too must make plans to defend ourselves against the inevitable backlash.”

“What shall we do, Cerdic?” Benjamin asked.

“We must gather together all of the weapons we have. Make sure that they are sharp. Benjamin, we entrust some of that to you, though every man must see that his own weapons are ready for whatever comes.”

“We would be no match for Norman troops as we are. We should use the land to protect us,” I said, “We must prepare to defend ourselves in the forests and by the rivers and wetlands.”

There were nods and mutterings of agreement.

“But what of the cities, Cerdic? Will they fight too, or will they give way to the Normans?”

“I do hear that York is simmering with disgruntlement. The Archbishop is calling for calm and trying to appease the people.”

At that point, Cerdic paused. We looked into his face to try to discern what would come next, though I think that many of us knew.

"I will travel, again, to York to see how the land lies, and, should I judge that an uprising is practical, then I will pledge myself to the cause. I would not ask that any man comes with me, but…"

We looked from one to another. Our thegn knew that we felt great loyalty to him, but he was loath to bring pressure upon us to leave our families and put ourselves in danger again.

"I will go with you, Cerdic," I said.

"And I too," said Benjamin.

"I enjoyed my last visit to that part of the world," he said, mischievously.

We grinned as we all knew what he meant. It was at York that we sacked the evil Earl Tostig's headquarters, and at Stamford Bridge that Benjamin finally took his revenge upon the vile man, who had once cut off the smith's ear in a fit of temper. More churls spoke up until we had a force of six men who would travel with Cerdic. We thought no less of the men who would not join us. They had families to care for. Why should they put their lives at risk again when the land was now occupied by our former enemies?

During that afternoon's toil, I tried to think of a way I would tell my mother that I was off with Cerdic again. I dreaded her reaction, and I was not wrong when I finally broached the subject over the evening meal.

***

When we arrived in York, we found Cerdic's information correct. There was great unrest in the city, and many men were secretly, and not so secretly, arming themselves for whatever might be their fate.

We tramped the filthy streets, dodging around scraps that had been thrown from kitchens and the stinking muck of human waste. Dogs ran around, picking up any remnants of anything edible. Kites soared in the sky, waiting to scavenge dead animals and offal thrown away by the butchers.

We eventually found lodgings at an inn and settled there for the evening to eat a meal and quench our thirst with the house ale. It was not the most wholesome inn I had ever seen. The rushes on the floor were soiled and should have been replaced days ago. The drinking pots and platters looked as if they had not seen water for some time, and I wiped old crumbs of what looked like bread from around the lip of my pot before I filled it with weak ale.

We listened to the conversations going on around us. It was a very varied story. Some men insisted that

William would never dare to come this far north and tackle the people of Northumbria. Others bemoaned the situation and forecast all sorts of miseries that they thought the Norman would inflict upon us.

"And how can we defend ourselves against the might of William the Bastard?" one man asked, "It will be the very death of many of us."

I looked across at the man. He was past his best and thickset, his face stubbled with a growth of whiskers.

"What sort of a man are you, Earh?" another asked, "Will you meekly bend the knee and lick the filth off the boots of the Norman without as much as a whimper of discontent?"

This man was much younger and big and rangy.

"I fear the Norman, Aglaeca, as any sensible man would. Has he not beaten us at every event? Has he not strengthened his cruel grip upon us so that we dare not so much as breathe too heavily, lest his sword comes down upon us?" Eahr replied.

"Do you never tire of flapping your gums, old man? You are a coward. We all know that. You wish things were different, but wishing is for those who don't have the gumption to go out and make things happen!"

At this, the older man rose from his bench and pulled a knife from his belt.

"You have insulted me once too often, Aglaeca," he said, and he lunged with the knife for the young man's chest.

The young man twisted away from the blade, but it caught him in the large muscle of his upper arm. He swore loudly and grabbed the wrist of his assailant with his good arm. He twisted it and, as he was a powerful man, the crack of Eahr's bone echoed around the alehouse. A terrible cry left his lips, and the older man looked incredulously at his arm, now twisted in a strange manner never intended for the limb when the Lord made it.

Aglaeca winced as he pulled the knife from his arm and hurled it at his attacker. It hit the old man solidly, with a deep thud, and penetrated his shoulder.

"You have killed me!" the old man wailed.

"You will live; more's the pity," spat Aglaeca, "If I had wanted to kill you, the knife would have been through your heart by now, and you would be on your way to meet your maker."

Some of the old man's friends, who had watched the whole thing as we had done, now rallied to his side and withdrew the knife from his wound. They pressed a dirty cloth onto the deep cut to help stem the flow of red that was staining his shirt front. Once they had done that, they took him from the alehouse, and we never did see him again. I cannot tell you whether the old man survived his injuries or not, though a cleaner cloth to bind the wound would have increased his chances.

The younger man —Aglaeca— took off his woollen shirt and doused the wound in his upper arm with ale from his jug. Blood and ale spattered onto the floor and made the stinking rushes even more filthy. The landlord brought him a clean scrap of cloth of linen, and his friends tied it tightly around the cut.

Cerdic spoke to the young man.

"You are a quick fighter, my man. Had you not been, I fear that you would have ended the night with the angels. Tell me, what do you see of the state of affairs we find ourselves in, here in Northumbria? Will there be an insurrection? Will the Norman come to engage in combat with us?"

The young man stared at us and glanced at his friends before answering the question.

"William will come. He will have to."

At this he leaned closer to us, across the bench, as if he was afraid of others listening (I found this quite amusing, as he had no idea who we were).

"There is a great uprising, even as we speak, in Mercia," he paused, "It is led by Edwin and Morcar," this we already knew, "And, I can tell you that…" and he paused again, "That Edgar Aetheling and

Gospatric are also amongst the number of leading men, who are involved in the struggle."

At this, we all started. This *was* news. We did not realise that Edgar was involved, much less Gospatric. Had he not purchased Northumbria from William not so long ago? Had he not sworn to be the king's man? And yet, he had broken his oath to support insurrection. Breaking an oath was a serious thing to do. And now, with two of his earls foully murdered and one betraying him by changing sides, William must surely have decided to intervene in the wilder north of his kingdom. What now?

***

We had been in York for some days, watching and listening to what happened. We sought to gauge the feeling and atmosphere before we committed ourselves to any cause. Cerdic, on occasion, disappeared for a while, coming back to our group very obviously with matters on his mind. We knew that he was meeting with other thegns and leading citizens of the city, but we never questioned him, simply relying upon him to tell us what he could.

On one day, we lounged in a square in the middle of the city, enjoying the warm sunshine upon our faces and admiring the comely wenches who bustled about their business when Cerdic returned to us from one of his 'disappearances'.

"I must speak with you," he said, with urgency in his voice.

We sloped off to a small plot of green turf within the city walls and sat in the sunshine to hear him out. He lost no time in telling us what he had gleaned.

"The king has ridden to Warwick and Nottingham, where he is building castles to suppress the local population and is leaving trustworthy knights to guard them," Cerdic continued, "From Nottingham, the Norman has sent a messenger in the form of Archbishop Ealdred, to York with a message. He is to march to the city but has promised safe conduct to all of the thegns of the city and its surroundings, provided that they gather here and swear their fealty to him. He has further said that they would keep their holdings of land."

"Why would William be so lenient to men who have threatened his rule?" I asked.

"It is hard to say," replied Cerdic, "But I am uneasy about the whole thing."

And here, Cerdic paused again for some time. We searched his face and knew that he had further news for us but was pondering how he could tell us.

He began again, "I have heard that Edwin and his brother have already surrendered, too afraid of the prospect of battle with William and that they have sought the king's pardon. It seems that William has granted his pardon, though it remains to be seen if he is as good as his word in this case. I, personally, doubt it. The man has not got a good record in such affairs."

We all looked at one another. Had Edwin and Morcar, who had trumpeted their resistance and promised to fight to rid us of the Normans, really lost their nerve?

"And what of our Northumbrian leaders, Gospatric and Maerleswein?" I asked.

"It is my understanding that all of the noble Northumbrians have decided to avoid the wrath of the king and the imprisonment that all must fear, and have sailed to Scotland, with Edgar and his family, back into the arms of Malcolm."

We were incredulous. Could it be so? Could the Northumbrians really have fled the field of battle? What would become of us now?

"We must pack our belongings and away home," said Cerdic, "I fear that, despite William's promises, we will be better at home when he arrives here."

And so it was that we hurriedly gathered our belongings and made our way back to our village.

***

It was but a few days later that Cerdic rode into the village. He sat his horse, refusing the hospitality we offered him.

“I must speak with you, and then I must go to see the Abbot. It seems that, when William arrived in York, he broke his oath to the thegns. He has imprisoned them to a man and distributed their lands to the Normans. We escaped at the right time.”

And with that, he turned his horse and rode off along the riverbank to the abbey.

Chapter 12

A Bishop and a King

"Ah Aethelwine," said William, as the Bishop of Durham entered his hall. Aethelwine was a short and stocky man whose head was as bald as an egg. He tended to sweat quite profusely, particularly when flustered and afraid, as he was on this particular day.

"My Lord, I made every haste here when I was told that you required my presence," and he pulled, nervously, at the collar of his undershirt.

His face was reddened, and beads of sweat stood out upon his forehead. But at least, he thought, he seemed to have returned to the king's favour.

"Humph! Quite so," muttered the king as he looked through scrolls of parchment on the table before him. He waved a hand.

"Sit down, Aethelwine," he said, and the Bishop hurriedly pulled out a stool and sat upon it.

He was still and quiet, not wanting to interrupt William whilst he hunched over the parchments. At length, the king looked up at the clergyman.

"Aethelwine, you are a loyal and trusted servant of the crown."

"Oh, yes, Sire. Yes indeed," interjected the Bishop.

William harrumphed again, a little irritated by the fawning clergyman.

"I would have you carry out a task for me."

"Oh, anything you require, Sire. I would be only too honoured."

By this time, the monarch was tiring of the obsequious little man before him. From the corner of his eye, he glimpsed a guard snigger. He shot a glance at the man, and his face immediately returned to a stern gaze.

"I want you to travel, yet again, as my emissary to the court of Malcolm of Scotland. I would know how the land lies with him. I know that many rebels have fled to Malcolm's protection, and I need to know what his intentions are. I have it on good authority that Malcolm has been wooed by the rebels, and that he has already prepared a strong force of men to join with them and give them aid."

Aethelwine bobbed his head in response to the king's orders.

"I will, of course, ride immediately, with an entourage, to Malcolm's court and ascertain exactly what his intentions are."

"I would have you point out to Malcolm that such a force arrayed against me would, of course, sour relations between our two countries, and I might need to consider what…action I might need to take as a consequence."

Aelthelwine bobbed his bald head again, and the light seemed to glint from its shiny surface.

"I understand perfectly, Sire."

"I have prepared this parchment with a letter to Malcolm, which I would have you deliver to him by hand."

The priest nodded his understanding again and sat on his stool, gazing at the king.

"As soon as possible, Aethelwine," William growled, and the little priest leapt to his feet and, backing away, took his leave of the king.

***

A short while after this day, William was informed by a patrol that his Bishop of Durham and an entourage of monks were returning from their mission to Scotland. In due course, a servant entered the room and announced the arrival. Aethelwine, as usual, shuffled busily into the room and bowed low to the king. With him was a group of Scottish envoys.

"What news, Aethelwine?" William enquired.

The priest stopped his bowing and scraping, and approached the king.

"My Lord," he said, a smile slashing his face with a look of self-satisfaction, "It is well. I spoke to Malcolm at some length and put to him the…'options' you outlined in your parchment. He listened to all I had to say, and we came to an understanding. He has no intentions of joining the rebels and has sent these ambassadors to swear obedience and fealty to yourself on Malcolm's behalf."

One by one, the Scottish ambassadors approached the king and bowed, and their leader presented him with a scroll from Malcolm.

"My lord, my king, Malcolm of Scotland greets you and assures you that he bears no antagonism toward the rightful King of England. He swears fealty to Your Majesty and is certain that our two countries can live at peace now and in the future."

William nodded to the envoys.

"It is good that there will be no rivalry and hostility between our people. I look forward to our future co-operation. You will, of course, join my court for dinner this evening, where we can further explore how we can ensure peace in the land."

The envoys bowed low and left the king's presence. William sat back in his chair and smiled to himself. He had Malcolm in the palm of his hand. That would seriously weaken any dissent in the north of his realm.

William now turned to his advisers, who had sat quietly, enjoying the performance of the Bishop of Durham and the Scottish ambassadors.

"We shall return home. Make immediate preparations. But we will not return directly. I wish to visit some of our regions to ensure that they are suitably strengthened so that our will is enforced."

He studied maps of the land before him.

"We will travel to Lincoln, Huntingdon and Cambridge on the way. Here, we will begin the erection of castles. Make provision for each to be garrisoned strongly so the Saxons are kept in their place. We will tolerate no further uprisings."

And so it was. William did everything he said he would, and his grip on the land was secure…for now.

Chapter 13

Eadnoth the Staller and Death in the Countryside

Did I say that the land was secure? When has it ever been secure? Certainly, there were people amongst the Normans who felt the land was anything but secure. I shall tell you further tales of the happenings in our land as I heard them.

It seems that many Norman families were torn apart by their Duke's venture into our land. During the turbulent times, many of the Normans serving William here had sensibly left their wives and families at home until the country could be subdued enough to be safe for their arrival.

But now, it seems, a number of the wives, left behind in Normandy, sent messages to their menfolk, pleading with them to return home. It is said that some of the wives, too scared to come to England, actually threatened their husbands that they would take 'other husbands' if their men did not return. Oh, but what a dilemma they faced, these men of Normandy.

If they returned to their lands across the sea and to their wives and families, they would be scorned and dishonoured as traitors to the cause, but what dishonour might be brought to them by their wilful wives? Several Normans did, indeed, leave our shores but were never to return to take up the lands that William had granted them.

I am happy to say that my own choice of wife has never presented me with such problems, but oh, how some men suffer at the hands of a spouse! Take careful note, my fine fellows.

***

But I digress. I cannot say whether William thought his new realm was secure or not, but I doubt it, as he was a shrewd man. And it came to pass, as they say in the Bible, that more trouble came to haunt him, this time in the shape of Harold's sons.

The sons and their families had fled to Ireland after the Battle of Hastings and the uproar in the land that followed it. They were taken in by King Dermot, who had given their father and Uncle Leofwine shelter in 1051.

The trouble began when a naval force, under Godwine Haroldson, sailed, unchallenged, into the mouth of River Avon. No one had considered that the family would pose any threat to the country now, but passionate men find it hard to give up on a long-held dream and a heritage that they believe is rightly theirs.

The ships were hauled up onto a secluded and deserted beach, and the Saxons disembarked, heavy with weapons, and made their way quietly to the surrounding villages. To their eternal shame, the men who had once been our earls and protectors were soon engaged in the plunder of what little the villagers had, leaving their kind in greater destitution as if they had not enough to contend with by living simply in these terrible times. Life was short and often brutal for the poor, and Harold's sons made it shorter and even more brutal.

The Saxon 'invaders' soon made their way to Bristol. They stood one morning, upon a small hillock, surveying the scene before them. The good people of Bristol, it seemed, knew nothing of their landing and pillaging the countryside, and appeared to be going about their daily tasks, blissfully unaware of the threat to them.

"I think that the good people of Bristol will receive us well," said Godwine, a look of quiet satisfaction spread across his face.

So far, this incursion had gone well, and they had encountered little opposition, save for a few 'stupid villagers' who had tried to defend what little they had.

His brother, Edmund, grinned.

"I am sure they will treat us with nothing but courtesy."

"Move forward!" bawled Godwine, and the band of warriors broke cover from the trees upon the hillock and began an advance upon Bristol.

Within the city, however, their progress *had* been followed, and a force of men-at-arms and local people had already gathered weapons and were ready to resist. The great gates swung open, and Godwine, a little surprised, thought that the people were about to receive him as the true heir to the throne. However, a steady stream of armed men began to emerge to meet the Saxon warriors approaching their homes.

Godwine held up a gloved hand, and the warriors halted.

"What is this?" he breathed, "It seems that the good men of Bristol are prepared to mount a defence against us."

"These are not simple villagers, Brother," said Magnus, as the steady stream of armed men became a flood.

The Saxon warriors looked at each other.

"This is a fyrd of levied men." (Levied men = conscripts)

"Nevertheless, I am sure that we can subdue such a rabble. We go forward."

And with that, the Saxons formed up and began to approach the men of Bristol.

Soon enough, the two parties came together.

"As the son of Harold and rightful king of this land, I demand entry to this place!" called Godwine.

"You have no claim upon this place," a voice replied, "We have heard of your pillaging across the countryside and are ready to repel you with all the might we can muster."

Godwine scowled.

"Shield-wall advance!" he cried, and the Saxon warriors tramped forward, their shields interlocked and weapons at the ready.

There was a great thud as the shields came together, and men screamed oaths at each other across the wooden wall. Axes and swords swung and came down upon shields and heads. Shields and weapons were ripped from hands, and men died where they stood.

The battle raged on for some time. The smell of fear and death invaded every nostril, and the ground became slick with English blood, spilt this time by Englishmen. But it has to be said that, as the battle went on, the death toll was greater on the side of the invaders than the men of Bristol. It soon became clear to the Haroldsons that retreat was the only option for their warriors, and they gradually moved backwards, fighting for their lives, until a call went up from the commander of the Bristol men to stand still. There was little point in pursuing the invaders, who were very obviously on the back foot, and no point at all in more Bristol men losing their lives. Godwine's men, shaken, retreated to their ships and put out again into the Bristol Channel, carrying away the plunder they had already taken.

And that, you would presume, was that. Oh, how little you still understand our land and people. Did you think that Harold's sons would meekly return to Ireland and lick their wounds? No, there was more bloodshed to come.

Godwine's men, once recovered from the battle at Bristol, sailed their ships to the coast of Somerset and began, again, with the plundering. Still, innocent men and women died. Still, they were little satisfied with what they had taken. The greed of men knows no bounds!

But it was in Somerset that they met their match again, in the person of Eadnoth the Staller. The 'staller' was the Constable of the area, and Eadnoth was a great landowner and a powerful man. It is said that he owned no less than thirty holdings from Devonshire and Dorset to Somerset and Wiltshire. He had been Harold's master-of-horse. And soon, he found himself, again, at the head of the fyrd, threatened by the sons of that same king. It must have pained him greatly, as he had watched these sons grow up into men and had known them closely. But fight them he must, if they were to threaten the fragile peace of the land and the lives of his own people.

On one fine day, with a gentle swell upon the sea, Godwine sailed his diminishing fleet into the mouth of the River Axe, near the small settlement of Bleadon in Somerset. The name 'Bleadon' means 'coloured hill' —I know not why it was named thus— and it lay within the Winterstoke Hundred. Its people were, in the main, of farming stock, like myself.

Magnus Haroldson stood on the prow of his boat and watched the countryside as the fleet ground onto the mud. Soon, the Saxon warriors were disembarked again.

"We shall see what the good people of Somerset have to offer us," he called to his men, "Since they seem not to desire our presence in the land of our birth, then they should, at least, provide us with some booty to make our lives more tolerable at the court of Dermot."

His men chortled at his wit and unloaded the weaponry they intended to use to their advantage. Soon, all was ready, and Godwine's men began to make their way inland, doubtless, dreaming of the plunder they might take from the poor souls unfortunate enough to be in their path.

Soon, the Saxons approached that small village of Bleadon and were there, taken aback, when a large force of the local fyrd rode and marched across their path, forming before them.

Godwine, a tall man, well-muscled and strong, his blond hair hanging to his shoulders beneath his helmet, stood and looked over the opposition that seemed to have appeared from nowhere. His eagle eyes scanned the faces of the leaders as best they could beneath the helmets each man wore.

"It is Eadnoth," he called to his brothers.

The Haroldsons, of course, knew Eadnoth well, as I have said. They had grown up with the man as he had served their father. He had been a loyal and supportive friend to their father, who had valued the man and his advice.

"Eadnoth would oppose us?" said Magnus.

"It is strange, but I thought I had caught a glimpse of the man at Bristol, but I told myself that it could not be," joined Edmund.

"Form up the shield wall," called Godwine, "I will not be denied my birthright by a servant of my father's court!"

And so it happened. The two armies, both English, formed up into the usual formation. Men locked shields and drew their weapons, sharpened for such an encounter. Slowly, slowly, the two sides approached, each man wary and wondering if this day would be his last.

Now Eadnoth sat his great horse behind the front line of the fyrd.

As the two sides came within hailing distance, he called out, "Godwine, there is nothing for you here now. Go back to Dermot and live out your lives there in peace. Only death awaits you in this new land of ours."

"I think that you are the one who should fear death today, Eadnoth," Godwine replied, "For my men will surely defeat you, and then no quarter can be given."

Eadnoth's head sank upon his chest, and he sighed. He looked up again at the forces of the Haroldsons.

"I have no desire for this battle against the sons of the king I loved, but I will defend this land from your pillaging. Be in no doubt of that."

At that, Godwine yelled an oath and called his men forward. Archers from Eadnoth's fyrd pulled back their great bows, and a flurry of arrows looped into the sky and swept down upon the invaders. The shields were lifted, and the deadly rain thudded into the wood. Another flurry followed, and some of Godwine's men fell prey to their sharp barbs.

Still, the forces moved toward each other. Now, each man could see the face of an opponent. But, again, it was Saxon against Saxon, and not against foreign opposition, and many men's hearts sank at the thought of fighting brothers, many of whom had fought at their side at Hastings.

A great thump rang across the field as the two walls came together. Now axes came down upon shields to pull them down and allow men behind to thrust spears and fire arrows at their adversaries. Men screamed as eyeballs were pierced and dragged from their sockets. Spears rammed into throats, and blood sprayed from mouths to cover the combatants.

Eadnoth, by now, had dismounted from his stallion and was fighting alongside his men in the shield wall. He was a large man with huge arms and chest. His great sword rose and fell, accounting for any number of enemy lives. His son, Harding, fought at his father's side.

The battle raged, with one side taking the initiative and then the other. Men fell, shrieking, to the turf, but others were lucky and were dead before they hit the ground. Heads were cut from shoulders, and skulls were split, showering the ground with blood and grey brains to fertilize the crops for years to come.

It was as Eadnoth was lifting his sword to strike a blow at the man before him that disaster struck. An arrow, fired from behind the lines of Godwine's invaders, caught the great man in one side of his neck. The arrowhead emerged from the other side, and the man looked shocked as his knees bent beneath him, and he sank to the ground.

"Father!" Harding cried, and he tried his best to push his way through the crowd of men.

But it was to no avail. When Harding finally managed to reach him, Eadnoth was dead.

Harding rose to his full imposing height and called to his men, "Eadnoth is dead! Avenge his spirit, that it might rest peacefully in the halls of God!"

The fyrd —now Harding's fyrd— redoubled their efforts and gradually began to slaughter the Haroldsons' forces in ever greater numbers. And now it was their turn to lose a leader. Magnus Haroldson, distracted by the death of his father's once loyal servant, glanced away to his right. A great axe came from nowhere and caught him in the shoulder, smashing his bones as a wife smashes an eggshell. He lurched to the side and turned to face his attacker, his arm now hanging useless at his side, just in time to see the axe fall again. This time, it took him on the side of his helmet, caving his skull and closing his eyes forever.

Godwine and Edmund looked on as their brother fell. Neither could believe what he had seen, and thought they must be in the middle of a terrible nightmare. But this was no bad dream, come to torment them at night; this was broad daylight and was very real. Now, their heart went out of them. Their shoulders sank, and each stood and stared at the spot where their brother had been just moments before.

"Retreat!" Godwine yelled to his troops, though his voice was not as strong as it had been, and every man could detect a quaver to it.

The Haroldsons' troops slowly backed away, as they had been forced to do at Bristol, demoralised and broken. Harding called back his men and allowed the warriors to leave with a little dignity. In any case, he was loath to lose more men to a retreating army.

That evening, Godwine's fleet sailed sadly out of River Axe. The Saxon sat on the prow and stared at the wooden floor of the boat. Men say that they could see the wetness of tears upon his cheeks as the boats sailed out to the safety of the sea.

But, although his fleet had been repulsed, Godwine still ravaged the coasts of Cornwall and Devon, determined to sail back to Ireland with enough booty to keep them in the manner to which they were accustomed.

It seems that Harding took over in his father's place, though I believe most of the estate was given to the new Earl of Chester. Harding still kept six manors —enough for any man— but I do wonder how the man felt; his father killed defending the new Norman kingdom, and much of his inheritance then taken from his grasp.

Chapter 14

Flames and Death Come to Durham

Now, you will recall, I have told you how we heard the news that Robert de Comines was to become our new Earl. And you will also recall that we were very resentful of this development. A Norman Earl of Northumberland? Never! I shall tell you a tale of fire and slaughter in the City of Durham and how I became involved in the rebellion.

But who was Robert de Comines, you ask? Well, from what I heard from the monks, he originally came from Comines, in Flanders. He had made himself useful to William and had secured the earldom after it was taken from the rebellious Gospatric.

On a cold, wintry day in January of 1069, a strange man rode into Cerdic's compound. He was not a man we had ever seen before, and we stared as we readied ourselves for a hard day in the woods, gathering firewood. Oh, I shiver, even now, when I think how cold that winter was. A hard frost had held us in its grip since Christmas, and we yearned for the long days of summer when we could lie in the fields in the evening and watch the white clouds scud across bright blue skies. It was a time when life was easier, and we were always warm. In that winter, I don't recall that we *ever* felt warm.

It was not long before the great bell at the church rang out, and, this not being the Sabbath, we knew that our thegn wished to speak to us on a matter of urgency. I think that we all, in our hearts, knew what was afoot. We turned our steps toward Cerdic's compound and were admitted to his hall by a serving girl who, it has to be said, I found rather pretty. I grinned at her as we entered, and she gave me back a shy smile.

The hall was bathed in the light from the blazing fire burning in the grate. Oh, how warm it felt against the bitter air outside. We all tried to manoeuvre ourselves as closely as we could to absorb its warmth into our bones. I could have stood there all day. I looked around at the great room we were in. It must be wonderful, I thought, to live in such a hall as this. Most certainly, it was much more comfortable than the homes that we lived in. But I didn't begrudge the thegn. He had always been good to me and had saved me from the outlaws. I owed the man my life.

Cerdic sat there at his table with the man who had arrived earlier. The visitor was a tall man, not heavily built, but wiry. I recall that he seemed to have huge hands. But then, I was just a boy, and my own hands still had some growth in them, though they were as hard as any man's due to the toil they had seen.

As we assembled, Cerdic and the man continued their low conversation, and we stood there, waiting until the thegn was ready to address us.

At length, the two men nodded to one another, and Cerdic turned and addressed us.

"My people," he said, "I am grateful to you for giving up your time in the fields and woods. I know how busy you all are."

Yes, we were busy, but the chance to warm ourselves was one that we were all enjoying, I am sure.

"The man here before you is Dreng. He comes from…another place."

Cerdic was, obviously, being careful in what he revealed.

"I must tell you the news he brings me. It seems that Robert de Comines rides to Durham in a few short days' time to take up the Earldom of Northumbria, at least north of the River Tees."

There was a good deal of muttering and grumbling from our assembled group, but Cerdic tapped upon the table, and the hubbub died down.

"He brings with him at least seven hundred heavily armed men-at-arms, supplied by William to keep the peace. But the opinion seems to be that there will be little peace for the people of this land of Northumbria. They do say that Robert means to rule us with a rod of iron and that many will perish and go to their maker, either by violence and cruelty or by starvation, as Robert and his henchmen seem to readily take what is not properly theirs."

This was a blow. The whole hall fell silent as men absorbed the information they had been given. Many stared at the floor, deep in thought. Others shook their heads in disbelief that what we feared would now happen. How could this be? What was to be done now?

As we stood there, Cerdic spoke again, "I am sure that there are many who will be wondering what to do and what will become of their lives now. Some of you might conclude that there is little left to do but flee for your lives. To move north and find some area where you will be accepted and might start again. I will stand in the way of no man who decides this is best for his family. Who am I to stop you? I know not what I shall do for the good of my own family as yet. I must ponder it in my heart."

It was a sombre group of men who exited Cerdic's hall that day and trudged to the fields. There were many worried faces, not just a few tears, when men told their wives and families what had been said. What were we to do? It was winter. Where would we go? How would we find food? We couldn't rely upon others to feed us through hard times. I thought of the outlaws who had murdered the tinker and took me captive. They had been moving north to avoid the Normans, just as we would have to do. Would our fate be like theirs?

Although we worked hard in the woods that day, we stopped frequently and discussed the situation laid before us. By the end of the day, most of us had decided that we should gather together what we could and set out at the earliest opportunity for the north. At least there, north of the River Tyne, in the hills, we thought we might be safe for a while until we could find a new home. What heavy hearts we had when we slunk to our beds that winter's night. All night, I thought I could hear the sounds of weeping and wailing drifting across our village on the breeze which had whipped up over the course of the afternoon.

On the following morn, few men went off to their tasks. There was a hustle and bustle about the village as people busied themselves collecting things they would need for their new lives as refugees in their own land. There was much discussion and argument about what should go and what would have to stay. There were the essentials of life, but also the small 'treasures' that all homes have, which the people were loath to leave behind for the Normans. Those small, sentimental things that remind us of our past and those who have gone before us.

As I left our home that morning, I shivered and pulled my cloak about me. I looked at the sky with some concern. The wind had risen even further during the night, and people were battling to hold onto the goods they were packing. Many a child was sent running across the village to catch something cartwheeling away from them. I studied the sky, and it seemed full of heavy white clouds that often foretold a snowstorm. There was a strange, ruddy glow on the eastern horizon. Another warning sign of bad weather to come. How would we cope with travelling if a storm hit?

During that day, we all worked hard, deciding what we should carry away and packing our goods as best we could. As night fell again, flurries of snow drifted across the land, and the air became even colder. We sat around our fire that evening, eating a meal of potage cooked quickly by my mother. But none had any appetite. I picked at it, pausing between each mouthful to ponder our situation until it began to grow cold. There was little conversation during the evening, and we all retired to our beds sooner than would be normal. What was there to stay up for?

I was awoken long before dawn by the screaming of a gale blowing down from the hills. I arose quietly, hoping not to wake my family, and put my head out of the door. Snow was falling thick and fast and drifting across the village to lie in banks against the houses and fences. I could barely see the wooded hills in the background. And I swear that it was the coldest night I can ever remember in all my many years.

As I returned to my bed, my mother spoke softly to me, "We shall not be able to leave now. Not with all of this weather to contend with. We would be dead within a few short days."

I nodded my head.

"We shall see what the morning brings."

When we arose a little before dawn, as we always did, we walked out of our homes upon a terrible scene. The children gasped. They had never seen snow like it in their lifetimes, and I don't think many of us had. Some of the houses had been damaged in the night, and thatch lay upon the ground, partly buried in a cloak of white. One of the pig sties had been blown down, and three dead pigs lay frozen in the snow.

"We cannot leave in this," Benjamin said.

I shook my head.

"No, we shall have to stay here. It could be days or weeks before the lanes will be suitable for travel. We would never survive."

"At least it might also slow down Robert de Comines and his troop of savages," said Benjamin.

And so most of the goods we had packed for the journey were slowly unpacked and returned to their places. I am sure that we all had mixed feelings about our fate. None of us wanted to leave our homes, but what would become of us now?

***

On a brittle-cold day in the deep midwinter, as we settled ourselves back into our homes with our possessions, waiting as we must to see what fate had in store for us, Robert and his troops made their way across the Tees and headed toward Durham, which was to be his headquarters. It was enough that Robert was a Norman, but his treatment of the people he encountered on his journey made us feel as if he was the very Devil himself.

The journey north was a bloody one, as Robert rewarded his men by allowing them to murder and pillage at will. Whole villages were entered and goods stolen, leaving the poor people with little in their already meagre lives. The people themselves, and I speak not only of men but also women and children, were slain, maimed, and abused in the most horrific ways, either because they protested or simply to 'entertain' the troops. I have no idea how many villages heard wails and weeping that winter, but it was many. But for the people of Durham, it was truly a nightmare.

***

It was upon yet another cold and frosty day, with the snow piling up even deeper, that we were huddled together again in Cerdic's hall to hear this terrible news from one of the senior brothers at the abbey. Brother Gerhard was a tall, spindly man with a long, mournful face. To my knowledge, he had never allowed a smile to cross his features. He twitched one side of his face at intervals as if he could not stop himself. He was the perfect person to bring us such grim news.

"...and Robert has even killed men of the church," Gerhard finished.

When we heard the news, there was a stunned silence. Why would the Normans kill us and steal from us, the people they were sent to govern? What point was there to this other than to terrify the people into obedience?

At length, one of our numbers spoke, "What can we do? We cannot hide or flee in this weather. We cannot fight them."

"That is why I have summoned you here today," put in Cerdic, "Fight is exactly what we must do."

We must have looked shocked.

"It will not just be our few men. More men are to gather around Durham to put an end to this. As soon as travel becomes easier, we will move. We shall either end the miserable life of our new earl or die in the attempt. Who amongst you is with me?"

A great cheer went up from the men. Cerdic looked at us and smiled.

"Ready yourselves."

***

Our plotting and scheming took shape in Brockford, at Aclet, the 'village on the cliff' south-west of Durham. Robert de Comines was to meet the Bishop. He had ridden north along the arrow-straight Roman road that was Dere Street. Now Dere Street entered our lands north of the Tees at the old Roman fort of Piercebridge. Here was a large bridge built by those very Romans to allow their troops to travel quickly toward the Great Wall. The next crossing for Robert would indeed be at Aclet, or at least, at the old Roman fort of Vinovia, near the village. At this crossing, the road branched off to the right toward the city of Durham.

The Bishop of Durham, Aethelwine, was already at the small, somewhat rundown inn in Aclet when Robert arrived. The Norman slid from his great horse and passed it to a servant. He strode into the inn, looking around him and curling his nose at what he considered were primitive conditions the English were prepared to live in. Looking down, he saw a dog lying on the floor of beaten Earth, and he savagely kicked it out of his way so that the animal let out a yelp of pain. As it slunk away to a corner, it looked back at him and snarled. Robert approached the Bishop, who stood and bowed his head to the new earl.

The landlord appeared, shuffled across to where the Bishop sat, and placed a large jug of ale upon the table before the two men, with clay pots for them to drink from. Robert took his and studied it carefully to ascertain its cleanliness. Again, he wrinkled his nose and rubbed the pot upon his sleeve before he would allow the landlord to pour the ale.

"My lord Bishop, it is indeed good to be in my earldom. I trust we can work together to hold the area and persuade the people that resistance to their new masters is futile. I have already worked to convince some of the people to the south of that."

"So I have heard," replied Aethelwine.

He had trouble disguising the revulsion at what he knew the man had done and allowed his men to do. He was far from the most popular Bishop of Durham and could be ruthless in his pursuit of power and wealth, but even he had his limits as to what he was prepared to do. The truth was, of course, that Robert paid the wages of his troops by allowing their savagery.

Robert looked at him for a heartbeat, considering the Bishop's words.

"The people must know who rules them, Aethelwine," he said.

"I am sure they are in no doubt, Earl Robert," the Bishop said pointedly, "But what I am bound to do is to warn you of a backlash to your methods. There are many rumours, and many of them will be true, that the people of this land are preparing to rise against you. You must not ride further. Durham will be a dangerous place for you now. You must not enter the city. Turn your men southward and retreat to safety."

"And tell William what?" Robert replied, "That I have turned tail before a rabble of peasants? I have seven hundred of the very best warriors that Normandy can provide. Our force will be invincible."

"My lord, I beg you. Your life is in danger here. I know these people. They are bred from the Norsemen and Danes who held this land before. They are wild and formidable warriors when they are roused. Every man in the city of Durham will be your enemy. Every man will be looking to do you harm."

"Will they indeed?" replied the earl.

He considered his Bishop for another long moment. Evidently, this man would be of no use to him. He had no backbone. Once settled in Durham, he would petition William to have this worm replaced by a real man.

"Perhaps the people of Durham need to understand who is in charge. We ride for Durham on the morrow."

The Bishop sank back into his chair. He knew what Robert meant by this, and he knew the people of Northumbria.

The landlord now approached with a platter of cold meats and bread. He bowed low to the earl before placing it upon the table. The earl looked at the offering for a second.

"What would you have me do with this?" he asked, "Feed it to the hound?"

The landlord glanced at him, fear spreading across his face.

"My lord, it is the best we have. We are not rich people who can afford the best in food. We must make do with what we have. I am sorry that it offends you."

Robert studied the plate of dried-up meat and rough bread. He rose from his place and strode over to the dog. It cowered in the corner. Robert took the meat and flung it at the dog.

"Here," he said, "Though this is hardly fit even for you."

The landlord fingered a large knife but thought better of it, and shuffled back into a room at the rear of the inn, humiliated.

The next day dawned with a brisk breeze blowing across the land. The people of Aclet looked on resentfully as the Norman troops mounted their horses and began to move out. The troops made their way along the road until they reached the steep inclines leading down to the River Wear. Horses slipped and slid, finding keeping their feet difficult on the frozen Earth of the slope. Beneath the wooded hill that slopes down from the fort of Vinovia, they crossed the shallow rapids, luckily not yet in spate from the snowmelt on the hills.

Through woodland and farmland, the troops rode, and more people in our land suffered as a consequence. At length, the procession of warriors neared Durham. Robert held up a gloved hand, and the troops grounded to a halt. He looked at the settlement, with its great promontory, with the River Wear wrapped like a snake around it.

"A good place to defend," he muttered to himself.

By now, the people of Durham knew that he was coming and feared for their lives. They had heard the news of the terrible carnage his men had wrought upon the land. Their hearts beat a little faster in their chests, and many a stomach churned.

Robert and his men moved on and eventually came to the houses scattered around the settlement. Not a person was to be seen. All were behind their doors and shutters, peeping from the smallest cracks. Robert looked from side to side as his horse picked its way up the slope until it reached a small plateau in the centre of the city beneath the summit of the promontory.

The city was silent. He beckoned for his captains to come forward, and five mounted men were soon by his side.

"Deploy the troops. I want every man, woman and child out of their filthy hovels and kneeling to me. How dare they not come out to greet me? They have shown their contempt for their rulers and must be made to pay for it."

The men rode off to brief their troops, and soon, men-at-arms were tearing open doors and wrenching the wretched citizens out onto the streets. Men, women and even tiny children, little more than babes, were roughly dragged to where Robert sat upon his stallion, lofty and imperious. When the space was filled with Saxon citizens, surrounded by Norman troops, Robert addressed the throng.

"I am Robert de Comines. I am your new earl. Let it be known from this day hence that I will tolerate no upheaval or disobedience from any man. I will punish any misconduct severely."

He nodded to one of his captains, whose troops were holding a number of men and women. The soldiers pushed them forward into the space before Robert and forced them to their knees.

"And now you will understand what I mean."

At a nod from Robert, the men-at-arms gored their swords between the shoulder blades of their captives so that they fell dead to the floor. A great wail went up from the captive crowd, and women sobbed. Some of the citizens pushed forward to fall to their knees beside their loved ones, holding them and begging them not to die.

"Now, I think, as I retire to the Bishop's house," said Robert, "My men will search this city for any hidden weapons and will confiscate anything that they see fit to remove. And I am sure they will find plenty to impound to show you snivelling wretches that I mean to maintain order in this city."

And as the Norman rode up the final incline to the house of the Bishop, his men did exactly as they were bid. Homes were ransacked. Larders emptied, and food and ale stolen. Any weapons were quickly seized, and even the tools that men used for their trades were often looted if they were of any use to the soldiers. Men who resisted were beaten to unconsciousness, and even women were slapped and assaulted in the most terrible way.

A child screamed as Norman soldiers entered her home, and a Norman gauntlet struck her to the side of her face so that the bones of her jaw snapped with a crack like a whip. It was a bleak and terrible day for the people of Durham when Robert de Comines arrived in their city.

I am sure Robert sat down that eve and allowed the Bishop's servants to fuss around him. I am also sure that he congratulated himself upon his performance that day. Had he not shown the Saxon rabble what would happen if they stepped out of line in his authority? He was convinced that the 'situation' in the north was now contained.

I am certain that, when he retired to his bed that night, he chuckled to himself at the thought of what his followers were up to in the streets and houses of Durham. If only he had known how his conduct would be repaid.

***

We made our way through the snow upon that bleak and frigid night. Our leather boots and breeches kept out some of the dampness, but, nevertheless, my feet were soaked and squelched whenever I put them upon the Earth. I shivered and pulled my woollen cloak about me, trying to retain what little heat I had left in my body. I wiped my running nose upon my sleeve. My eyes stung with the cold. And still, we marched on.

“Tis a terrible night to be abroad, John,” said Luke, a churl of our village.

“Aye,” I replied, “It would be better to be huddled around the fire with a pot of ale and some of my mother’s honey cakes.”

Luke chuckled at the image of it, and we battled on.

It was not too long until we began to see the outline of Durham against the sky. We left the lane upon which we had approached and made our way down, through woodland, toward the city. We approached as close as we dared to the gates before stopping at the woodland edge to survey the scene.

We could see Norman guards posted around the reinforcements. Slowly, they wandered up and down, peering out into the darkness to catch sight of anything that might be unusual. They looked as cold as we felt. We were almost near enough to hear as they stamped their feet, blew upon their hands, and cursed the winter chill in Norman French. And there we settled, shivering, for the rest of the night.

Very early in the morning, as a crisp dawn broke in the eastern sky, the gates of Durham were opened, and a few of the peasants made their way out to go about their daily chores. The birds roosted for the night against the buildings and began to chatter and call to one another. A red kite soared across the city’s skies, waiting to see what the citizens might throw out that might be scavenged. Dogs barked in the streets, and calls could be heard between the people. What voices we could hear sounded tense, and no laughter carried upon the breeze.

Our leaders began to deploy us in groups to the gates of Durham. A horn blew, and we all knew this was the signal we had been waiting for. We arose and pressed through all the gates and ran through the city streets, seeking out the Normans who had so cruelly mistreated our people. The group I found myself in included Luke and Benjamin, along with a group of men from other villages whom I didn't know.

We ran, hither and thither, along the winding streets, calling to the locals that we meant them no harm, and that they should join us, which a good number did.

We rounded a corner, Luke slightly before me, to pull up sharp before a number of Norman soldiers. They were armed, I recall, with swords and spears, and held shields before them. They were dressed in chain armour and us in leather jerkins. What were we to do?

They looked as startled as we must have done, and time seemed to stand still. Slowly, the Normans, perhaps coming to their senses more quickly than we did, began to move forward, beating their swords upon their shields, a look of determination in their steely eyes. We, for our part, began to retreat along the narrow alleyway, not knowing what else to do.

Suddenly, seemingly from nowhere, another band of Saxon villagers poured around the far corner behind the Norman troops. I permitted myself a smile as I realised that the Normans were now pinned into the alley with no means of escape. Of course, the Normans also realised their plight, and some swivelled to meet the new distraction.

Now, we pressed them. Slowly, slowly, we moved toward them, our shields up before us now, and our weapons banging out an ominous beat upon them. Eventually, both of our groups had forced them into a tight space before a tanner's shop. And then the killing began.

We could see the fear in the Norman eyes as our two walls of warriors met. We hammered shield upon shield and, as the pressure was coming from two sides, it caused the Normans to fall back against each other. Men lost their grip upon the frozen street and lurched backwards to the floor. Axes fell heavily upon shields, which were wrenched from Norman hands. Our spears came into play, and we aimed them at the parts of the body not covered in mail. Spearheads pierced flesh and were ripped out again with a sickening squelch, and men screamed upon the trodden Earth.

Now, we were close enough to deploy swords, and my own, taken from the battlefield of Senlac Hill, was gainfully employed. Time after time, I slashed at flailing Norman arms and legs, inflicting terrible injuries and severing limbs to the bone. Blood flowed onto the frozen Earth, as it does in battles such as these, and the street soon became slick with it. Now, down and at our mercy, I fought my way forward and used my short seax to send men screaming to their deaths.

As the last man died, we turned again and left the blood-soaked alley for other streets. What we found was much the same as the scenario we had left behind.

Norman bodies were strewn across the narrow lanes, many with terrible injuries that spoke not just of killing the enemy but of making him suffer before he left this world. Body parts lay in filthy gutters. Men lay with their guts exposed to the chill winds. Empty eyes stared up at the heavens, where their spirits soon would be.

As the Normans fled, trying to seek sanctuary in the Bishop's house, slingers hurled rocks at their retreating backs. Men fell to the ground, their wind beaten from their chests, and Saxons and citizens alike fell upon them, slaughtering them where they fell like pigs in a pen.

We made our way through Durham, up to the Bishop's house upon the hill. Every street was covered with the slime of blood and human offal and filled with dead bodies. But when we arrived, at last, at the bolt-hole of Robert de Comines, we found a considerable number of the earl's associates and soldiers guarding it. We tried a number of assaults upon the building but to no avail. We were beaten back at every attempt, and the Saxons were dying in each attempt. Clearly, another tactic must be used. We fell back to a safe distance and considered our position.

Cerdic had now joined us with his little band of men. I was relieved to see that all of our village men in his group had survived, though others of his number from other villages, I noticed, were missing.

"What shall we do?" I asked as the thegn stood, pondering.

"We could lay siege, I suppose," he replied, stroking the grey beard which covered his chin.

"Or we could burn them out," chipped in Benjamin the smith, "It would not be difficult to throw fire at the house, and it would burn like tinder."

Cerdic smiled.

"Then make up a goodly fire, Benjamin," he chortled.

The smith did just as he was bidden, and, in a smithy a short distance away, Benjamin and the man who owned it were soon busily stoking the fires. It was not long before men were bringing lumps of burning wood to the Bishop's house. Men had wrapped cloth around their arrows and now lit them and sent them flying into the more easily burning parts of the house. Other men ran forward with fire held in tongs and on spikes and threw it at doors, over walls and onto the roof. In a very short time, smoke began to rise from the building, and flames licked around it.

As the house burned, sparks flew upward from the roof timbers. Many were blown upon the wind and alighted on the west tower of the church, which lay nearby. We looked on in horror as a terrible tragedy began to take shape before our eyes. Would we destroy God's house, along with the evil Norman? Men and women fell to their knees in prayer and begged St. Cuthbert to intervene and save his church from burning. And then a miracle happened.

I would not have believed it had I not witnessed it with my own eyes. I swear that the wind changed to the east and drove the sparks and flames from the church, and the fire upon it died. The house, however, continued to burn with an ever-increasing ferocity.

Now the doors opened, and some of Robert's associates, along with those of the Bishop, spilt forth, coughing to free their chests of the suffocating smoke. But Saxon men waited for them at the doors, weapons in hands, and slaughtered them as soon as they emerged. Bodies fell and blocked the way of men behind them. Many went back into the blaze they knew would surely end their lives.

When the house was little more than charred timbers and broken walls, and some heat had left it in the chill January air, we moved in and picked our way through the ruins. Men found odd things amongst the rubble that would still be of some value, and took them.

As we stirred the ashes with our swords, I came upon many bodies, now almost unrecognisable as the people they once were. I moved a fragment of timber beam to reveal another corpse in the ashes. Little of its human form was left, but a number of metal articles, some melted and twisted out of shape, remained. I picked them up and showed them to a man from Durham beside me.

"They belonged to the earl," he said, "I saw him with them only yesterday. That is the sword he carried, though its scabbard is long gone to the flames. And that is the brooch that held his cloak. I would know it anywhere. He wore it as he struck my daughter and broke the bones of her jaw. May he rot in hell," he added.

And so the earl was dead. Of the Bishop, we could see no sign, though men said that they were unsure if he had returned home.

All at once, a voice cried out, "We have won!"

A man of Durham had found a Norman soldier crouched within an outbuilding. He was wounded and a little scorched by the ferocity of the flames but was otherwise alive.

"Kill him!" yelled another man, and men ran with swords raised, ready to execute their prisoner.

"No!" barked Cerdic, "Let him be. Let him crawl back to his master and tell him of what happened here today. Let us see how he likes that."

And so it was that the Norman soldier was stripped of all belongings, except for the few light clothes that he stood up in, and was cast out of Durham into the bitter cold of winter to make his miserable way back to William with our message.

As we trudged back through the littered streets of Durham, the local people were beginning to clear away the bodies before the dogs, the crows and the kites could begin their grisly feast. Some men were trying to dig a shallow grave through the frosted Earth outside the city, and others simply stripped the corpses of anything of value and then threw them into the river to float downward with the current to the sea. We stopped for awhile and helped in the gruesome task.

As we toiled, some of the men began to look up. An apparition appeared upon the road. This was no ghostly presence but the Bishop of Durham. With a small troop, he rode into the city and sat his horse, gazing down at the carnage before him. He shook his head sadly.

"I tried to turn him in his tracks," he said to the now assembling crowd, "I told him that it was folly to come here. That the men of Northumbria would not accept him, and that there would be bloodshed."

A man of Durham, who had ridden with the Bishop to Aclet, confirmed this.

"Aye," he said, "What the Bishop says is true to the facts. The Bishop should shoulder no blame for the deeds of Robert and his barbarians."

"People of Durham," the Bishop called, "I have news. Edgar the Aetheling comes with the exiled Northumbrians to York. How many of you will follow me to York, where we will meet up with them and take back that city?"

A great cry went up, "To York!"

Chapter 15

York —again!

It was a little while later, in February, having gathered our weapons and a few useful belongings about us, that we marched off south.

This time, our destination was York. To his credit and perhaps 'drunk' from his own success, the Bishop had gathered together quite a force of men. News of what had happened in Durham had spread like wildfire across the region. Even in the snowy conditions we had to bear during those bitter winter days, which made travel difficult. As we walked, men joined us now from other villages, emboldened by what we had achieved. Perhaps they now felt that there was hope and that we could take our fate into our own hands and resist the Norman invaders.

I did think of my own family at that time. We had told everyone in our own village the news of what had happened in Durham when we returned, and my family were overjoyed that I had survived again and was well, and I hoped that, perhaps, they were at least a little proud of me. I also knew that my mother would sleep little while I was away again. She tried to show a brave face to the family, but I knew that deep inside her, like any mother, her heart was sore with the worry of it all as we had made preparations to leave again.

And so, we assembled again in Durham, from where the road ran south —the same road that had brought Robert de Comines to his fiery death. The distance was a little over 75 miles, and, in good conditions and walking hard and fast, we could have done it in three days. Now, in the grip of winter, it took us five days to complete our journey.

And what deprivations we endured. Men's toes froze in their boots and became blackened. Our faces were pinched with the cold, and my eyes were sore from walking in the bitter wind. The little food we had was provided by Cerdic and the Bishop and by kindly villagers as we passed through their settlements, though Lord knows they had little enough to share.

We were always pleased if villagers took us in at night, where we could huddle around a warm fire. But there were many of us to accommodate. Nights, crouched in a woodland glade in the bitter cold of February, were little more than a nightmare.

As we approached York, it soon became clear that Edgar, Maerleswain and Gospatric were already in the city and had made a treaty with most of the leading citizens. Under William Malet, the Norman garrison was holed up in the new wooden castle that the king had erected and under heavy siege. Not a mouse could stir from that tower or around it without someone seeing it, I thought.

At the gates of the new Norman castle, I glanced briefly up at a man who appeared to stand there as if watching us. But then I looked again, realising that the man was looking at us with empty eyes.

Robert Fitz Richard, a Norman commander, was propped up on a stake, seemingly staring out at us. But those eyes would never look out over York or any other city again, for his throat was cut, and Robert was dead.

And this is how we found York when we became part of the besieging army of the Norman Castellan, William Malet, and his troops.

***

I later heard that William Malet, the Castellan, was a great companion of the Conqueror and had been at the Battle of Hastings. He was, of course, a wealthy man with lands of great beauty, men said, in Normandy. He owned a great castle at Graville-Ste-Honorine, at the mouth of the River Seine, near Harfleur. Legend has it that William Malet's mother was English and that he was no less than the uncle of King Harold's wife. I don't know whether this was true or just men's gossip.

Malet did fight for William at Hastings. Of that, there was no doubt. Indeed, the story has it that when Harold's broken body was brought into the Duke's camp, the Conqueror gave it to Malet for burial and would not permit it to be given to Harold's grieving mother —by now a broken woman— who had offered her son's weight in gold for its return.

And so it was that this self-same Malet was confined to his keep in the city he was supposed to rule as Castellan. But still, the man was not without influence and cunning, for a Norman soldier was, I heard, smuggled out of York under the cover of darkness by some of the townsmen who favoured the new regime. He was sent, with all speed, to William to tell him of the situation and to beg that the king would come rapidly to relieve the garrison before he was compelled to surrender.

And so, we settled in and took our turn at besieging the castle of York. All in all, life was cold and boring, and men sat around in the inns and houses, and played games, drank, sang, swore and fought amongst themselves. I longed for my own village and family again, for clean air and a warm fire, but knew that I must stay, at least for a while, until others were mobilised and arrived to relieve us of our duties.

It was a short while later —I don't know how many days— that a rider galloped through the gates of York and came to a halt before the hall where the leaders were accommodated.

"I bring news!" he screamed, "William comes with many troops!"

Well, that threw everyone into a frenzy of confusion. Men urgently called to each other, spreading the news, and talked about what this news might mean for us. Confidence suddenly seemed to fade in many men. Could we stand firm and resist William, or would we all be murdered where we stood when his troops entered the city? The locals, too, of course, were in a state of dread. What would become of them? They were, after all, the ones who began this state of affairs.

As we stood around in the streets, not knowing what to do, Cerdic rushed into the hall to attend a meeting of the leaders and the thegns. It was but a short while before he emerged again into the spring sunshine. His face was flushed, and he seemed flustered by what he had heard.

"Gather together what you will. We must leave York within the hour."

"Will we not stand firm?" Luke asked.

"It seems the earls have decided that we cannot hold against William and his troops," Cerdic replied, "They have decided to abandon the mission and return to Malcolm in Scotland."

"What?" I gasped, "We have come this great distance to stand firm with the people of York and the earls, and now they say that they will abandon us?"

Cerdic looked forlorn.

"I am sorry, my friends. I have brought you here, along with the Bishop, to try to reclaim Northumbria from the invaders, and this is how you are rewarded. Collect everything you need. We must leave now or face death."

And so it was that we left the city, packs over our shoulders, along with a steady stream of men from other villages and even some of the residents, to escape the wrath of our new king. However, some men remained, determined to resist the Normans at all costs. I wished them luck, but now I thought them foolhardy. I had a terrible feeling of disappointment at what we were doing, and not a little cowardly, but I had to think of my family.

As we were emerging from the city gates and turning our steps back to the north, we heard a great noise. It was as if a great thunder was drumming in our ears. It was the sound of horses' hooves on frozen ground. Still from a good distance, across the Vale of York, we could see mounted men approaching. Banners flew from great poles. William was here.

“To the woods!” Cerdic cried, and we all turned and ran for the cover of a nearby copse at the edge of a wood.

There was little cover in the woodland, at that time of year, from the bare branches of winter, and the icy winds whistled through, unbroken, chilling us to the bone. But still, we lay there, looking around the trees from ground level, where we were less likely to be seen but could observe at least something of what was about to happen.

The great army now approached the city, and men still in the open fled in all directions like headless chickens. At a call from their commanders, the Norman soldiers fanned out and pursued every living being. Oh, the carnage! Men were brought down by great swords, wielded from horseback, and fell like autumn leaves upon the Earth. Spears and lances pierced leather jerkins and brought men screaming to their knees, only to fall upon their faces, dead to the world. I tried to turn away from the scene but found that I couldn’t. I was almost in a dream-like state, and my eyes were riveted on the orgy of blood-letting.

William’s men now entered the city, and the carnage continued. It seemed not to concern the Normans that innocent men, women and children alike were sent to their maker that day. We were later told that the death toll of men ran to many hundreds.

Once the city was overpowered, the Normans began a rampage of looting, burning and violence.

We could not see this bloodbath, but we could certainly hear it, so close were we to one of the gates of York. I shall never forget the shrieks and wails that carried on the cold afternoon air as men were put to the sword and sent to their God in all manner of unspeakable ways. But still, we lay there upon the bitter ground, hardly daring to breathe in case a Norman soldier should detect our presence. Some men, and I am not ashamed to admit that I was one of them, wept bitter, silent tears onto the Earth that day.

By evening, the city was quiet, and little seemed to stir other than the smoke from many fires that told not of cooking, but of burning buildings. We could still hear occasional laughter and calls in Norman French. Even St Peter's Minster was looted and left a ruin, and most of the city was plundered, trampled upon and despoiled. Why would a Christian king desecrate a Minster? Perhaps to further punish the people of the city, I suppose.

When darkness truly fell, we dared to move again, collected what we could carry and made our way toward safety. We felt it best to travel west at first, through the thick woodland, before we turned to the north toward home. I remember, upon that frosty night, my heart leapt into my mouth whenever one of us stepped upon a twig or sent roosting birds to shriek their alarm calls. Men have many fears in life, but the fear of imminent death is unlike any other. All warriors know it, but a man who has never stood in a shield wall can never fully understand it.

The king, it seems, spent a goodly while in York and built a second castle. Now, these two castles were cunningly sited to control access to the city from the river. They were constructed on either side of the River Ouse so that a great chain could be stretched between them to prevent ships from passing up and down. It confirmed that this city was important to William, as it was the only city outside London with two castles.

Once the new defences were almost complete, William rode off to Winchester to celebrate Easter there, leaving William Fitz Osbern as Castellan. We later heard that English forces had made one further attack upon the city, but were soundly beaten by the garrison. Those who escaped with their lives were the lucky ones.

…and Edgar Aetheling went back again to Scotland.

***

Our arrival back in our little village of Brockford was, at first, celebrated. The people gathered around us, chattering and laughing, to hear our tales of great success against our oppressors. But there were glum faces when we told them what had taken place there.

We had failed. Would we ever be free of the Norman Yoke? It looked doubtful. We now had to live with the prospect of Norman earls ruling over us and, no doubt, making us pay a heavy price. But just what a price we didn't yet understand, and we probably couldn't imagine.

My mother and family were delighted at my return, of course, and my mother made a special meal for us all that night, probably using up scarce supplies we could barely afford. But at last, I sat before a roaring fire, warm and dry, and with my family around me. It was well that I had returned, as the year was beginning to change, and there were many tasks to do in the fields and woods.

My grandfather and siblings had managed the pruning of the trees in February, and now March would be a time for digging and sowing. As we worked together in the fields, my mother paused and looked at me.

"John, will you promise me that you will not go off again, with Cerdic or the earls, to spend more time in fruitless conflict and perhaps lose your life in this hopeless quest to return to happier times?"

I looked at her, and I thought she had aged since I last saw her before we had gone to Durham and York. I could see the worry behind her eyes and behind that kindly smile of hers. I knew what she was thinking —I was the man of the house, and what would they all do if I didn't come home? My brothers were still too young, and though my grandfather tried so hard to fill the role, I could see him failing in health and strength. And, of course, I was her son.

I smiled at my mother, hoping that it was a reassuring smile.

"I doubt that I shall leave again, mother," I said, "I can see no way to fight the men who have stolen our land. We must accept what comes to us and make the best we can of our lives."

I thought she seemed happy with that and returned to her work with a little more enthusiasm.

But I found it hard to accept the failure of what we had tried to do. I brooded upon it, both in the fields by day and at night, around the fire. It burned into my belly and spoiled my dreams.

The year moved on, as always, and I have to say, things appeared more settled. We were not persecuted by the Normans, and life seemed to have returned to normal. Perhaps our adventures in Durham and York were just pointless violence, and our rulers would, indeed, forgive and forget and leave us in peace.

In April and May, we tended our sheep. They had done well this year, and we had a good birthing of new lambs to gambol in the fields. My sisters loved this time and fussed over the new-borns like little mothers. Sometimes, a lamb dies, and its mother still has milk in her udders. Then I would skin the lamb and wrap the pelt around another that had been born as a twin or triplet to another ewe. If the bereaved ewe could smell its own lamb, she would take it to her and rear it as her own.

Spring turned into summer, and the days grew long and warm. In June, we cut wood from the forest to build or repair our buildings or to burn upon the fire when the nights grew colder.

Life became much busier when July came in. Now, the mowing was to be done. We were in the fields from first light until the sun began to dip below the hills on the western horizon. The great scythes would swish backwards and forwards, slicing through the sweet grasses and myriad wildflowers that grew in our hay fields. There was quaking grass and foxtails, lady's mantle and harebell, with its pale blue flowers. There was meadow saxifrage and knapweed, bird's-foot-trefoil and purple-orchids. The animals would relish the sweetness during the cold days of next winter.

How I loved to lie there in the fields on a warm summer day, watching the birds flying backwards and forwards, looking for a meal of insects, grubs or seeds. I would watch the swallows and martins as they swooped and dived upon their insect prey. I would watch the bees as they flitted from flower to flower, collecting the sweet nectar they would turn into honey. Life was busy in the summer months, but in other ways, it was much easier. At midday, we would break from our work and lie in the new-mown hay, eating cheese, pies and sausages my mother brought to the fields in her basket. There would be a jug of ale to wash it down with. All in all, life was hard but wonderful.

It was in late August, on a blisteringly hot day, that fate took another twist. Now, it was the turn of the barley and oats to be harvested. We moved across the fields like a line of shore crabs, our backs bent and our arms slashing the sickles through the stalks of the grain. Once cut, it would be gathered and tied into sheaves to stand and dry in the fields. The children followed us and gathered any spilt grain in baskets —we could not afford to lose a single grain, if possible. Of course, the birds flitted in and out of our feet, dashing in to peck up a seed that fell upon the ground. The dogs ran about, growling and barking, trying to chase them off, but only succeeding in moving them on for a short while before they returned to their task.

I had stood up, stretched and leaned back, trying to ease my aching muscles, when a cry went up. I turned and looked in the direction of the caller, who stood transfixed, looking at the hillside, over which spilt an army. Mounted men led it, with foot soldiers to the rear. They were all heavily armed, and banners flew from spears. The great tide of men poured over the brow of the hill and cascaded downward towards the ford in the river.

We grabbed the children, left our tools in the field and made our way back to the stockade, where Cerdic was just arriving, having seen the wave of men from his own hall.

The army picked its way over the ford, which was running very low at this time of the year, and crested the bank on our side. I looked carefully at the banners. It was Edgar and the northern earls. What could bring them here? The earls approached, and Cerdic greeted them, framed within the great gateposts of our village.

"My lords, to what do we owe the honour of a visit from yourselves and your men?"

"We would speak with you and your men, Cerdic," Edgar replied, "We have urgent news."

I looked around for my mother and caught sight of her standing before the doorway to our home. I knew exactly what the look upon her face meant. It was a look of terror that her son would be marched off again to do the bidding of the earls, putting his life in mortal danger again, and to what purpose?

“Let us go to my hall,” Cerdic said, “Where we might eat and sup.”

Chapter 16

A Broken Promise

The Saxon soldiers lay wearily on the banks of the river, eating what little rations they had and watering their horses in the gentle flow of summer. In the meantime, we all trooped *again* at Cerdic's hall, this time to hear what the earls had to say. Many of us exchanged glances and looks that said, 'What is the point of this? We will not march off to war again with the earls who so easily deserted York the last time the enemy stirred their feathers.'

Inside Cerdic's hall, the nobles sat at the long tables, and servants ran hither and thither, bringing out the best food and drink Cerdic could provide. We clustered around, contemplating the fine foods and remembering how they tasted from last Christmas's feast that Cerdic had kindly provided us. I had flashed a smile at the young serving girl as she hustled and bustled about her duties. She had repaid me with a shy smile of her own. I had found out that her name was Edyth, which I heard, in Anglo-Saxon, means 'Joyous'. She had come to us from the household of another thegn, but I never did find out why that was. She would never tell me except to say that she had been unhappy at her previous home.

At length, Edgar rose from the table and scrutinised us. We all bent our heads. He was, after all, of royal blood. He was quite a tall man, I recollect. His long face was rimmed by a neatly cut stubble of a beard.

"Englishmen!" he called, "I know there are men amongst you who followed us to York. I know how disappointed you were that we were not able to stand firm against William and his troops."

Heads nodded, and there were not just a few mumbles and grumbles from our number. Edgar was obviously aware of it and paused a while in his speech.

"I have to tell you that the intelligence we received about William's arrival pointed to the fact that we could not prevail in battle against so many hardened troops. It was decided then that we should withdraw to fight another day."

"You can fight another day! What of the poor wretches who died that day supporting your claim to the throne of this land?" came a voice from the back of the crowd.

A great gasp went up, and Cerdic's face was a mask of horror. To address a noble like this was unthinkable!

"My Lord," Cerdic gabbled, "I must apologise. The man who spoke those words will be severely punished, I swear!"

"He will not, Cerdic," replied Edgar, "For I sympathise with him. It was a terrible time and a major miscalculation on our behalf."

And he wafted a hand at the assembled earls and commanders, who looked decidedly uncomfortable at their leader's words. Cerdic was dumbstruck, as were we all. To hear that from the potential king of our realm was incredible, and I think it began the softening of the feelings of all those gathered toward the man addressing us.

"If you will allow me, I would speak to you all again of a new situation and an endeavour to rid our land of the Normans. And this time, it cannot fail."

'If we would *allow* him…' We had never heard such a thing. It was not our place to *allow* a highborn noble to speak to us. I scanned Cerdic's face, and I must say that I chuckled to myself inside. It was a picture of shock and confusion.

"Will you allow me?" Edgar asked.

A good many confused voices said, "Aye."

Edgar smiled at us and began.

"The lords I have with me, and a good number more, are to ride to York again. But this time, it will be different."

A few mutters came from the back of the hall, and Edgar looked toward them, which silenced them immediately.

"This time," Edgar continued, "We shall not be alone in our quest. Sweyn Estrithson's sons have already sailed with an army. They are to sail into the River Humber and march across the land to York to meet up with us. With a Danish army at our backs, how can we fail to take York and use it as a capital city of Northumbria, from which to fight back against William?"

"How many men do they bring, my Lord?" interjected Cerdic.

"I have no certain knowledge of the numbers, but it is a very large fleet," Edgar replied.

There was muttering again from the hall, and men looked at one another, again unsure what to think.

"What would you have us do, Lord?" asked Benjamin the smith.

"I would have you join me and bring about the beginning of the end of William and his Norman brutes," Edgar replied.

Again, men scanned each other's faces. The muttering began again, but this time, Edgar sat and allowed it to continue. Cerdic tried to rise, to put a stop to what he obviously felt was poor behaviour in front of the Saxon aristocracy, but Edgar stretched out a hand and prevented him.

After some discussion, Benjamin stepped to the front of the huddle and bowed low to the table of nobles.

"My Lords, some of our number will not march to York with you. They say that they owe it to their families to remain and care for them. Some say they have little confidence that this venture will end any better than the last."

Cerdic's face clouded, and a purple flush rose in his cheeks.

"Others have said that they will march with you and lay their lives in the hands of God again to gain the freedom of this land from its oppressors."

He bowed low again and retreated back to the crowd of assembled men.

Some of the nobles exchanged glances as Edgar rose again.

"It is good that men take responsibility for their families seriously, and I applaud it. No less shall be thought of the men who would stay behind," And at this, he looked at Cerdic, "I thank the men who will march with us. I am certain that this time, with the backing of the Danes, we will triumph."

I think what persuaded those of us who chose to go was that Danish warriors would be there. We still harked back to our Danish culture, and many a man would have welcomed Sweyn and his sons to rule over us again.

But now, I had another problem. Had I not promised my mother that I would not go with Cerdic and the earls again? How would I break the news to her that I had agreed to go? How would I survive the wrath that would be unleashed within our household? What would my grandfather's face reveal? Concern, no doubt, that I had tempted fate too far this time and would never return. In truth, the odds were beginning to be stacked against me. I had survived a number of battles by now; how many more times would I be lucky?

The earls left us and made their way to the coast. They would sail down the coast and meet the Danes in the Humber.

***

During the last few days of August, we worked hard to bring in the harvest. Once it was safely in, I could relax as much, as I would know that my family would have enough to eat for another year…regardless of what happened to me.

Oh, what a time it was. The atmosphere in our home was funereal. My mother wept often and openly. I had never seen her weep like this in front of my younger brothers and sisters. She was usually the strong one who kept everything together. But now I knew that she felt betrayed. I had broken my promise to her, and nothing I could say or do seemed to lift her mood of depression and gloom.

I listened, one night, in the darkness, as she said her customary prayers.

At the end, when she had prayed for all of us in turn, she halted a moment and said to my dead father, "Aelric, up in heaven, look down upon our son and keep him safe in the perils he faces. I love him so dearly and couldn't bear to lose him too. I understand why he feels that he must go, and I burst with pride at the young man we have brought forth and nurtured. God protect him."

I wept quietly in my bed that night.

I watched my grandfather, too, in the evenings, as we sat around the fire. He stared for long periods into the flames and told fewer stories to the little ones than he used to. We had heard them all before but still enjoyed the telling. Even my brothers and sisters, usually so boisterous and full of fun, seemed subdued in those last days. I tried to jolly them along, but it was to no avail.

***

Soon —too soon for my family— on a scorching September day, as the year rolled from summer into autumn, we were ready to depart. There were six of us villagers, and also Cerdic, who arrived at the village with a small troop of his own retainers. The last embraces were exchanged, and tears were shed. We shook the hands of the men who would not be coming with us. My mother held her apron to her eyes and dabbed at them. My brothers and sisters looked forlorn.

"Must you go, John?" my youngest sister, Cathryn, asked me.

I looked down at her little face and smiled.

"Cathryn, I will be home again before you have grown another inch."

At least, I comforted myself, that my family would eat well. The harvest had been good, and September's main task was to take the swine to the woods and let them grow fat on the fallen nuts and fruit. That would be a simple task for my brothers and my grandfather to carry out.

And so, we set off.

We had not yet arrived at the time of the shrivelling of the leaves, and I listened to the wind breathe amongst the trees as we marched. We quickly emerged from the hill country and arrived at the flatter land nearer to the east coast. There, we turned our steps south again, toward York. At least we weren't trudging through thick snow now. That was a blessing. But all seasons bring their problems.

As the sun rose higher and shadows shrank, Luke appeared at my side.

"I shall be glad to get into the shade of woodland, John," he said, "Out of this Devil's breath of a wind."

I nodded, and we strode on.

After two days of hard marching, we began to meander to the east, the better to bypass York, and where our leaders told us we would meet up with the Danes. This, of course, would add to our journey, and many were footsore by the time we made camp for the night. It was upon that evening when one of the 'wolves' rode into camp with news.

The 'wolves' rode to the front, the sides and rear of a moving army, looking out for danger and reporting what was happening in the countryside. We stood around whilst he delivered his message.

"My lords, it is good that we have skirted east, for a Norman patrol has left York and is heading north, towards Northallerton. It seems that they think we are there. They intend to engage us in battle, and then proceed to Durham."

"Then we must allow them to think it," said one of our leaders, a large man called Grimbold, a fierce and bold leader of men with a huge red beard.

"How far distant are they?"

"My lord, they will be very near to us within the hour. We must take action."

"Get yourselves to the folds of the land to the east and lie up there for a camp. It is better if we avoid this band of soldiers. There are others following in our wake who might meet them and give them battle."

"It will be all the better for us, as there will be fewer men to guard York," another said.

And so it was that the Norman patrol approached us but knew nothing of our presence, hidden in the landscape. None of us dared move or breathe as the squeak and rattle of harnesses and the thud of hooves on the land were borne to us on the breeze. As the troopers drew level, one of the young lads who had come with us to help could not contain his curiosity any longer. Slowly, his head rose from the land and peeped over the ridge. A Norman soldier, at that very moment, was casting his eyes around, perhaps uneasy in the seemingly deserted landscape that he thought was 'too quiet'. He called to his fellows, and the troop drew to a halt.

"Come here, boy!" the man bawled.

The lad rose from the ground and, warily, dragged his feet over to the troop of soldiers.

"What are you doing here?" the trooper asked.

"My lord, I mean no harm," the boy said, "I make my way to York."

We all gasped and held our breath. Would he uncover the plot in his terror? Would we be found and have to fight for our lives, still short of York?

"And what would you want in York?" the soldier questioned, a little suspicious of a boy, seemingly alone in the empty landscape.

"My lord, I am running away from my home and my cruel master. He beats us daily. I can take no more. I am off to seek my fortune in the city."

We all chuckled inside at the tale and began to relax just a little.

The Normans laughed.

"You would seek your fortune, then?" the soldier said, amused, "And we might even be able to do you a service, my good man," he said, a little mockingly, "For we travel north to punish those in Northumbria who would defy us. We'll have to see if we can root out your master."

With that, the Normans reined their horses again and continued on their journey, chuckling. It was a while, though, before we dared to rise, and the boy re-joined us. We travelled on and, eventually, began to walk into a thick mist that seemed to descend upon the land from nowhere. By early evening, we had settled into a little woodland, whilst the mists swirled about us and made everything damp and ourselves miserable.

But strange things can come from the mist. After a dank night, huddled in the wood, we awoke to find the sun up, and the fog disappeared. Had we known then what had happened in that mist, we would have been astonished. But we were not to hear it for some time. It seems that the Norman troops had also been engulfed in the thick fog and the terrible darkness that had descended to the north, so that a man could hardly see a comrade riding before him. None could determine the way to go. They had dismounted and sat down at the edge of a field, not knowing quite what to do.

A treacherous Saxon scout who travelled with them was, I heard, terrified at their plight.

"It is the saint!" he cried, "We are damned!"

"The saint?" the commander asked, "What saint?"

"Why, my lord, it is Saint Cuthbert. He is the protector in adversity of all in Northumbria. This is his doing. He has sent this terrible fog to engulf us and bring us to certain death!"

The Normans looked from one to another as best they could in the gloom. The commander pondered the Saxon's words.

"We will not wage war upon Heaven," he declared, "We return to York as soon as there is light to see the road."

And so it was. People still refer to it as the miracle of St. Cuthbert, even today, though we could have done more with help from the saint in the days to come.

The following evening, we found ourselves in a wood between York and the Humber, a little way from Stamford Bridge, where I had fought the battle against Harold Hardrada and the hated Earl Tostig. It brought many memories back to me, not least that of my father, who fought by my side at Stamford Bridge and Hastings. I could see my father in my mind's eye. I could see his long fair hair blowing in the wind, and his ruddy face from long hours in the fields. I could hear his reassuring voice.

We sat there, on this, the final evening of the march, eating cold food and supping warm ale. We were not allowed fires to cook, in case it alerted the Normans to our presence, though I have to say that I was fairly certain they knew exactly where we were. They would have patrols moving across the landscape, ensuring that the people behaved and toiled hard at their labours.

A messenger rode into the woodland. He dismounted and made his way to our thegns.

"The Danes and the earls are landed in the Humber, my lords," he reported.

The ships of our time were designed for entering a river or landing their men on a beach. They were broad of beam, but shallow of draught. They would be rowed right onto the beach until they were grounded there. The thegns then made it their business to come around to their own men and speak to them of the situation, and to inspire us all to the task that lay ahead.

I knew that many of the men were still uncertain as to the wisdom of this venture, and I have to admit that I, too, had misgivings. What were we doing there? Why were we not at home, caring for our families and ensuring that all of the tasks upon the land were completed before winter took the upper hand?

After some time, we heard the tramp of feet and coarse voices through the gloom. We could hear low conversations in both English and Danish as a troop of men entered our wood. The reinforcements were here, just as Edgar had said they would, and I think that, at this point, spirits began to rise. Perhaps it would come to pass that the Saxons and Danes would drive the Norman invaders from our land and install some sort of Danish rule to replace them.

On the following morning, when I had slept a fitful night in the wood and arisen to another cold breakfast, we, with the Saxon earls and their men and the Danish warriors, arrived a little way from the boundaries of York.

From our positions, we could peer through the trees and bushes and see the ancient walls of the city. Along the top of the walls paced Norman guards, who looked out at intervals over the surrounding land.

Although we were still hidden by trees and scrub, which, I noted, the Normans appeared to have cleared back for some distance, they must know that we are here, I thought. Even if just by the noise we made. No matter how softly a man treads, when hundreds of men tread, it can be heard at a distance. And then there were the horses that whinnied and snickered from time to time.

At one point, Cerdic's gloved hand brought us to a halt as a patrol of our men rode carefully toward us through the woodland and scrub. The soldiers had taken care to muffle the hooves of the horses with cloth and wool, but still, there was a dull thud upon the Earth as they picked their way forward. At its head was Gospatric, and behind him rode Saxon troops and Danes together. They reined their horses to a halt.

"Cerdic," said Gospatric, "It is good to see you and your warriors again. We must now fan out and spread ourselves around the city. Most of the men will be posted at the great gates to see if we can gain swift entry."

I doubted that, but Cerdic nodded, and we moved on toward the city walls. So, here we were again, at the gates of York. But this time, Sweyn Estrithson's sons were also here with their forces. Many faces in our own troop had been brightened by their arrival, as the Danes were always welcomed by most people in the north. We had, after all, been part of the Danelaw for many years.

At a signal, we emerged from the trees and began the approach across the cleared land toward the walls. Now, many more Norman soldiers appeared along the walls, watching and waiting. Of course, they had known we were coming. How could it be otherwise?

As we began to move forward, a rain of arrows suddenly flew from the walls of York. We drew up our shields over our heads and felt the thud as the Norman arrows struck them and implanted themselves in the wood. I grew concerned when one arrow pierced the lime wood of my shield and peeped out at me from the inside like a mouse from a hole.

Some of our men were hit and cried out in agony and terror. Still, we moved on. Still, arrows bombarded us with their threat of sudden death. Still, we moved on. When we were closer to the walls, our archers, who, up till now, had hidden behind our cloak of protection, stood up and showered their own arrows and a few scavenged Norman arrows back toward the city walls. Now, it was the turn of Normans to cry out and fall from the walls where they stood.

And then a very strange thing happened. I noticed some of the Normans upon the walls suddenly stop their hail of arrows against us and turn to look inward to the city. Some began to point and run toward the gates. And then, the great gate that stood in our way began to creak open. As it opened, we could see local men pushing at it, all the while fighting off the Norman troops now behind them.

Now, more Normans left the walls to scramble down the steps to the ground below. As the gates parted, we pulled our shields up to the front of us and over our heads to create a great 'shell' around us and made our way as rapidly as we could to the gaping entries. And then we were within the walls, and great bloodshed followed.

As we entered the city more easily than we had thought, much to our surprise, the local people actually met us with a variety of reactions. Many cheered us on. Backs were patted, and cheery welcomes called out as we pursued what Normans we could find as they made their retreat to their defences. Some, however, met us in silence, their faces full of fear and anger. I could well understand that many would be fearful of what was to happen and that some were, perhaps, quite happy with the rule that the Normans had brought.

Perhaps, I mused, they thought to profit by it. As we continued, I noticed that many of the houses in York seemed to have been sacked and burned. The Normans had burned and destroyed the houses near the castles so that they provided no cover for attackers and could not be used to fill up the trenches around the castles. People crouched, hiding from the fray, near the smouldering ruins of where their homes and businesses had once stood.

But now, the fire was spreading and attacking other areas, burning to the ground the homes and businesses of the citizens of York. This was not what we had planned. We were here to liberate the city, not destroy it. Even the monastery of St Peter was consumed by the flames. It was a mournful sight.

A short while later, as the Norman resistance was fading and the troops fought their way back to their castles, Gospatric, Waltheof and Maerleswein arrived with more Danish and Norse troops. Some were on horseback and others on foot, but all were heavily armed. For what reason, I shall never know, the gates of the castles opened, and a good number of Norman troops sallied out to engage ourselves and the Danes within the city walls. What folly!

I was immediately thrust into the very jaws of the battle. I rubbed my eyes and coughed to rid my throat of the smoke that billowed across the city. And then I found myself looking straight into the eyes of a Norman soldier. His nose-guard divided his face into two, and I could see both fear and ferocity in his eyes. Like all men entering into battle, his stomach was churning as mine was. His bowels felt loose, and he wished himself anywhere but there.

The man came at me, his sword drawn and a snarl upon his lips. I thrust up my shield and parried his first blow. I stepped to the side, and he strode forward a little further than he had meant to. I turned and thrust my own sword into his thigh, below his coat of mail. He screamed and pulled himself off the skewer of my sword. He grasped the leg where my sword had been, and blood spurted through his fingers. Now that he was off his guard, I stabbed my sword again. This time, catching him in the eye, I thrust the blade into his skull. He fell to the floor, dead, taking my sword with him.

I snatched at it and drew it free from the corpse just as another Norman loomed over me. I had little time, but I lunged with my seax into his groin, where the mail coat was split to allow movement. He stopped and stood there, like a scarecrow in a field, staring at me with disbelief. He was a hardened soldier and he had been mortally wounded by a boy; it was surely not the end he had imagined for himself. I withdrew the seax and lunged again. This time, his bowels gave way, and their contents spread down his legs, creating a stink within his breeches. He sat down upon the ground as if to eat a meal in the fields. Again, he looked down at his terrible injuries and then up at me as I now stood over him. It was as if time stood still for me. I knew that I should move on for my own safety if for nothing else, but I couldn't.

The Norman took off his helmet and pulled back the mail hood over his head.

"Finish it," he whispered so that I could hardly hear it over the din of battle.

I knew what he meant, and I swung my sword, almost slicing his head from his shoulders. I looked down upon his bloodied and lifeless form. 'Is this what we have become?' I asked myself. Slaughterers of other men? Why? It all seemed so pointless, and yet there was a point to it: *Freedom*.

The battle raged on for some time. Most of the Normans were massacred that day on the streets of York, or what was left of them. Some managed to reach the relative safety of the castles, but our forces marched on.

Now, our forces were split. The Danes began to assail the castles on one side and we, the Northumbrians, on the other. We made a number of sallies under fire from the castles, and some of our men died in the attempts. But soon, we were able to approach closer, ever closer to our target. As we cleared soldiers from the walls with our constant fire, we were able to bring forward great ladders that had been made for us, and lean them against the walls. Men ascended and threw grappling ropes over the walls. Now, they could pull themselves up to the battlements and clamber over to engage in hand-to-hand fighting with the remaining troops.

I was amongst the last of our men to enter the castles that day, being a young boy, and I was able to enter through the gates opened by our troops as they overwhelmed the guards. The scene was terrible. Bodies littered the Earthen floor —Normans, Saxons and Danes. Blood pooled in the uneven Earth and seeped downward to the worms. Danes and Saxons alike were plundering the castles and carrying off whatever loot they could find.

As I stood there, gazing at the scene of horror and carnage before me, a group of men emerged from the castle keep. With them, they roughly handled a man, a woman and two children. They were followed a little later by another man, bundled unceremoniously from his hiding place.

"Look what we have found!" cried a huge Northumbrian, whose speech revealed that he was from the far north of our territory.

"What shall we do with them? Why, she is a pretty young thing," he leered at the woman, who pulled the children to her.

The man tried to stand between them.

"I am William Malet, the Castellan. This is my wife and family. You will not harm them unless over my dead body."

"It can be arranged," replied the Northumbrian, grinning with a mouthful of rotten teeth and gripping the handle of a great sword.

"But it will not!" barked a voice behind us.

We turned to see Gospatric, now astride a stallion.

"These people are my prisoners and will not be harmed. Besides," he added, "They are too valuable to waste."

The other captured man, I later heard, was one Gilbert de Gant.

And so we retreated from what was a broken city, though some parts stood untouched by either flames or violence. We camped in a little green space not far from the Coppergate. The Danes returned to their ships, which they had now brought further up the river, loaded down with untold booty from the campaign.

Once we were settled into our green space, which had once been used to hold livestock, and we had eaten a meal in almost total silence, I arose and meandered back to the walls of York. Somewhat reluctantly, I entered and wandered along one of York's still-standing narrow, twisting streets. I tried to talk to some of the city's people, though most had nothing much to say. As I turned into one narrow alley, I was met with an unpleasant scene. A group of Danes were assembled there, laughing and joking. A huge Dane had hold of a young Saxon girl by the wrist.

"Come, give a man some comfort," he said.

The girl shrank from him and tried to free herself, to the amusement of the Dane's friends.

"You are a pretty little thing," he said, "And I would enjoy your company."

Again, the Danes chortled.

I could never understand a man who would want to harm a woman or torment her in such a manner. It is a cowardly thing to do, I have always thought. I quietly drew my seax from my belt and, holding it under my cloak, I approached the scene. As I drew near, I produced the short sword and pushed it into the Dane's back, just enough to prick the skin and cause him pain.

"Ouch!" he cried and tried to turn.

I pricked him again.

"Stand still!" I ordered him in as deep a voice as I could muster.

"Release the girl, or I'll gut you like a trout!"

The Dane's grip released, and the girl pulled her arm free.

"Run!" I called to her, fearing that another Dane might grab her.

She looked at me for a heartbeat and smiled.

"Thank you, Sir," she called and ran off down the alley to safety.

What do I do now, I thought? The big Dane was still standing with his back to me. By this time, his friends were rolling in the dirt with mirth. Tears ran down Danish faces with laughter at what had just taken place. Even some of the local Saxons were now chortling and slapping their thighs. Slowly, the Dane began to turn. Imagine his surprise when he saw a young lad pointing the seax at him. He stared in disbelief. Surely, he will attack at any moment, I thought, still pointing the seax in his direction.

The Dane looked down at the finely honed blade of the weapon and obviously thought better than to attack me. He just looked at me with anger in his eyes.

"I don't know who you are, but we will meet again," he growled, "And when we do, it will be you who lies gutted like a trout. Look over your shoulder every moment of the day," he warned, and then strode off, the laughter of his friends still ringing in his ears.

When I returned to my band, I was a much sadder man than I had been that morning. I sought out Cerdic. He was sitting upon a barrel, staring into space around him, and lost in thought. He looked up as I approached and must have seen the look upon my face.

"You are troubled, John," he said.

"I am, my lord," I replied, "I have spoken to some of the good citizens of York, and theirs is a sorry tale."

I told him of the incident with the big Dane, and he smiled at the thought of it.

"Aye, it is a bad day, John," he replied, "We have caused death and devastation to this city again, and now, it seems, our own men must make it worse with their looting and pillaging."

"But why?" I asked, "We have won the day. Let us celebrate with the people of York, who will soon be free of the Norman yoke when we liberate Northumbria."

"It seems that some of Sweyn's men are a disobedient rabble, and Edgar is little more than a figurehead rather than a leader. Edgar's men and their Danish allies are here, it seems, not just to free our land but to cause pain and sorrow and to make themselves richer for it."

"What are we to do?" I asked.

"What can we do? We cannot challenge such men as Sweyn, Edgar and Gospatric. But I am a much sadder man tonight."

I sat at his side and pulled my cloak around me. A thin yellow dog snuffled around, picking up what scraps he could find. He pressed his nose around Cerdic's boot.

"What do you smell there, my friend?" asked Cerdic, "I have nothing to share with you. We have little enough for ourselves, and I will not take more from your master and his fellows."

The dog rooted and unearthed the carcass of a dead rat from the mud and greedily gobbled it down.

"Well now, was that a tasty morsel?" asked Cerdic, but the dog just shook his shaggy head and was upon his way.

And so it was done. York was 'liberated', though it had suffered greatly for its freedom. On the following morning, we packed our belongings to begin the long march home again. The earls and their men were confident that they would have no trouble holding their prize now with the help of their Danish and Norse allies. We, it seemed, were no longer needed and would return to the land to begin winter's tasks.

As we left the city for the last time, I glanced around at the scene. Men and women were slowly beginning to clear away the debris of the carnage. Charred wood was piled in heaps. The Earth was swept off the rubbish of battle and fire. Bodies, bloated now and beginning to buzz with flies, were carried out to hurriedly dug mass graves beyond the walls. Families wept over their departed loved ones. Other men were cast into pits without a tear —their families were far away and unaware of their demise.

Would I ever see York again? Perhaps, but I hoped it would be in happier times when it was truly the capital of Northumbria. And so we turned for home. *I had survived.*

Chapter 17

What Price a Promise?

Upon my return to Brockford in the September of that year, I found plenty to do to occupy my mind. In October, we thinned a good deal of the woodland and built great bonfires of the wood that was of no use to us. There was little point in keeping it, as it burned too quickly in the hearth and was only used as kindling. But we had another use for the wood as we cleared and burned it. The women would sit for hours, coiling pots from the clays of the ponds and river bank. We would build a clamp kiln, and the new pots would be fired in the heat.

The children always loved this time. They would sit around the fires and the kiln, sing songs and rhymes and play games. I would stand and stare into the flames, remembering the terrible fires I had seen in York. It brought it all back to me, and left me feeling hollow and uneasy.

***

It was at this time that we heard what had happened in York after we left. Cerdic told us that the force we left there under Edgar and the other nobles was an unruly mob, and were responsible for a good deal of trouble in York. I remembered well, my brush with the huge Dane whom I had found man-handling a young girl in the narrow streets of the city. I wondered what had happened to the man. I had never seen him again after that day and hoped it would stay that way. I thought of the girl. Was she well? I hoped so.

Edgar, it seems, had decided to foray into the lands south of the Humber. He led a seaborne raid into Lindsey to see how the land lay and, no doubt, to profit from the plunder. The ships had beached upon a spit of land in the estuary, and Edgar and his men set out across the country.

They arrived at the edge of a woodland clearing, where a few small huts lay, smoking from their vent holes in the early morning. The people of the village were stretching and yawning as they began the day's chores after breakfast. Women made their way down to the banks of a small stream to fetch water. Men stood around and studied the skies to determine how well the day's work would go, and whether they would complete them without a drenching. Small children ran hither and thither, shouting to one another at the start of another day. A couple of dogs barked, and a cockerel crowed.

Edgar looked at his band of men and smiled.

"Let's see what might be palatable to break our fast," he said.

"And also what trinkets we might find," mumbled one of his troops, to the amusement of the others.

Slowly, the men emerged from the woodland and made their way toward the tiny hamlet. It was a young woman who saw them first. She dropped her water jug and yelled a warning to the villagers. Children ran to hide behind the adults. Women scurried into the huts, dragging the young ones with them. Men stood, fingering their working tools and watching the arrival.

As the troop neared the centre of the hamlet, Edgar called to the group of men now facing them, "Good morrow my men. We have come to breakfast. I am sure you have enough to allow us a bite on this cold autumn morning."

"My lord, we have scant supplies enough, so that we must often go hungry. I wish it were otherwise. We would be happy for you to sit with us and tell us what happens in the world, but we have little food or drink to spare for a troop of men," one of the leading men replied.

Edgar looked him up and down. He pondered. These people were Saxons, true enough. But they were not his own Northumbrians. Should he simply take what he could find or leave these poor people in peace? Would his men leave with nothing to show for it? He was not confident that he could do anything to stop them should they demand food or anything else. He took a chance.

"Then we will not trouble you to feed us, but tell me, are there any Norman patrols in the area?"

His men looked at him, askance at his refusal to simply take the food available, and more than one stomach rumbled its complaint.

"We have seen one or two patrols over the last few days, Lord," the man replied.

The man was wary, still not certain to whom he was talking.

"What of their strength?" Edgar probed.

"I would say, as many as you have, and again and again," the man replied, obviously unsure as to how many men that was.

Edgar was about to ask when they were last sighted when he stopped suddenly, the words unable to come as he looked at the Norman horseback patrol entering the clearing from the opposite direction. The leading horseman held up a gloved hand, and the patrol halted in its tracks.

The Normans stared at Edgar and his men and then waved the same gloved hand as he urged his horse forward. Edgar's men began to draw swords, whilst the village men retreated to their hovels. But

Edgar saw the situation they were in and yelled at his troops to run for the thickest part of the woodland edge. The Saxons quickly pushed their way through the tangle of bushes and branches, where no horse could follow, and tried to cut their way back to the river and their boats. The Normans dismounted and followed them into the woodland, slashing at branches to clear a better path.

It soon became obvious to Edgar and to the men he commanded, that their position was a difficult one. They could not stand and fight such a large group of soldiers, but flight was difficult. They would have to fight a retreating position until they reached the river. But now, the Normans were quickly catching Saxons, and the first clash of metal and the thud of swords on shields could be heard echoing around the woodland.

Woodland birds took flight; their raucous alarm calls alerting every animal within a mile of the danger. Now, the cries of injured men could be heard, intermingled with the snap of twigs and the swish of branches as the two sides fought a desperate battle.

Edgar himself was retreating backwards toward the safety of the river when two Normans emerged from behind a tree and stared at the nobleman. It was obvious from his clothing and weapons that this was no ordinary foot soldier. This was a man of substance and could be a valuable prize.

"Take him alive," growled the larger of the two men.

The other nodded, and they approached Edgar, still wary of the sword in his hand. Edgar backed into a tree and stood there. At least one side was covered. Just as the men approached within three paces of him, a Saxon arose from a blackberry bush and thrust a sword through the uncovered neck of the Norman nearest to him. The man's eyes bulged, and his face became puce as he slipped to the floor, lifeless, with blood coursing from his wound. The second Norman was taken by surprise and lifted his gaze from the Saxon earl for a split second. Edgar lunged forward and slashed his sword across the man's throat, sending him gurgling to the leafy floor.

Now, the rest of Edgar's men fought their way to the boats and began to push them out into the stream. A few of the stragglers, including Edgar, arrived and had to wade out to the boats, now almost in mid-stream. The Normans didn't pursue their quarry into the flow and just stood, watching the boats sail off downstream on the current. They had killed a good number of Saxons that day, and they would be satisfied with that. As for Edgar, he sat on the bow of one of the boats, quickly working out just how many men he had lost that day. It was an unhappy group that finally pulled their boats into their own camp that autumn afternoon.

***

When William heard what had happened at York, his headquarters in Northumbria, he was filled with sorrow and despaired of his northern subjects. But it was the anger that filled him that was to be feared.

"What must I do to quell the rebellions in this land?" he roared, "I could trust a rat not to bite me before I could trust these people!"

The assembled Normans stood quietly, not knowing quite what to say to their master. William pored over the map of the country, sketching the rivers with his finger and contemplating what he would do to put down these infuriating uprisings.

"I have trusted the northern earls, and this is how they repay me!"

William sat again in his great wooden chair at the head of the table. He picked at the food that had been laid there by his servants. Somehow, the cheese simply didn't taste as good as it usually did, and the bread seemed stale to him. In truth, nothing could please him at that moment. The king's face was a dark mask of fury, as he thought of what his reply must be.

“Gather together as large a force as we can safely take with us without leaving the rest of the kingdom undefended. We ride for York as soon as possible. I will show these barbarians they may not try my patience with their puny insurrections! There will be great suffering across this land until they know I am the ruler here!”

And so there was a great commotion of preparations, with commanders and noblemen dashing this way and that, giving orders, counting supplies, checking weapons and preparing horses for the journey from Nottingham to York.

During this time, when the storms of war appeared to be rising on every side, William sent his cherished wife, Matilda, back to Normandy so that she and their son, Robert, would be safe and could ensure that the Duchy of Normandy was secure. Matilda would also be able to give up her time to her religious devotions in peace.

William’s army marched swiftly toward York. It was a difficult journey, as the year had turned and the leaves were now fallen from the trees. Heavy rain turned the tracks into pools of mud, which clung to the feet of those who trod them. Hail beat from the helmets and hoods of the troops, and they pulled their cloaks tightly around them. We shall never know what misery and depredation the soldiers endured on that forced march, but we can only guess at.

Meanwhile, in and around York, Edgar was brooding about the ill-advised journey into the Lindsey side of the Humber. He had felt the eyes of his followers and the other nobles boring into him, reproaching him for his foolhardiness. He knew that they were right, of course. He also knew that he was losing what respect he had from his followers, and it troubled him deeply. Would he ever truly be the king of this land? Perhaps.

It was on a bitterly cold day, with the sky empty of clouds and a thick hoar frost upon the grass, that the news arrived about William's march north. In the hall in which Edgar was accommodated, the Danish leaders filed in across the rush-strewn floor. Edgar looked at them and wondered just how well he could now depend upon the Danish army when William approached. The other Saxon nobles sat around the table; all seemed lost in thought but looked up as the Danes strode in.

The Danes took their seats around the table, and servants brought jugs of ale. Edgar spoke to them, though not perhaps in his most authoritative voice.

"You will know as I do that William has collected together as many men as he can safely muster and is marching toward York as we speak. I have heard that he approaches Pontefract. We must decide the best course of action to repel and defeat him."

The Danish leaders looked from one to another.

"We have heard much of William's strength of arms. He brings a good many hardened warriors with him. Our boats are drawn up on the Lindsey side of the Humber, out of his reach. I think that is the best place for them," replied one of the Danish king's sons.

"But your men are no good to me standing on the southern shore! I need every man here to fight alongside me and the other Saxon lords."

There was an uneasy silence. A young serving boy entered but saw the scene before him, felt the tension, and quietly backed out of the hall. He was too cautious to approach the assembled warriors at that moment. Word had spread to all levels of society in York, and all feared the firestorm that was to come.

"If we stand together, we can defeat William. Divided, we will lose, and William will take Northumbria and England as his own," reasoned Edgar.

The Scandinavians looked from one to another. They were thinking of the booty that was already loaded onto their boats. If they stood and fought and lost, those riches would be forfeit. If they sailed to a safer haven, they could watch proceedings. If they thought Edgar had the upper hand, they would sail back across and join in behind the Normans. But if

William had the better of it, they would sail away, back to Scandinavia with their loot. A bitter argument followed, with persuasions and recriminations from the Saxons, and excuses and evasions from the Danes and Norsemen assembled.

At length, the Scandinavians left and sailed back across the river to their ships. Edgar and his followers sat in the hall, their faces clouded, staring into the embers of the fire. Gospatric broke the silence that had descended like a black cloak over the proceedings.

"Edgar, what say I take my troops and meet William first at the crossing point of the river at Pontefract? We might be able to inflict losses upon his troops there before retreating to York to defend the city."

Edgar mused the point.

"Hmm, it is a thought. It would certainly be a good point at which to meet him in battle before he is allowed to surround this city. Do it, Gospatric, with my blessing."

The following day, Gospatric and his troops, along with Maerleswein and his followers, rode out toward Pontefract to the crossing of the River Aire. Upon their arrival, the men tied up their horses and were assembled by their captains along the bank of the Aire, with bows strung tight and swords sharp. The wind was bitter, and men blew upon their hands and rubbed themselves to keep out the winter chill from their bones.

After two hours of shivering and foot-stamping, the clinking of horse harnesses could be heard in the distance, and the steady thud of hooves was brought to the Saxons on the wind. It was not long before the Norman column hove into sight around a bend of the stream. Slowly, it made its way across open fields toward the crossing.

"On alert!" bawled Gospatric, and the command echoed down the line as captains brought their men to their stations.

"There are not as many as we had thought, Maerleswein," observed Gospatric.

"Then where are the others," pondered the tall, rugged Saxon, "Our intelligence tells us that William has many more men than this in the field. Is this some sort of trap?"

Gospatric didn't reply but stared into the distance to watch the approach of William's troops. The men rode palfreys, coursers and rounceys, all of which are strong breeds for travel and war. Pennants fluttered in the breeze from a forest of spears of the conrois of troops. These conrois were groups of up to ten men who would live, train, compete and fight together. One of their favourite forms of attack would be to charge the enemy infantry with their long spears pointing downward like a lance, spearing their prey like fish in a barrel.

Soon, the Normans approached the river bank, within around twenty yards. The Saxons scanned the scene, but of William, there was no sign.

"Where is William?" breathed Gospatric.

"Perhaps he is tucked behind the housecarls."

"Not William! He would be in the forefront of his men. It is not his style to hide behind his men. I smell a rat. Where is he…?"

A rider emerged from their front line and cantered up to the edge of the river bank. He looked down at the swollen flow of the river and contemplated the possibility of an easy crossing. Then he looked up and scanned the Saxon faces and weapons arrayed against him and his troops. He sat his horse for a moment and then rose in the saddle to call across the water.

"My commander requires you to leave peacefully and return to your homes. In that way, your lives will be spared, and we will be able to proceed to York to carry out the king's business."

Gospatric now spurred his horse forward and trotted to the opposite bank.

"Tell William to turn now and return to Nottingham. Northumbria is ours and shall remain so under Edgar the Aetheling. You cannot defeat our combined armies with the scant forces you seem to have brought with you. Many men will die in vain."

The Norman shook his head.

"Then it seems that many men will die," he shouted and turned his horse to return to his men.

The Normans now formed into waves of troops. Shields were taken from the saddles where they had hung, and longbows and crossbows were readied for an assault. The first wave approached the river bank and raised their shields just as the Saxon archers unleashed a stinging swarm of arrows across the stream toward them.

Some men fell from their saddles and splashed into the foaming waters of the Aire. Others continued across this, the only real crossing point for many miles. Soon, the Norman archers were trading arrows with the Saxons, and men were dying on both sides. And still, they came, their horses slipping and sliding upon the wet rock and straining against the flow. They were big animals with hugely muscled hindquarters that drove them forward.

It was not long before the Normans began to clamber up the opposite bank, and swords and axes were unsheathed for hand-to-hand combat. There was a great clash of iron and wood, and men battled bravely to gain the upper hand. The battle raged first one way and then the other. The River Aire ran red with the blood of those who met their death that day.

Bodies floated upon the current, face down in the swirling waters. The air was filled with shouts and screams, curses and oaths and the snickering of the horses. Free horses ran between the two sides, their eyes bulging, their only thought to escape the melee. The Saxon army was now in retreat to a short distance from the bank, driven back by arrows and horses. They formed up into a shield wall; the usual way of Saxon battle order. Shields were interlocked and spears thrust forward whilst the archers continued their aerial assault on the Normans. But still, the Normans came. And still, the shield wall retreated.

As more Norman cavalry reached the north bank of the river, they began to fan out and to harry the very edges of the Saxon lines. Slowly, the cavalry began to wrap around the Saxons to bring death and destruction to the flanks. Now Gospatric saw the situation they were sleep-walking into.

"Retreat to the horses!" he bawled, and the message was sent down the line.

Small groups of Saxons now broke away and began to fight their way back to the woodland where their horses were tied. Now, the conrois saw their chance. An order rang out in Norman French, and the cavalry lowered their great spears and raced after their retreating foes.

It was but a short time before the fleeing Saxons were caught by the horsemen, and spears penetrated the leather jerkins, and spines were cut and broken. Men threw up their arms and collapsed to the ground, their legs of no further use to them. Men were trampled under the hooves of the attacking horses, and skulls were broken, spilling grey brain matter over the soil for the crows to enjoy later when all would be still. Any man found alive by the Norman infantry that followed was quickly put out of his pain and misery. No prisoners were to be taken.

As the remaining Saxons began to reach the cover of the trees and the horses tied there, the Normans slowed their charge. A horn blew, and the Normans left the chase altogether and wheeled their horses to return to their column. Gospatric and his Saxons were allowed to take their horses and make their escape. The earl wondered how much time that had bought for York and just how much damage they had inflicted upon the Normans. But where was William, he wondered?

***

As the bedraggled and depleted Saxon troops entered York, they were struck by how many Danish warriors also seemed to be entering the protection of the city walls in a similar condition to their own. Gospatric and Maerleswein twisted in their saddles, looking at the dishevelled Danes and Norsemen, wondering what had happened to them. It was not long before they found out.

The two earls entered Edgar's hall, to see some of the Viking leaders sitting there, with heads down and concerned looks upon their faces. Edgar, too, looked strained and worried. They approached the great table, causing a wolfhound to rise from the rush-strewn floor and slink into a corner. It circled itself a couple of times before settling again, its chin on its paws, watching the assembled men.

"Edgar, what has happened here?" Gospatric asked.

"William has attacked the Danish camp on the other side of the river. He and his men arrived without warning and have taken a huge toll on the Scandinavians who were camped there. William knew the Vikings had made camp there and hastened to the spot with his knights. He hunted out those who had taken refuge in what we thought were almost inaccessible marshes, and has put many of them to the sword and wiped out their hiding places. The Danes who escaped his wrath have escaped back to this shore and are now planning a suitable opportunity to avenge themselves and their countrymen."

"So that is where William was," said Maerleswein, "We wondered why he did not lead his army at Pontefract. It seems his spies are better informed than ours."

Edgar nodded.

The two earls outlined what had happened on the banks of the River Aire, and the men sat to consider what would be their next move. It was a long and serious conversation that lasted far into the night. Rushlights and torches were burning low before the meeting ended, and men went to their beds with a terrible, uneasy feeling in the pits of their stomachs.

***

Two days later, a messenger arrived in the Danish camp, now on the northern shore of River Humber. He was a tall man, rugged, and with his short crop of dark hair and a neatly trimmed black beard, he was an impressive sight. He was accompanied by two other Normans —evidently men-at-arms. If anything, they were even larger than the messenger, and their faces bore the scars of many battles. One man's ear was crumpled up like a piece of old parchment, discarded and ready for the fire.

The messenger wore a fine linen shirt under a hauberk of mail that reached to his knees. It had three-quarter length sleeves to protect the arms and a split from hem to crotch to allow easy movement. Beneath the hauberk, the man wore baggy breeches that tapered in to fit tightly just below the knee. Criss-cross bindings wrapped his lower legs, and a tunic and cloak covered it all. Upon his feet were leather laced-up shoes. This sort of armour and clothing is expensive, both in terms of the time and skill to make it, so the common foot soldiers were rarely equipped with it.

The three Normans seemed to have little fear of the Danish warriors who began to surround them, and perhaps knew that their imposing entry had impressed their hosts. The Danes were always impressed by bravery, and this entry was obviously well-planned to take advantage of the fact.

Upon reaching the centre of the rough and ready camp, the three men sat their horses and looked around them. Quickly, a group of the leading Danes, including the king's sons, made their way to the centre of the melee.

"You are either very brave or very stupid," a huge Dane commented.

"Brave we might be, but stupid, never," replied the Norman, "We come with a message for you from our king. He would come to terms with the Scandinavians rather than both sides lose many men in a futile battle, for William *will* prevail. It will be your decision; leave now with enough riches and booty to satisfy your men and your king, or fight on for a lost cause and be driven out with nothing except your lives...*if* you are lucky."

The Dane looked him up and down. He glanced at his comrades, who each gave an almost imperceptible nod of the head.

"I think that we must speak further," he said.

The Normans dismounted, and their horses were taken to be cared for. The party then made its way into an old hut that was serving as a hall for the higher ranking Danes. A rickety door closed behind them.

***

The following morning, a brittle cold wind blew into the streets and yards of York. The Danish contingent approached a gate in the wall and filed in on horses that showed the effects of long nights in the chill of the night air. A more miserable string of animals cannot be imagined. The Danes atop them looked almost as miserable as they drew their cloaks around them and bent into the wind. The people of York and the Saxon warriors watched them pass by with concern.

They approached Edgar's hall and dismounted, their horses taken by boys. The men pushed their way into the cold and miserable interior of the hall, warmed only by a single fire in the centre and the torches that burned along the walls to provide a little light. Edgar and his men looked up as the bitter cold barged through the open doors. The Saxons made no attempt to rise as they watched the Danes cross the earthen floor.

"What news?" asked Edgar, unable to think of anything else to say to his foreign allies from across the North Sea.

The leading Danes —Sweyn Estrithson's sons and a handful of the more prominent warriors— sat down without speaking. Each man had made sure his cloak was pulled back so that his sword was readily available to him, should he need it.

"We have met with William's men."

Silence.

"We have agreed terms with him and will leave our camps along the river and from our fortified encampment on the Isle of Axholme, near Doncaster, which William has also attacked, and we will sail for home."

"You would desert us because William has attacked you? Will you leave this land empty-handed, after all of the effort and the wasted lives of your men who have died?" questioned Edgar, incredulous at the thought of his allies deserting his cause.

There was another uncomfortable silence until one of the Danish princes spoke up.

"As we have said, we have reached terms with William."

Another long pause.

"He has agreed to pay us a large sum in Danegeld for our departure."

"Ah, so that is the truth of it!" cried Edgar, "You have been bought by the Normans and will now desert your allies and scuttle home with your tails between your legs for his thirty pieces of silver!"

"The winter is here and is becoming more bitter by the day."

That much was true, as all of the men could feel the cold sneaking in through cracks and underdoors to chill their bones.

"We will dismantle our camps and return to our ships. Then we will sail on the next good tide."

And with that, the Scandinavians rose from the table and turned to go. It was at that point that Maerleswein leapt to his feet and drew his sword.

"What sort of men are you?" he roared, "You submit to William at the slightest setback. You haven't the stomach to stand and fight alongside Saxon warriors!"

At this, the Vikings whirled and drew their own swords. The air was thick with tension as the two sides eyed each other across the table. The Saxon guards were armed and ready, and each side glanced around them warily. The prince who had spoken glared at Maerleswein.

"You would be better to watch your mouth, Saxon weasel, or I might find the stomach to skin you alive!"

The Danes were now arranged into a tight circle, back to back, the better to fight off an attack from any direction.

Edgar rose from his seat. His very demeanour was that of a broken man, a man whose dreams had been shattered again by a broken promise.

"Go! Get you from this land."

He could find nothing more to say. He signalled for the guards to put up their weapons, and the Danish delegation slowly retreated from the hall, all the time watching, waiting for a sly attack that never came. They mounted their horses and slowly made their way from York to their camps to pack up what they could salvage and sail away from England's shores.

Now, the Saxon lords looked from one to another.

"It is finished," said Edgar sadly.

He shook his head and stared at the doorway through which the Danes had left.

"What now?" asked Gospatric, "Do we meet with William in battle, perhaps for the last time?"

"No," replied Edgar, looking into the earl's face, "We cannot defeat William in battle. If I am any judge of the man, he will not attack us directly, now that the recent break in the weather has closed like a trap around us again. He will try to cut off any chance of support and supplies of food and weapons. No, he has us and the longer we remain here, the more chance he has of squeezing the life out of us. We have no choice but to flee again to Scotland."

And so it was that Edgar and his followers broke camp the next day and fled to Scotland — *again*.

A few days later, William rode in, unopposed, through the gates of the city and occupied it again, after viciously despoiling the land around it in punishment for any man who had supported the Saxons. He would spend Christmas there. And then the terror would really begin!

Chapter 18

Slaughter

We had spent the Christmastide in contemplation of what might happen to us, now that William held York. I have to say that it was not the most joyful Yule that we had ever had. There was little merriment, and even the church services seemed muted. Every face carried a worried look, and it was evident to all of us that efforts to be happy were somewhat forced.

After the Christmas celebrations were over, the terror really started for us as William began his barbarous punishment of the good people of the North. The king was determined there would not be any more rebellions in the north. When they arrived there, the Norman adopted a scorched Earth policy, as they had near York.

The early morning frosts had not yet lifted when William stalked into his hall, a look of fierce determination on his face. He was a tall man and stocky, with a shock of red-blond hair just visible under a fur hat. He settled himself in a large wooden chair at the head of a table. A fire roared at the end of the hall, behind William's chair, casting its flickering light around the daub walls. The room was quiet. The servants had not yet had the time or the opportunity to place food and drink on the table for the monarch. William sat there, his hand rubbing his stubbled chin, pondering his course of action.

The door was opened by a man-at-arms and the weak morning sunlight flooded the entrance to the room. A number of commanders entered and filed up before their king. They bowed their heads in unison and stood to receive their orders.

William looked up at them and took a moment to study the faces. Would they do his bidding in this? He knew what his plans were, but they did not.

"Henry, you will take out a troop of cavalry. You will go west from here for a five-day ride. That should suffice. You will kill anyone and everyone you find in a village or town. And I mean everyone! No Saxon or Dane is to be spared —men, women *and* children. You will burn to the ground all homes and property. You will destroy all crops and stored food. You will seize all wealth. The countryside will be a wasteland. The whole region north of the Humber will be stripped of all means of sustenance. I will make these people realise that I am the ruler of this country, and they will bend the knee and obey my commands. It is the only way in which these people seem to learn."

The Normans looked at one another, shocked by what they had just heard. Surely, the king could not mean this. He was a cruel man, to be sure, but surely not this cruel. Their faces must have betrayed their feelings.

"My lord, the children? Surely, they are innocent of the insurrection."

"Nits turn into lice! I mean everything I say!" William bawled, "You too will follow my commands or explain to me why not! Robert, you will take a troop to the east and do the same. Bernard, you will travel north-west to the hills. Gilbert, you will travel to the north-east. Eustace, I will join your troop and move directly north. Once the troops have mopped up resistance to the east and west, we will all travel north. I intend to lay waste to this land from York to Durham and on to the Tyne. Now go about your duties."

And with that, the king arose from his seat and strode from the hall in order to ready himself for the slaughter that was to come.

The Norman commanders just stood in the middle of the hall, too shocked to do anything. Each man was lost in his private thoughts. None had foreseen what this invasion would become. It was supposed to be easy. They would simply invade, fight a few battles against Harold, and, once the Earl was dead, they would simply take over the running of the country. It wasn't meant to be this way.

The stunned silence ended when Gilbert shook his head and muttered to his companions, "We must be about our business."

Within two hours of the orders, the men sat upon their steeds —William clambered up on a great black destrier— and they slowly made their way out through the gates of York, watched by the few ragged and cowed residents left in the city. Each troop was equipped for a journey, with supply horses bringing up the rear. Each man was equipped with mail suits and had a selection of weapons at his disposal. It was a grim sight for any Saxon who saw the terrible procession.

Saxon spies, still in York, left as soon as they could after the troops, and made their way with the greatest speed to warn the people of the movement of William's troops. Some refugees fled north and south, from the killing that was to come and also from the resultant famine to come. Of course, many could not leave their homes and farmsteads or simply didn't believe or imagine the scale of the slaughter to come and stayed in their homes and villages.

Once outside the city walls, the Normans put their horses on a trot and began to fan out in all directions. William and Eustace began their journey north. The first two settlements they encountered were Haxby and Wigginton in the Forest of Galtres. William sat his destrier and looked at the settlement of Haxby. Haxby was an old Danish farmstead named after a man called Hakr, who must have lived there many years ago. A great Viking cross stood in the churchyard of St Mary's Church. The wattle and daub huts lined a lane, and small piggeries and gardens stretched out from the rear of every home. Each man needed to provide for his family and ensure they had enough to eat throughout the year.

The sun had risen over the top of the trees, and the frost was disappearing from the grass and the leaves where the feeble warmth of the winter rays could reach.

William signalled to move forward, and the troop walked their horses calmly toward the settlement. The locals stood and stared at the troop approaching. Some disappeared into their huts, whilst others just stood, not quite knowing what to do. The soldiers were simply walking their horses toward them, and although heavily armed, there appeared to be no cause for worry. The sight of armed men was far from unusual for the residents at that time.

As the troops rode forward, William made a signal with his arm. Now, the troop, riding in twos, split so that one man went one way and the next another. The soldiers began to encircle the village, and it was at this point that the residents began to fear what was to happen. Now, anxious faces looked around them at the ring of steel.

Eventually, the Norman soldiers had encircled the village and turned their horses inward. At another signal, they drew weapons and began to trot inward toward the houses. Now, screams began to rend the air, and a great wailing could be heard.

The carnage was terrible. People began to realise what was happening, and some hid within the dark recesses of their huts. Others tried to run for safety, through the advancing lines, toward the forest, but soon realised that the deadly circle was tightening around them like a noose, and that flight was not an option.

Now, the Normans were upon the people and cut down both men, women and children without a second thought and seemingly without emotion. They just killed, killed, killed. Men lay upon the ground, some split from shoulder to waist by the great swords of the Normans, wielded from horseback. Headless corpses wept their blood into the soil. Women were caught and dragged, screaming, to the centre of the village, where they and their clinging children were put to the sword. And all of the time that this murder took place, William sat, imperious, upon his black stallion and watched —a grim look upon his face. To his great shame, he made no effort to control his or his troops' fury and punished the innocent with the same zeal as the guilty.

Once the villagers outside had been killed, William ordered that the houses should be burned to the ground. The soldiers lit torches and began to move from house to house, setting ablaze the thatch of the roofs. Now screams could be heard again, this time from within the buildings, and villagers emerged from their doors, their clothes in flames. Many simply burned to death in their own homes.

When the killing was over, and William was satisfied that no one was alive, he ordered his troops to commit further devastation.

"All crops will be destroyed. All herds will be killed. Tools found in the ruins will be broken so that they can no longer be repaired. Find every last scrap of food, and it is to be burned to ashes."

And so the killing continued. Pigs were put to the sword in their stys. Sheep and cattle were cut down where they stood, their eyes widening as they began to smell blood and saw their number slain. At length, the troops looked around them. Nothing of any worth or use was left untouched. The village was a wasteland.

Some of the soldiers stood, their heads bowed, looking at the ground, considering what they had just done. William's strategy was an act of genocide that none would have believed could happen just a few short years ago. William had always been a cruel man and offered or asked for no quarter from his enemies, but this was on a totally different scale. These were not enemy soldiers, met upon a battlefield, but innocent men, women and children who offered no resistance.

The other troops were committing similar barbaric genocides across the countryside.

Once the destruction was complete, William's men sat at the edge of the village and ate some of the food and drink they had salvaged for themselves from the village. Cheese, salted meat and cakes were enjoyed, along with jars of beer. Once they had satisfied their hunger, they mounted again and rode out of the devastated village at a walk toward their next target.

And so, this was William's progress across the land. Wherever the king's army spread over the countryside below the Tees was to be found a land of continued solitude; the dwellings everywhere were deserted, as many inhabitants sought safety in flight or by lying hidden in the woods or the protection of the mountains.

As the king neared the boundary of the land divided by the Tees, a messenger rode into the camp, where his troops were enjoying a well-earned rest from the killing they had been ordered to carry out. The messenger, a 'wolf' —one of William's scouts— dismounted and approached the king. Men-at-arms moved toward their master, with spears at the ready. William waved them away.

"What is it, Fulbert?" he asked the man, who wiped the mud of the road from his face and clothes as he approached.

"My Lord, it has been noticed by some of the locals who are more inclined to your rule that an enemy band is hiding at a place called Tod Point on the south side of the Tees. It is near Coatham."

"Indeed," answered the king, "Then, tomorrow, we shall do them the courtesy of paying a visit."

He gave orders to his captains that the men should bed down and be ready to leave shortly after the dawn broke to the east. On the following morning, the troop ate quickly and saddled up, leaving the woodland glade that had sheltered them from the winter night.

Later in the day, the troop approached the position where the enemy had been sighted, but their prey, it seems, had been aware of the situation, and had fled under the cover of darkness. William dismounted and walked amongst the remains of the Saxon camp.

"We shall remain here for a while to replenish ourselves and allow the other troops to reach the

Tees. Then we shall cross the river and deal death to the inhabitants there, at least those who remain."

William spent fifteen days camped along the banks of the Tees. He knew that Saxon messengers were taking the story of his devastation far and wide, warning the people of what they might expect should they remain upon the land.

Upon one afternoon, a guard watching the river bank entered the camp.

"A troop of Saxons approach. I think it is Waltheof and his troops."

In an instant, the Norman soldiers leapt to their arms and arrayed themselves around the camp. The Saxon approached slowly, indicating that this was no attack but an attempt to parley. William arose and stood, arms folded, before his tent. Waltheof held up his hand, and his troop halted. He then moved his horse at a walk toward the king. A few paces from him, he halted and dismounted. He approached William and fell to his knee.

"My lord king, I wish to submit to you and take the oath of fealty."

This was the same Waltheof who, just a short time earlier, had killed many a Norman in the battle of York, cutting off their heads one by one as they entered through the gates.

"I also bring the oath of fealty from Lord Gospatric by proxy."

William looked down upon the Saxon earl on his knees before him.

"And where is Lord Gospatric? Why is he not also here?"

"My Lord, he is in Bamburgh."

"Had he not the stomach to meet me? I had thought he was a courageous man, or so he would have us believe."

William mused a while, whilst the Saxon knelt there, unsure what his fate would be.

"Arise Waltheof, I pardon you of the crimes that you have undoubtedly committed against myself and my rule and accept your oath of fealty. I also accept the oath of Gospatric, even though it seems he lacks the courage to meet me in person to repent of his sins. But I will issue this warning. There must be no repeat of this uprising, or my justice will be terrible upon yourselves and your supporters."

"It is understood, my Lord," the Saxon replied, rising to his feet.

He bowed low.

"I will leave my king in peace and return to my lands. I will inform Gospatric of your decision. I know he will be gladdened and relieved by your magnanimous decision."

And with that, he retreated from the king and rejoined his troops, turning with a final nod and riding off toward the ford of the river. And so it was. Indeed, in 1070, Wlatheof married Judith of Lens, daughter of Lambert II, count of Lens and Adelaide of Normandy, Countess of Aumale. But his peace was not to last…

And it was similar for Gospatric, who was allowed to keep his possessions around Bamburgh, where the king left him undisturbed till 1072. But nothing lasts forever.

Chapter 19

The Grim Reaper Calls

After the short break for his soldiers on the south bank of the Tees and to allow his other troops to convene, William, again, issued his orders, and the soldiers crossed the river and moved into the mid-section of Northumbria, between the Tees and the Tyne. This was my area, and news of the atrocities spread around the region like wildfire in a summer meadow.

As William made his way north, we watched as floods of refugees passed by Brockford, fleeing the atrocities that he was inflicting upon the land and people. We spoke to them as they passed and begged for food and drink from us. Their advice was always, 'Get out now, whilst the going is good.'

There was a good deal of discussion amongst the villagers. Cerdic appeared in the village more and more frequently, giving us the news he had heard and discussing what he thought we should do.

"The villages that have been attacked, I am sure, will be those not defended by a thegn and his men. I pledge that I will do everything in my power to protect the good villagers of Brockford and their possessions. I am certain that William will see the sense of it, and if we pledge obedience, then he will be reasonable."

"And what of the towns he has attacked?" asked a villager, "He seems to have overwhelmed whatever defences they had. Why would he listen to us, mere villagers, and pass us by?"

Cerdic pulled at the collar of his shirt in discomfort. He knew what the man had said was true.

"I am sure that much of what we have heard is exaggerated by the telling. Why would William kill the very people he means to rule over, and who will keep his coffers full with the taxes he imposes?" And so it went on.

In the evening, sitting over a meal of pottage in our home, gathered around a roaring fire, I spoke to my mother quietly.

"Mother, I have been thinking about what the refugees have told us, and also of what Cerdic has said. I think that we must pack up as much as we can carry, take the milk cow and leave Brockford. It is surely too dangerous to put it off any longer. I cannot see any other way out of it."

"But where would we go, John? William moves north with every passing day."

"I think that we must cross the River Tyne and head into the hills to the north and west of the river."

“We couldn’t do that. Your grandfather is very frail. He would never stand such a journey and would surely die along the way. And the children are still very young. How would they cope with such a long journey, especially in the middle of a bitter winter?”

I stared into the flames, pondering what she had said. She was right, of course. Grandfather would never make it over the River Tyne to the safety of the hills, and I certainly would never leave him to his fate. He couldn’t survive for a week alone. And what about that which Cerdic had said? Would he —could he— protect us from William and his marauding soldiers? And why would he kill the very people who paid him taxes? And so, we stayed in Brockford and continued to work the land that fed us.

At first, all was well. We lived in the more remote western part of the land, where rolling hills and moorland sweep down to the fertile valley of the River Wear. We ran our sheep upon the hills, our cattle in the valley, and our pigs in the woodland. Of course, during a bitter winter such as we were experiencing, the animals were down in the valley, where they could shelter.

We busied ourselves with breaking up the frozen ground and working hard to put the first ploughs of the year onto it. The children followed us, picking the stones from the surface. We often picked strange objects from the soil. There were often shards of very fine pottery, deep red in colour, and often decorated with fine scenes. Cerdic told us that this was Roman pottery from many centuries ago, when the Romans ruled our land.

On one occasion, I picked up a beautiful brooch. It was of fine metal, though the jewel it once carried was now long gone. I was always fascinated by anything that a villager found in this way. It was a look back in time, I thought, to another life long gone. I wondered if the Romans were like the Normans. How was it for the local people in their day? Certainly, they built wonderful buildings, and their goods were exceptionally fine. What would life be like for us now if they had not left our shores to return to Rome?

It was upon such a day that the Normans came. I had just hitched the ox to the plough and was ready to begin to cut the first furrow when my attention was caught by movement. I looked up to see a troop of mounted soldiers approaching along the river bank from the direction of the abbey. Other people became aware of them at the same time and stood as I did, not knowing quite what to do. A few began to make hurried steps toward the village, and I followed their example.

The Norman troop approached Cerdic's compound just as the thegn, and his men tumbled from the doors of his hall, quickly strapping on swords and grabbing for other weapons. The Norman column turned and rode in through the gate of the compound. We could not see what happened next, but shouts went up, and we all scattered to our own homes.

I called to mother, grabbed the children, and, as quickly and as calmly as I could, led them out of the house toward the gates of our village compound. I shouted again to my mother to follow us. I looked around me warily. No Norman soldiers had appeared here. They still seemed to be busy in Cerdic's compound. I dragged the smaller children by the hand and led them all to the river bank, where I pushed them under the roots of a great tree, where an otter has often lain up after his night's foraging for fish.

"Don't move!" I said, "And don't make a sound!"

I scrambled up the bank and peered over the top, frantically searching for signs of my mother, aunt and grandfather. But they were nowhere to be seen. Had they hidden somewhere else, or were they still in our house? Across the field, from Cerdic's compound, I saw a figure. It was a slightly young girl running for her life from the Normans. It was Edyth, the serving girl from the thegn's household. I raised myself above the cover of the bank, perhaps stupidly, and waved at her as she ran. I whistled loudly, and she looked up and saw me there. She changed her course and quickly covered the ground between us until she leapt like a goat over the edge of the bank and landed in a heap at the bottom, where the waters of the River Wear lapped against her, soaking her clothes.

"Get under the roots!" I called to her, and she scrambled up from the river cobles and disappeared into the hole like a mouse in the wattle.

I remained on the lip of the bank, watching and waiting to see what happened.

As I lay there, my breath coming in short gasps, I saw the first curl of smoke over Cerdic's hall, and I knew what must be happening. My stomach churned. That day had dawned with a grey sky and the river the colour of pewter. Now, I could see fire coming from Cerdic's compound and from the village, and the red flames seemed to stab at the underbelly of clouds. Pillars of greasy, black smoke crawled skyward. And still, there was no sign of mother, aunt or grandfather.

What was I to do? Should I go back to the village and search for them? Would I be alive to see the sunset that day? Should I stay with the children and protect them as best I could? If they were left without mother, my aunt, grandfather and me, their older brother, they would have no one. They would surely never survive.

As I lay there, I could hear shouts and screams coming from the village, and my skin crawled at the thought of what was happening to the people I had grown up with, loved, and loved still. So, the tales we had heard were true. William had no pity. The idea behind this slaughter, I later heard, was to show, finally, that the Norman king was very much in charge, and that there was no one else who could or would come to the aid of those considering rebellion. William had now stopped trying to merge his followers into the Anglo-Saxon people, their power structure and their way of life, and decided that he must, instead, fully replace the old ruling classes with his new one, which he knew to be loyal.

More castles were built across our land in order to dominate the country and oppress the people until life became little more than terrifying slavery in many areas of the country —particularly those areas that William felt were still liable to a flare-up of resistance.

I later learned from an elderly monk, that William was criticised for his cruel methods of oppression in England by no less than the Pope, and although William was a man capable of such barbaric events, he was also very concerned about his fate in the afterlife, which led to him richly endowing the church in order to find favour with God, to gain his absolution. I can only hope that the Lord could see through this man and his evil.

When I think, even now, of helpless children, young men and women in the prime of life, and the elderly, succumbing alike to murder, hunger and disease, I am still moved to pity, and I still shed a tear in my own old age, many years on from the events I relate to you in my tales.

The admirers of William the Conqueror must confess that in cruelty, no pagan tyrant ever surpassed, and few ever have equalled this, supposedly, Christian destroyer.

Chapter 20

Devastation

It was quiet now. It had been for a while, but I wouldn't venture out, even by half a head, or let my brother and sister move a muscle. I'm sure if I could have safely stopped them breathing hard, I would have done so. Whenever Aelfled whimpered, I put my hand over her mouth and gently rocked her. Edyth wrapped her arms around the others.

There was no sound from the village nor from the compound of Cerdic the thegn that reached us in our bolt-hole beneath the tree roots at the riverside. At length, I slowly, slowly thrust my head up between two great roots, my heart pounding at the thought of discovery by the Norman troops. I reached the lip of the river bank, and I gazed around me, taking in every item of the scenery around me. Nothing stirred except the lazy smoke that twisted its way into the air above the buildings. It was still thick and black, and I knew what that meant.

I pulled my head back down and whispered to Edyth and the frightened children who huddled, shivering beneath the tree, where an otter had once lain up in its holt.

“Don’t move from here,” I said, “And don’t come out until I return, no matter what happens.”

They looked up at me, their tear-stained faces tearing at my heart. Edyth gave me a forced smile that was meant to reassure, but she couldn’t hide the pain and sadness behind it.

I quietly clambered out from the root shelter and stood behind the tree, scouring the landscape again, hardly daring to breathe. When I was satisfied that no living soul was moving except the birds on the wing, I ventured out and, bent double, ran across to the stockade gateway. I stopped and flattened myself against the gate, waiting to detect any tell-tale sound that might signal danger. There was nothing except for the low moaning of the wind in the trees and the gurgle and swish of the river behind me.

I entered the gateway, softly treading, and gazed around me at the utter destruction of the place that had always been my home. The acrid stink of smoke and roasting flesh filled my nostrils and stung my eyes. Lying before me were the dead. People I had spoken to only that morning as we went about our chores.

Luke, a churl like myself, lay staring into heaven, a rose patch of blood spread upon the front of his shirt. His wife lay behind him. He had tried to protect her. Benjamin the smith leaned against a post of his smithy, his head hung low. A spear protruded from his body and held him fast to the post. It was the very spear that he had brought back from York. Others lay scattered in random fashion around the compound. All were dead.

I walked in a daze toward my own home —what was left of it. The thatch had gone, but the walls still stood charred but firm. My father built it well. I didn't want to enter its doorway but knew I must. The inside was now open to the sky, and I could see the carnage within clearly. My mother, aunt and grandfather lay prone upon the ground. I went from one to the other, looking vainly for signs of life, but their sightless eyes and gaping mouths told me they were in a better place.

Tears streamed down my face, and my body was racked with sobs as I dug a large hole in the middle of what had been the floor of my home. I gently eased each body into the pit and laid it as comfortably as I could before covering them again and brushing the rushes over them to disguise their resting place. It wasn't much of a grave, but it was better than leaving them out there for the crows to pick at.

I stood over them and muttered a short prayer.

"Oh Lord, protect my family, now in your care..." I broke off.

Why would any God who loved us all and protected us bring such a horrific end to people who had never hurt a living soul in their lives? My life was shattered.

Then I looked around me to see what we could take with us, for it was certain we could no longer remain safely in Brockford. There wasn't much left: a little corn and beans that had not been scorched or spilt and a dead chicken I found in a corner.

Now, I knelt down beside a corner post and dug down into the packed Earth with a knife. I lifted the package from the dust. I unwrapped it and belted on the sword and seax that had been buried there. I had taken them from the bodies of dead warriors in the battles I had fought when I was just a boy, when I should have been innocent of killing and carefree.

Peeping around the door, I left my home and began to drag the remaining bodies of my fellow villagers into the smithy. I pulled the spear from Benjamin's chest and dragged him inside to join the others. I pulled the straw from the thatch and covered the bodies with it. Then I broke off lengths of wood and threw them on, too. Lastly, I went to Benjamin's fire and scraped out the burning embers that still glowed with a little warmth.

I carefully placed them around the straw and wood until they began to catch alight. I couldn't bury them all, but this was the next best thing, and better than leaving them to the wild beasts. And so, more smoke rose above Brockford.

Cautiously, I made my way back to the bolt-hole and whispered to the others to come out. They hesitated for a few moments, terrified, but I coaxed them gently, and they emerged.

"Can we go home now?" Edmund asked, turning toward the stockade.

I grabbed his shoulder.

"No! We need to move away from here."

"But what about mother and the others?"

"They have already moved on," I told him.

I couldn't tell him the truth, could I? The children stood and stared at the compound and at the thick pall of smoke now rising from the smithy.

I looked up at the Sun. The Normans were spreading from the south, so the north was probably as safe a direction as any other. We left the riverside with what we stood in and the small amount I could carry and headed up the hill toward the woodland. I would try to stay within the forest as much as I could. We would need to keep away from ridge lines and travel over open country only by night.

As I looked around me, the tell-tale columns of smoke rising into the crisp winter air told their own stories of the harrying of the people of the north. Many villages, it seemed, had suffered our fate.

Slowly, we tramped on, day after day, dodging from one stand of trees to another. We passed villages like our own, which had been burnt and raised to the ground, their inhabitants slaughtered mercilessly by the invaders, the conquerors of our land.

I wouldn't let my brothers and sisters enter the villages, but hid them safely in the forest whilst I scavenged for what little food was left behind by the Normans. In one hut, I found a bow and a quiver of arrows, which would be useful in providing a meal. Why the raiders had left them behind, I didn't know, but I was grateful for their oversight.

I sat with Edyth in the evening, watching the children sleep, huddled together against the winter chill, and wondered. What would we find in the north? A new life or just death at the hands of our enemies, for that must now be what the Normans were —enemies. But I couldn't let the worst happen. As far as I knew, we were all that were left of our family. I must protect my little brood. We must survive this terror.

Chapter 21

The Crone

We moved on through the countryside until our feet blistered, and we stopped to cool them in the bubbling streams that ran down from the hills. We sat and rested on the banks, watching the dippers bobbing their heads and disappearing beneath the water to hunt. Our shoes were beginning to wear a little thin, and we stuffed them with grass to make walking more comfortable and soften our footfall.

Most often, we travelled by night, whenever it was possible to see by the light of the moon. We avoided towns and villages wherever we could. Much of the woodland around us was higher up on the hillsides, as valley bottoms had been cleared to grow the crops vital for our survival. Rivers, though, did sometimes offer a useful track as we could move along the banksides where tree cover allowed it.

Often, we peered from the woodland edge and stared at the devastation we saw before us. Towns or villages, it mattered not to the Normans, it seemed. Most were raised and burnt to the ground. Sightless bodies stared up to the heavens, their eyes taken by the crows and limbs chewed upon by wild beasts. I tried to shield the young ones at first, but I soon realised that I couldn't. I simply couldn't protect their tender youth from the carnage in our landscape.

Sometimes, when I came across a settlement that looked deserted and where there might be some small pickings that would provide us with a meal, I would venture out of cover, leaving the little ones hidden, and cautiously explore. The Normans were nothing if they were not thorough, and often times I would scavenge nothing. But sometimes, I would be lucky. There might be a dead animal lying bloated in the sun, from which I could cut some of the meat that had not yet begun to decay. Stale bread was to be found in the ruins of some houses. Salted fish and fruit were a rare luxury.

It was on one such scavenging search that I met with more than I had bargained for. I emerged from a thicket and looked around me. Nothing stirred. It seemed as if the whole countryside was dead. It occurred to me that even the birds seemed to have stopped singing. The only murmur was from the breeze through the trees and the whispering grasses.

Slowly and steadily, I made my way down the hill, watching, glancing, staring in every direction. I could feel my heart beating in my breast. My stomach churned and knotted.

Eventually, I reached what was left of a stockade fence. I stood a while, sheltering behind the gateposts, listening for the slightest noise from within. Hearing nothing, not even the birds, I ventured around my shelter and entered the village.

It had been quite a large settlement and must have had a goodly number of homes. All were now in ruins —their walls pulled down and the thatch merely dark stains upon the Earth. It struck me that there were no bodies lying there. Had the people managed to run away? If so, where were they now? Perhaps, like me, they were moving north to seek safety.

I peered around the door frame of what was left of the first hut. Nothing stirred. Lifting my feet and gently placing them on the ground, I entered. There was nothing. Not one useable item could I find. I left the ruin and made my way to the next house in line. I repeated my cautious inspection of the building and, finding nothing to alarm me, I entered. And that was when the world went black. All I remember was a blow to the back of my head and a bursting of stars before my eyes.

I awoke sometime later. The sun had now tipped over from its climb into the sky and was falling again toward the horizon. I shook my head, and the pain returned. I blinked my eyes and strained to see where I was. I tried to get up from the floor but found my arms and legs were bound behind me. I turned my head as far as I could and stared as my eyes fell upon an old crone chewing on a piece of meat that looked as if the dogs had left it in disgust. A pot of ale stood on the floor beside her.

"You're alive then?" she said, though I thought it was fairly obvious, "I'll soon change that!"

"Who are you?" What have you done to me? Why?" I asked.

"I am but an old woman. You are a Norman, and one less Norman will surely be a blessing in this land. But I want you to know that you are dying, like my husband and son did when you raided our village."

"But I am not a Norman," I protested, "I'm a Saxon."

"With weapons such as these at your belt?" she snorted, pointing to my sword and seax she had stripped from me whilst I was unconscious.

"I took them from Normans and Norsemen in battle," I explained.

"Battle? Battle! You have been in battle? Against whom? Saxon people?" she asked.

"Against Normans. I was at Hastings. My father was killed there, fighting for Harold. I was one of Cerdic's fyrd. I'm trying to escape from this bloodshed and madness with..." my voice trailed off.

"With…?" she probed.

"Ahem, with whomever I can find who is also escaping," I blurted.

"There are more of you?" she questioned.

I sighed.

"I have my younger brothers and sisters and a young girl."

She sat and considered me for a while.

"If I untie you, there would be nothing to stop you from filleting me like a fish."

"True," I replied, "But you will either have to trust me or kill me. But to kill me would probably condemn four children to death, too."

The old woman rose from the floor and picked up my seax. She approached and held the point of the blade to my neck. I felt the blade cut my skin and the blood run down my neck. I gasped, thinking that this might be my last breath on Earth. She stood awhile, running the flat of the blade against my throat, considering her next move. My breath came in short gasps. My stomach churned, and tears began to well up in my eyes.

Suddenly, she took the blade from my throat and moved behind me. She cut the bonds on my wrists and then leapt back with the seax levelled at me. I sat up and untied my feet. I stood and stared at her for a while.

“My name is John Aelricson,” I said, “I will not harm you.”

She seemed to relax a little and lowered the seax to her side.

“Let me leave, and I will bring the children back, as long as you promise not to harm them.”

She nodded, and I turned on my heel and left. Some minutes later, I re-entered the ruined house with Edyth and the children. They stared at her, frightened by her appearance. She stared at them, and her face softened.

“You spoke the truth, John Aelricson,” she murmured and laid the seax on the ground.

“Be seated,” she said, gesturing to the ground, “I have little food I will share with you.”

The old woman scuttled off to the back of the house and returned with some flat bread and a little pottage. We ate greedily, making sure that the children had the best of it. She watched us intently.

When we finished the meagre meal, I turned to her.

“Thank you for sparing me and for feeding us with what little you have. Will you not travel with us to the north and safety?” I asked.

She shook her head.

"I cannot. My husband and son are here. How could I leave them?"

"It was you who cleared and buried the bodies," I said.

She nodded.

"You are welcome to come with us," I repeated the invitation.

She shook her head again and looked at the floor. I knew she could not find it in her heart to leave her home, though it was now just a ruin. How would she survive? Surely, this would be her final year in this life.

We rose and gathered together our few belongings. We turned to her again and smiled. She simply stared at us.

"Go," she said, "Before the Normans return to finish their task."

We left the village with heavy hearts and trudged on our wandering journey.

Chapter 22

Flight to Safety

For a few days more —I forget how many— we journeyed on north toward the River Tyne. Travel with the little ones was slow, much slower than it had been with the fyrd. We were careful, as ever, to avoid anything or anywhere that might prove to be dangerous. In truth, the whole land was dangerous!

Wherever we travelled, we found nothing but devastation. In every settlement, houses were burnt to the ground, and food stores and livestock were destroyed so that anyone lucky enough to escape the terrible massacre would simply die of starvation over the bleak winter. I thought often of the old crone we'd met in her deserted village. Surely, this winter would bring her end.

Men said that the land was 'salted' to destroy its use for food production for decades to come. Whether the land was actually spread with salt to prevent plants from growing or not, I don't know, but it symbolised the destruction of the Earth. I do know that it was a custom in far-off lands to purify a city destroyed in war and was a curse on anyone who dared try to rebuild it.

In Spain, it is said that a traitor's house is demolished, and salt is poured onto the land owned or farmed by him, who is executed, and his head is stuck upon a pike. Truly, we live in *barbarous* times!

As we progressed north, I began to change direction toward the northwest. Common sense told me the river would be more shallow and narrow toward its source than its end. Surely, we would find a ford where I could safely herd my brood across the water to the safety of the far hills.

At length, on a bitterly cold day, we approached a small village on the banks of the river, which I assumed to be the Tyne, as it was at least as wide as our own River Wear this far into the hills. I looked ahead, always wary of any new situations, and was struck by the lack of movement from the village. No one was working the fields. No smoke rose from the smith's forge or the houses. No noise came to us on the wind of men's calls and children's merry voices. It was cold, but surely they were not all indoors. And yet the village houses seemed to stand undisturbed. There was no sign of fire damage. All *seemed* well, but that only made me the more cautious. Was it a trap set by the Normans to attract fleeing Saxons like wasps around a honeypot?

I motioned to the children to sink to the ground and shelter behind a fold in the land. Edyth gently pulled them to her, and they settled in like hares in a pasture. Slowly and cautiously, I made my way forward, keeping low in the pelt of rough grass and glancing to the sides to detect any movement that might signal danger.

A little way from the village, I stopped again and listened. I knelt behind a leafless bush and tried to mimic its shape to make my outline blend into the background. No sound came from the village other than the rush of the river behind it. I waited. Nothing.

I looked up into the grey sky and watched as two buzzards and a kite floated in lazy circles above the village. The great birds would often come down for carrion —a dead sheep or pig would be spotted quickly lying upon the ground. A murder of crows suddenly flew up from the centre of the settlement, as if startled by something. I lay a little longer to see if they would settle again, which they did. They'd probably been quarrelling over something. I knew in my heart that it was a baleful sign.

Slowly, I arose from the Earth and made my way across the remaining land, my form a flitting shadow, until I stopped behind the first house in the village. Here, I stopped again to listen. Silence. I craned my neck to look around the side of the building and was shocked to the core at what I saw.

I had seen many terrible things in my short life, but this turned my stomach, and I wretched what little food I had had that day onto the cold Earth beneath me. A great black rat looked up at me, disturbed in its grisly feast of human flesh.

For some reason which I have never fathomed, the houses were mostly intact, unburned but ransacked inside. But around the houses and in the lanes were human carcases, swarming crows, pecking at the flesh dissolving in putridity, and discharging a horrible stench. It seemed that none were left alive here to cover them in a decent burial, all seeming to have perished by the swords of the Normans. It seemed that not a single house was left inhabited. It was a wilderness without hope, left only to the wild beasts and robbers, who might terrorise the honest traveller.

I entered the village reluctantly and began to look through the wrecks of the houses to see if there was anything worth scavenging. There was nothing. Not a scrap of edible food was left. Not a tool was left undamaged. Not a cooking pot was left unbroken upon the floor.

I left the confines of the village and went to look at the river to determine whether there was a suitable means of crossing. I noticed a small jetty jutting out into the waters with a hitching pole for a boat. I approached the bank and stared down into the stream. There, lying beneath the water, I thought I could see the vague outline of a small boat. I presumed that it had been sunk there by the Normans. I wondered —could I drag it to the surface and make use of it to row my family across the winter torrent of the Tyne? Not without help. I would need Edyth and the boys to help me.

I returned to my family and took Edyth aside.

"We must make our way to the river bank. There is a boat there that I might be able to salvage from the river and re-float, but I will need help. We must not take the children through the village."

"Why not?" she asked, and then, by the look on my face, understood the reason.

We gathered the children together and told them what we must do. We skirted the village, trying to distract the children from its gory sights, and made our way to the river bank. We looked down into the muddy-brown waters, and I explained my plans.

Knowing how cold it would be, I gently lowered myself into the current, clinging to the jetty, and made a grab for the rope at the front of the boat. I thought I knew how cold it would be, but I had underestimated winter's icy grip, and I gasped as the water came up to my waist. I managed to reach the rope and pulled upon it, trying to lift the boat toward the surface. I had also underestimated the weight of the water-bearing down upon the little vessel.

Desperately, I hauled upon the boat but couldn't move it so much as a hand's breadth. After struggling with it for some time, I decided that there was only one option. I took a gasp of air and plunged under the water. Battling the current, I grabbed the boat and hauled upon one side in an effort to turn it over. My lungs burning, I held my breath as best I could and heaved at it. Slowly, slowly, I began to lift one side. With one huge effort, I finally managed to turn it onto its back. I rose to the surface and took a huge breath of fresh air.

"John, we thought you were gone!" shouted Edyth.

"You can't be rid of me that easily," I grinned, "I've managed to turn the boat so that the weight of water will be less upon it. I need to go back down and try to drag it a little further up so that I might pass you the rope. Once you have it, I will need you all to pull hard whilst I lift so that we can raise it."

They nodded their understanding. I took another deep breath and dived again beneath the surface. Slowly, I managed to raise the boat until its prow was out of the water. I surfaced and grabbed the rope, pulling on it until I could raise its end enough for Edyth to grasp it. Once done, we worked together to haul it up. As the rope rose, the boys grabbed it and helped Edyth. Gradually, and with much puffing and panting, we finally dragged it to the surface, where I was able to turn it so that it floated upon the water. Edyth now quickly wound the rope around the hitching post and tied it tightly.

I was delighted to see that there seemed to be no damage to the boat that would make it unusable. I dived for the last time and picked up the oars, held fast upon the bottom of the river.

I crawled out of the river, shivering, with my teeth chattering in my head.

"You must get warm and dry, John," Edyth said.

"We will return to the woodland and build a camp there. We will have to risk a fire to make some sort of warm meal for the children. Take the children into the woodland edge from which we approached. I must make a final visit to the village."

Edyth hurried the children away, and I entered the village again. I searched through the wreckage of the houses until I found what I was looking for — clothes. A short while later, I returned to my family, dry and re-clothed in the apparel of a dead man.

***

On the following morning —another bleak and cold one— I took my family back to the shore, where the little craft waited for us. I clambered into the boat, and Edyth and I carefully helped the children down until she finally descended herself. I untied the rope and grabbed the oars to steer the boat out into the stream.

It was at that point that I realised that I had bitten off rather more than I could chew! The little boat began to drift rapidly downstream under the force of the swollen winter current. The prow of the boat was forced upstream as the current pushed upon the sides until we were floating down the river backwards.

Desperately, I hauled upon the oars to try to push us further into the bankside. Slowly, gradually, we began to make some progress until we rounded a bend, and I saw the trunk of a fallen tree jutting out over the waters. I pulled hard upon the oar, aiming for the tree, and I was relieved when the back of the boat smacked into the trunk with a loud bang. The children and Edyth lurched as the boat came to a sudden halt. I grabbed the rope and quickly tied it to a branch. Now, I was able to push the boat towards the shallower water and, holding fast to the branches of the tree, we were able to help each of the children to safety.

I lay for many minutes on the bank, gasping for breath, and with my head pounding after my exertions against the river. Gradually, I recovered and was able to lift my aching body and lead my family back into the safety of a spruce copse on the north bank of the River Tyne.

After a short rest to let our hearts calm down again, following our watery adventure, I knew that we must set off again on our journey to safety. And so we raised the children again and encouraged them to put one foot in front of the other on our trek to another life.

As we began our long walk north of the Tyne, I began to guide us again to the east. In the western distance, I could see a faint smudge of the great rolling hills that I hoped would become our refuge, but I wanted to be further north and thought that it might be easier for the children to walk on the flatter land that lay to the east of the highlands.

And so we followed the northern bank of the River Tyne until we came to a place that I was later to learn was Hexham, at the confluence of the South Tyne and the North Tyne.

At Hexham, we turned our steps north again and trekked further into the landscape along the eastern edge of the hills. We had not gone far when we came across a great wall stretching across the land as far as we could see in either direction —east or west. It stood there, of squared stone and around seven feet across and, in some places where it had not tumbled, around ten feet high.

"What is this place, John?" Edmund asked.

I looked out at the great stretch of stones that disappeared into the distance.

"I think this must be the great wall of the Romans, which they built here when they ruled this land."

"But why did they build it?" asked Arthur.

"It was to protect our land from the savage tribes to the north," I replied.

"Are the people here savage?" asked a clearly worried Cathryn.

"No," I replied, "The people here are our friends now, and I am sure they will give us sanctuary from William and his Normans."

We all stood there, gazing at the great structure that curled like a snake around the curves in the land, and twisted its way through the hills, marvelling at how men could have raised such a construction. Truly, it was a sight to see, with drifts of snow still piled against its grey stones. I could almost see the Roman soldiers standing upon it, pulling their cloaks tightly around them against the bitter winds.

Eventually, I pulled my thoughts back to the here and now, and we helped each other clamber over the tumbled remains of the wall and down the other side to the safety of the grassy bankside. After turning for one final look at the wall, we went on our way north. The land here was reasonably flat, and the skies seemed to stretch forever. Grey clouds scudded over us, with the odd crack of blue sky peeping out from behind them.

As we journeyed on, we came upon another river confluence with the North Tyne, which I later learned was the River Rede. It seemed to flow through the flatter land, north, whilst the North Tyne turned sharply west into the hills. I decided that we would continue to follow the banks of this lesser river, further north, before we took shelter in the hills.

After many hard days of walking, our feet blistered and raw, and the children crying with the pain and the cold, the River Rede finally began to meander west into the hills itself. I stood there, pondering what to do. How much further north should we travel? Should we face the bitter winter weather that the hills had to offer us? Which would be the safer option? It was at that point that my mind was made up for me.

"Look!" cried Arthur, and we all turned to look in the direction in which he was pointing.

It was toward the east, and, on a small rise in the land, some way away, was a troop of mounted men. They hadn't seen us, I hoped, but I quickly threw the children to the ground and, with Edyth, followed them.

"That hurt, John," Cathryn complained, an indignant look upon her face.

"It will hurt more should they find us," I murmured.

We held the children hard to the Earth whilst I peeped around a rock to watch the patrol go by. They rode at a canter and were soon out of sight behind a copse of trees.

It was at this point that I decided to accept the refuge that the hills offered us despite the weather, and we turned west up through the valley. Here, the hills seemed to be folded together —first one way, then the other— like sheaves of straw in a rick. In the distance, the peaks frowned down upon us, brown as the Earth, with scattered white blotches. The weak winter sun shone its feeble rays upon the south-facing slopes, whilst those facing north lived in deep shadow, not allowing the sun to melt the winter snows that still littered the landscape we could see in pockets. The clouds cast their own shadows on the countryside as they scudded across the sky. And so we ventured upward into the Northumbrian hills.

As we walked, constantly looking around us at the changing scenery and always on the lookout for trouble, Aelfled suddenly let out a little squeak and said, "Look! Look at the stoat!"

From behind a boulder emerged a stoat, its brown fur now white in its winter camouflage, except for a little fur around its face and the black tip to its tail that never changed, no matter how fierce the winter became. In its mouth was the corpse of a thin rabbit, which it had caught off-guard as it tried to find sustenance in the barren land. The stoat stopped, astonished to see us standing there. It looked for a heartbeat and then scampered off again, as quickly as it could manage with its prey between its jaws.

"Wasn't he lovely?" Cathryn observed.

"But he'd killed the poor rabbit!" Aelfled cried, "I like rabbits."

"All animals, large and small, have to eat, Aelfled," I said, "It is no different to us eating mother's rabbit pottage."

At that moment, I realised what I had said as I looked upon the crestfallen faces before me.

"When will we see mother, aunt and grandfather again?" Arthur asked.

"One day," I said, unable to think of anything else to say.

I looked at Edyth, and she smiled a sad smile back.

For days, we struggled on, up and down through the hills, through patches of snow and bare barren moorland. We reached a plateau covered with a hand's depth of snow, and I began to regret my decision to climb into the hills. I stared out over the undulating plane. A single tree stood before me, its bare branches bent by the wind so that it leaned to the side like a drunken man. Boulders peeped their blackheads out from the snow that drifted against them.

In the middle distance, there was a thread of evergreen woodland that obviously marked the valley of a stream, as it tumbled over the hills on its journey to the sea. Behind it, the hills rose again to a sky of brilliant orange and grey. It looked for all the world as if the Earth itself was on fire, and had I not been so cold and tired, I could have stood there and looked at it for hours. But I knew we must journey on to some sort of shelter as the sun began to dip toward the line of hills to the west.

I lost count of the number of streams and bogs we crossed and how many descents and ascents we made as we made our way to what I hoped was safety. We passed through upland forests and over heather moors, trudging, often soaked, cold and miserable. The children demanded more and more resting breaks, which slowed our progress, but I knew they were essential if we were to continue.

It was during one of these breaks, behind a large boulder, where the snow had melted, and the grass showed through, and where the children could shelter in a large cleft in the rock, that I noticed a sign of life. To the east was a twin-peaked hill. It seemed to be encircled by the ruins of a wall, for they were in too regular a line to be random falls.

The walls seemed to enclose a large area of some sort of oval settlement, which appeared to have been carved out of the very hillside. As I strained my eyes to look, I thought I could make out a few stone huts. Could it be that this place was inhabited? Could we find shelter here? Was it safe? All of these questions, I could not answer.

I looked around at the children, huddled in their little stone refuge. I looked at the little worn and wind-burned faces, haggard and tortured by our escape from Brockford, and I came to a decision.

"We must make for that great hill," I announced, "I think that we might find shelter there."

And so, we rose again for what I hoped would be one last push for a little warmth and comfort. We made our way across the boggy plain and through deepening snow until we reached the slope of the hill.

As we neared the base of the hill, Aelfled suddenly called, "Look, I think I see goats."

And sure enough, a small herd of goats was grazing on the poor foraging upon the hillside. Before us, I could see a hole, an entrance, in the tumbled wall. With the last of our energy, we climbed up to it.

As we neared it, a man rose from behind the rubble, a spear in his hand.

"Stop!" he cried, "Who are you?"

I stopped in my tracks and looked at the form that had risen like a ghost before us. He was a tall man with long, straggling grey hair cascading from under a fur cap and blowing wildly in the wind. A grey beard masked his lower face. Around him was a cloak which looked to me like goatskin. I thought his eyes pierced into my very soul.

"I am John Aelricson. This is my family. We have fled from the south to escape the massacre being carried out by William and his men. We mean you no harm but would simply ask for some food and shelter."

The man stared at us for a while, obviously weighing up if we could be trusted. But what was to mistrust about a young lad, a slip of a girl and four tired and ragged children?

"Hm," he grunted, "Follow me."

And we did so until we reached one of the huts. The man threw open a rough wooden door and ushered us inside. A woman looked up in surprise as we entered. She, too, was grey-haired but as thin as her husband was stocky. Her gnarled hands were sewing a patch onto an article of clothing.

The interior of the hut was sparse. There were a few slabs of stone, strewn with skins and bits of old cloth, for sitting and sleeping on. The rough walls were of stone. Most were grey, but some I noticed were bright pink. The roof was thatched with reeds from the moorland bogs. In the centre of the room was the most important thing from our point of view —a fire. Hanging over the fire was a bubbling cauldron, giving off the most delicious smell.

"I found them half-frozen at the bottom of the Bell," the man said to his wife, "I am Aidan. This is my wife, Eldrida."

I introduced my family, and the man gestured for us to sit.

"You look hungered and frozen," Eldrida suddenly spoke up.

"We are certainly that," I replied, as we all huddled as near to the fire as we could, trying to thaw the chill in our bones.

"It's only goat broth," Eldrida announced, "But I think we have enough to spare, should you want some."

"It would be the most wonderful meal that we have eaten in many a long time," I replied, "I thank you for your kindness."

And so we ate from Eldrida's wooden bowls, the most wonderful hot broth I had ever tasted. Edyth and I tried to restrain the children from gulping it down but to no avail. After the meal, Aidan poured us all pots of ale, and we sat back and enjoyed the warmth and comfort that we had missed for many a long day.

"So, what's your story?" asked Aidan, and I told him of the happenings in our village and in every other town and village we had travelled past. He and his wife shook their heads sadly at our tales.

"We had heard that it was bad. We have not seen Normans here yet, and may God grant that we never do."

That, at least, was a comfort; no Normans. Perhaps we had finally reached safety.

"Tell me about this place," I asked Aidan.

"This is Yeavering Bell," Aidan replied.

"I have heard of Yeavering," I answered, "Wasn't it once a royal place?"

"Aye, it was," he replied, "At the foot of the hill, on the other side, stood the royal palace of old King Edwin. It was called Ad Gefrin in those days —the Hill of the Goats."

"We saw the goats!" cried Aelfled, now much revived by her meal and the warmth of the hut.

"Aye, you would," said Eldrida, "They are wild. No one owns them. You ate one in your stew."

At that, Aelfled looked a little crest-fallen again, though why I could not say. It was not the first goat she had eaten.

Aidan continued, "The settlement, up here in the Bell, has been here from before men could count time. It was the largest hill fort in Northumbria. They say there were once 125 houses here, between the peaks. The old fort had four entrances, with a guard house. When we came up here, we were all set to rebuild some of the old huts. We live here in safety, hidden from the gaze of anyone in the valley. We can only be seen from the moor, as you yourselves found out."

"There are more than you living here?" I asked.

"Five families spread across the site. Some of them have gone down to the valley to hunt and forage for what food they can find. I dare say you will meet them in the morning."

"You can see as far as the sea from the top on a clear day," Eldrida said to the children, and their faces brightened even more.

They were red with the glow of warmth now.

"We've never seen the sea," said Arthur.

"Tonight," Aidan continued, "You will stay here with us. Tomorrow, we shall move you to one of the spare huts, should you want to stay here a while."

"That would be wonderful, Aidan. I thank you again for your kindness to us. We would be happy to stay here."

Aidan grunted and went back to his ale.

On the following day, the morning dawned cold but with clear blue skies that showed hardly a whisker of cloud and, true to his word, Aidan introduced us to the other families as they emerged from their huts, and we cleared out some stored goods to make the spare hut habitable for the family. The children went up to the summit of the Bell with Eldrida, and stared out to the ocean in wonder.

At last, I thought. We have reached safety.

Chapter 23

Nightmare!

During that day, Aidan, his wife and all of the other members of the community, who, it has to be said, turned out to be the most welcoming community I had ever seen —even in my long travels— helped us patch up and make comfortable the spare hut that had been used for storage.

Some people donated skins and thin bolsters to make the hut habitable. Pots for cooking and eating were readily loaned to us. Holes in the walls were packed with rushes and mud to keep out the winter chill. We lit a roaring fire in the central hearth from the timber hauled from the forest below the hill. The girls went out onto the boggy land, under strict instructions from me to keep close to Edyth, and picked sheaves of rushes to cast upon the floor. All in all, we were very comfortable in our new home.

***

The scream woke me from my slumber. It was a piercing shriek that seemed to cut through me and chilled my very bones. I leapt from the rough skins covering me and grabbed my seax from its sheath.

The embers of the fire were still casting a ruddy glow around the hut. Now, the others were rising to see what the trouble was.

I paced around the hut, probing into the dark recesses, whilst Edyth scrambled over to the children to calm them.

"Shh, my lovelies," she crooned and wrapped her arms around them.

I could see no intruders, so threw a few more sticks onto the fire and stoked the embers until they took hold and cast their warm glow around the room.

My youngest sister, Cathryn, was sitting up with Edyth's arms folded around her, sobbing. Edyth glanced up at me as I approached.

"A bad dream," she said, "Nothing more."

My younger brothers were now by my side but unarmed, and as young as they were, I'm not sure how much help they would have been had we been under attack.

At that point, the rough plank door flew open, and I whirled to meet the interloper, my seax pointed at his gut. But it was only Aidan, his sword by his side and a look of fear on his face.

"John," he said, "What is it?"

"Just Cathryn having a bad dream," I replied, "She'll be fine now."

He breathed a sigh of relief and relaxed.

"She will not be alone in her fearful dreams this night," he said, "And there will be many nights like this to come."

With that, he closed the door behind him and left for his own bed.

"What was it Cathryn?" Edyth asked my sister, gently rocking her, "Tell us about it, and you'll feel better."

"I saw our village," she said, "I saw the bodies —Luke and Benjamin. There was blood running from their mouths. Then they sat up and grinned at me."

Edyth glanced up at me with a pained expression.

"And then I saw mother and grandfather. They were standing by our house and shooing me away. They wouldn't let me run to them. I just wanted to hug mother."

I looked around at the other children. The boys had sunk to the floor now, and, in the firelight, I could see tears streaming down their faces. Edyth's eyes, too, were moist, and she rubbed away the beginnings of a tear and rocked Cathryn gently.

"Cathryn, what happened was terrible, and none of us will ever forget it."

And then I made a decision. Edyth could see me fighting within myself and nodded her head.

“I have something to tell you that is not what you want to hear, but I fear it must be said. Mother, aunt and grandfather were…were…killed in the Norman raid.”

There, I had said it. The children looked up at me, and tears welled in their eyes until they burst in a torrent down their little cheeks. Oh, how they sobbed. How Edyth sobbed. How I sobbed! We took them in our arms and held them tightly, rocking them and soothing them as best we could. At length, we had all cried ourselves out and just lay there, exhausted.

After a while, I found the strength to talk to them.

“The pain will become less with time. What we must all remember,” I said, looking at all of the upturned faces, “Is that mother, aunt and grandfather are safe in Heaven now. They weren’t shooing you away from them, but telling us that we must get as far from the village as we can. You see, they are still watching over us and guiding us from Heaven. And we were never afraid of Benjamin and Luke when they were alive, so why should they harm us now?”

Heads were nodded, and eyes dried.

“But why must we have bad dreams, John?” Cathryn asked, “Why can’t the bad dreams be caught in a net, and only the good ones get through?”

"Ah, but it wasn't a bad dream," I replied, smiling and trying to sound happy, though I didn't feel it.

"It was a good dream. Mother and grandfather came to see you. They were here, protecting you and keeping us all safe."

I hoped it sounded more convincing than I felt.

"Oh, yes," my sister replied and began to brighten.

"Mother, grandfather," she said, "I'm sorry I was afraid of you. You can come back to see me any night."

Now, my eyes began to water again. Edyth looked up at me and hugged Cathryn more tightly to her. She smiled a thin smile that said, 'Well done'.

"What will we do now, John?" asked Edmund.

"Well, we will stay here a while with Aidan, Eldrida and all of the other lovely new friends we have made. I think we are safe from the Normans here; they have never found this settlement. After that, we'll have to see."

"Could we go to the sea?" Edmund asked.

"Someday, when the weather is fine, I promise we shall make our way to the sea," I told him.

The children's faces brightened.

"I've never really seen the sea," Arthur said, "Only from the top of the hill. It looks so nice."

"None of you have," I replied, "Only I have sailed upon it. You will like it. It is a wonderful sight. You will see many strange things. And the smell — oh, the smell!"

After a little coaxing, the children returned to their Earthen beds and Edyth and I sat around the fire until we knew they were asleep again.

"Will it be safe at the coast, John?" she whispered.

"I don't know," I replied, "We shall have to see how far north the Normans penetrate. It might be that once they think they have subdued the land, they will go back south and leave us in peace. If they do, then, one day, we shall take ourselves to the Holy Island of Lindisfarne, where St. Cuthbert lived. Perhaps he will protect us from the Normans."

On the following morning, I stood upon the great hill of Yeavering, above the ruins of Edwin's palace of Ad Gethyn, and gazed out to the ocean. Would this hill and the coast beyond be the place of safety we all dreamed of or just another chapter in the nightmare we were all living?

Chapter 24

Lindisfarne

We stayed with Aidan, Eldrida and our new-found friends for a while until winter released us from its icy grip. We lived by hunting and collecting what edible plants we could find. We often dined on goats. It was not an easy existence, but it seemed safe, as far as I could tell. How I longed for the days in Brockford, where we grew our own food and enjoyed my mother's cooking.

Winter turned to spring, and the weather gradually warmed —something I was grateful for. The weather in this part of the country seemed much colder than I remembered it at home. The winds seemed brisker and more bitter. It had snowed, on and off, for most of the winter. It would build and then melt again as a slightly warmer breeze blew up from the south. But it was always windy at the summit of Yeavering Bell.

One particularly warm and pleasant late spring evening, when even the wind at the summit seemed to be calmer than usual, I sat within a hollow between the two peaks, gazing up at the myriad stars strewn across the heavens. Why was it that we sat on our Earth, unmoving at the centre of this wonderment? Why did the stars move around us in a circular motion, with the Moon at the centre? Were the stars really angels in God's Heaven, as my grandmother told me? Were mother, father, grandmother, grandfather and my aunt up there somewhere? Were they looking down upon us? What would they tell me to do?

As I pondered these questions, I became aware of a presence approaching. It was Aidan.

"John," he greeted me, "It is a wonderful night to be out, gazing at the wonders above us."

He sat down beside me in the hollow. (We did try not to spend too much time on the summit ridges in case it attracted unwanted attention).

"Tell me your thoughts," he said.

"Oh, I was thinking of what is best to do now. It seems to have become more peaceful here in the north. We haven't heard nor seen a Norman patrol for some weeks."

He nodded.

"I was wondering what to do. Should I take the children home and try to rebuild our lives, or stay here, living on the Bell? I have also thought of taking the children to the sea. I have heard of the Holy Island of Lindisfarne. I heard that it is wonderful there. Perhaps we can build a life there, near to the old monastery. I hope St. Cuthbert might protect us. I have asked God for his advice, but he doesn't seem to be listening."

"I fear God has not been looking at our part of the world over the last few years."

I nodded.

"Why would a kindly, loving God allow William and his men to carry out this sort of butchery?"

Aidan sat lost in his own thoughts for a while.

"It has been a terrible slaughter," he replied, "And it has made me wonder too."

Another long pause followed while we both pondered our own thoughts. I stared, again, at the heavens above me. Was God really there? Was he watching me now? Why would he not tell me what to do for my family? At length, Aidan spoke again, at first hesitatingly.

"John, I once spoke with a very wise man. He put something to me that I have thought deeply about, particularly since the invasion and the terrible happenings in our time. I shall tell you as I heard it, and then you too can ponder it."

"It went something like this:

If God is willing and able to defeat evil, whence then is evil?

If he is willing, but not able, then he is impotent.

If he is able, but not willing, then he is malevolent.

If he is neither able nor willing, why call him God?"

I was astounded at this.

"What do *you* believe, Aidan?" I asked.

"In some ways, I have returned to the old religion, John. I now think of Woden and Thor, the Lord of Ogres, as my guides."

And with this, he pulled from his shirt a pendant in the shape of Thor's hammer.

"It is the religion brought to these shores by the Danes and Norsemen, and I can only hope that Thor and Woden might be powerful enough to rid this land of the foul Normans who now pillage it and slaughter our people."

I was left speechless for some time whilst I considered his words. He sat there beside me, lost within his own thoughts. As the night air began to chill, I wrapped my cloak more tightly around me, but I would not go to my bed. I wanted to talk more with Aidan.

"What else do you believe, Aidan?"

He sat a little longer. I think he was unsure what was best to say to me.

"Have you heard of the Woodwose, John?" he asked.

"I have heard of him from tales my grandfather told, but I know little about him. He is the Wildman of the Woods, isn't he?"

Aidan laughed.

"Some would call him a *wild* man, but I would call him a very *wise* man. The name 'Woodwose' comes from the language of long ago, from the words 'wuda' meaning wood or forest, and 'wasa' meaning 'being' or 'to be alive'. You might also have heard him called the Green Man."

"Tell me more, Aidan," I begged, warming to the conversation more and more, and wanting to hear everything Aidan had to tell me.

"Some say he has leaves for hair, with a leafy beard. He is the powerful Force of Nature. He is weakened and almost killed by winter, and yet he is born again in springtime, refreshed. He is the lord of the seasonal cycle and the struggle for life that all animals and plants suffer. He has been a centre for worship and sacrifice throughout our old world and is as immortal as the very land itself."

Now, I was fascinated. I sat there, wrapped in what Aidan was telling me.

"Tell me more," I urged him.

"He is the life force of rebirth. Spring must return and bring with it the Sun and new growth and plenty. Our lives are never certain, and many times, we have few comforts."

This was true!

"All men yearn for a plentiful harvest, and many still believe in the power of the Green Man. I did hear that some peasants once tried to capture the man of the woods by getting him drunk and tying him up in hopes that he would give them his wisdom in exchange for freedom. I don't know whether they ever became more wise or not."

"What you have said makes sense to me, Aidan."

I knew that I must ponder this much longer and decide upon my own feelings.

Aidan nodded and smiled.

"You must think it through for yourself, John," he said, almost reading my thoughts, "The next time you are in the forest, with the trees coming into leaf, the woodland floor strewn with flowers and the animals bringing forth their young, pause a while where the sun breaks through, and look around you at the magnificence of Mother Nature. I know that you, too, will see the glory of the Green Man."

"Aidan," I said, "You seem to have great knowledge of the world, more than most men. Where did you learn all of this?"

Aidan chuckled.

"I have not always lived like this, John. I grew up in the great monastery of Jarrow. I was to be a monk but decided that there were too many unanswered questions and that I must answer them myself, out in the wide world. I am still learning and deciding things —even now."

I knew he was right, and I thought about his words long into the night, huddled in my rough bed. There was much that I had to think about and decide for myself.

***

A few days later, I was hauling timber up the great hill to our camp when a man passed me by, descending from the Bell. I didn't recognise him and wondered what his business was with our community.

As I arrived at our hut, near to the summit, Aidan emerged from his hut and beckoned to me.

"I have news," he said.

I left the great pile of wood and sauntered across. He entered his hut and beckoned me to follow him. Once inside, when my eyes adjusted to the diminished light, I was aware that the other men of the community were also there, sitting around the edges of the house in anticipation.

"That man you saw was a messenger. He brings news. It seems that Bishop Aethelwine and many of his monks have tried to flee to Lindisfarne with the body of Cuthbert and much of the treasure from Durham. However, the Bishop was caught by the Normans pursuing him and has been outlawed and imprisoned."

(I was later to hear that the Bishop would die in prison during the winter of 1070/72. William later appointed the French William Walcher as the first 'Prince-Bishop').

Aidan continued.

"It seems, however, that some of the monks escaped capture and have reached Lindisfarne. They say that the tide was at flood when they approached the island, but that it ebbed as they approached the shore and the safe passage across the sands. The monks have proclaimed it as a miracle of St. Cuthbert."

So, St. Cuthbert was at Lindisfarne. Was this the sign I had waited for? Should I now take the children and make my way across to the coast and see if we could make a better living there, in the protection of the saint? And yet, my faith had suffered a blow recently. During that evening, sitting around the fire, I made my decision.

I turned to my family —Edyth too, as she was now regarded as one of the family by both myself and the children— and announced, "We must pack all of our belongings. We will be leaving Yeavering soon to go and try to find a better living on the Holy Island of Lindisfarne, under the protection of St. Cuthbert."

They had all heard the news of the escaping monks and the saint. The children's faces showed a mixture of excitement to reach the ocean, but also the worry and uncertainty of leaving our new home and the community on the Bell.

Edyth smiled at me.

"I think it is a good decision, John. We could not have withstood another winter at Yeavering. Life has been a struggle and little more than an existence. I think we will do much better on the island, where proper food might be more plentiful."

And so it was that a few days later, we said our goodbyes and left Yeavering Bell. We were never to return. I heard no more of Aidan and the little community that had taken us to their hearts and probably saved our lives during those terrible days.

Chapter 25

The Sanctuary Island

We descended from the Bell at the western side, the eastern side being very steep and open to all eyes for miles around. A small flock of wild goats scattered from their foraging as we passed them. We meant them no harm today, but it was not always so. We had dined upon them on a number of occasions, and they were wise enough to regard us as dangerous.

The day had dawned fine and warm for the time of year. The sun beat down upon us from a clear blue sky. Not a cloud was to be seen. When we reached the plateau, we all turned and looked back up Yeavering Bell, past the old fortress walls to the small hut that had been our home for many weeks. Then we turned again and made our way around the foot of the Bell until we reached its towering eastern side. Now, it was a straight trek northeast. It was, Aidan told me, around twenty miles, and I hoped to do it in two days, but with the children, it might be three. Only time and the conditions would tell.

As the day wore on, we were making good progress, and came upon the River Till. Here, I decided to spend the night. As the children rested with Edyth, I scouted the river bank and finally found a wooden bridge across the flow. Clustered in a small clearing near the river crossing was a small settlement. Some houses had been burned to the ground, but some still stood, perhaps rebuilt. People were busying themselves around, trying to attend to their daily needs, and smoke curled from the roofs and into the blue skies. As I approached, a man looked up and watched my advance warily. As I closed the distance, more villagers turned and watched me.

"Good day to you," I said, trying to sound friendly.

"What would you want?" the man replied.

"I am looking for somewhere for my young family to spend the night. We are on our way to Lindisfarne."

"Young family, you say. How many?"

"I have two brothers and two sisters, and we also have a young woman with us."

"We want no strangers here!" the man exclaimed.

I must have looked a little surprised and crestfallen. An elderly woman stepped forward.

"You can stay with us," she said and glared at the man, "We will have no man say that we refused hospitality to children in need."

"Thank you," I said, "I will bring them."

The man spat and turned on his heel to wander into the woodland.

At length, I returned to the settlement with the family, and the old woman showed us what must have been an old pig sty.

"Best I can do," she said, "There will be a little food at sundown."

"Thank you," I replied, "We are grateful for any help."

She turned and left us. We tried to settle in as best we could, with the few belongings we could carry, and then went out and sat on the river bank, watching the current and the trout as they flitted back and forth from beneath the cover of the bankside vegetation.

Occasionally, one would rise to the surface to take the odd flies that were now beginning to drone above the water. It was not a large river, and it ran with the brown colouring that I had always known from our own River Wear.

As the Sun began to dip to the western horizon, the old woman emerged from her house and called, "We have a little food."

I had noticed the smell of roasting meat during the afternoon, and my mouth watered at the prospect. We entered her house. An old man sat in the corner. He stared at us. I nodded, but there was no reply. We sat down around the edges of the house, feeling a little uncomfortable. The old man simply stared at all of us in turn. I could tell that Edyth was a little uneasy, and the children just sat with their heads lowered.

In the middle of the room was the hearth, and, as I had thought, a large piece of meat was hanging from a spit, roasting slowly over the flames and dropping the odd splash of fat to sizzle upon the logs. It looked to me a little like pork or the flesh of a young calf. Had they killed an animal, or had the Normans slaughtered it in their terrible butchery?

The old woman took the sizzling meat from the fire and laid it upon a large platter of wood. With a knife, she carved slices and served them to us on smaller platters, along with a few roots and herbs from the countryside that she had collected.

"Thank you," I said, and the children all muttered their own thanks.

Edyth nodded and sniffed at the meat. I took my knife and immediately cut off a chunk. I stuffed it into my mouth greedily. It certainly had the taste and texture of young beef, but perhaps a little sweeter and softer. I decided that it was not pork. There was no thick rind to it that I always savoured from pork. It was good, without the strong taste of goat or game.

"There is nothing else," the old woman announced, "Except a jug of ale."

"Thank you," I replied, "We are more than grateful for what you have given us. These are bad times, and food is scarce everywhere."

We had savoured our meagre meal and when finished, the children took the platters to the river to be cleaned.

"Was the meat from a young calf?" I asked.

"Calf? We have no calf!" the old man suddenly exclaimed.

His sudden burst of life surprised me, and I jumped.

"It was not calf," said the old woman, quietly.

She said no more.

"Oh," I said, "Then what was it? It was very tender and full of taste."

The old man sprang to life again.

"It was an accursed Norman," he cried, "I shot him from his saddle not two days ago!"

Edyth looked at me with horror. She leapt up and fled the small building. I had no doubt in my mind why.

“Are you truly telling me that we have just eaten human flesh?” I asked, stunned by the old man’s revelation.

“There is no other use for a dead Norman,” the old man said, his voice bitter.

I sat, still stunned by the statement. Surely, this was not real. Surely, it had not come to this.

“It is happening all over Northumbria,” the old woman sighed.

“There is nothing else to eat. The Normans have slaughtered animals wherever they could find them. Not a beast is left. We hunt in the woods and manage to get some food that way, but then so is every man. Cannibalism is rife amongst our people. There are certainly plenty of dead to carve from.”

I looked down at the ground. The children must never know, I thought. That night, we huddled up in the deserted pigsty of the old couple, and I tried to get some sleep. Edyth had returned, looking a little grey, and I had no doubt where her meal had ended up. The wild beasts will pick at that, I thought.

And then I thought of the Norman, whom we had just helped to eat. His family would never know his fate, other than that he had been killed by the barbarous people of Northumbria. It was well that that was all they would know.

On the following morning —another fine and warm one— we gave our thanks to the old woman, whose name I never did ask, and set off again on our journey to the coast. It was a long trek and seemed to go on forever across the flatter land, until we finally could look east and see the sea before us. This hastened our step, and soon, we could see the island of Lindisfarne before us.

The island was, I estimated, around two miles out from the coast. It seemed quite flat except for a great mound at the very end of the land. Like a single tooth in an old crone's jaws, it protruded to the sky. Here, the mist was still heavy, and the great posts for tying up the fishing boats stood like sentries at the shoreline. The charred ruins of what must have been the priory, stood, just visible, in the centre of what looked like rough huts. It had been built entirely of wood, and so little of it remained.

The children stared out over the sand, entranced by the sights and sounds. They watched as white gulls floated on the breeze and swooped down to look into the rock pools. Edyth, too, was fascinated by the sea. I took hold of her hand and led them all down to a line of weed that lay where the tide had left it. I scooped up a handful of the weed and held it for them to smell.

"Oh," said Cathryn, "What a wonderful smell!"

The others sniffed it in turn and agreed.

The only access that we had to the island was by crossing the sand and mud flats, which are covered with water at high tides. These sand and mud flats carry an ancient pilgrim's path. I looked out to sea to determine how far from the land the waves were breaking. It seemed to me to be quite a distance.

I led my party to the beginnings of where I could see the crossing. We started out across the mud, watching the waters of the ocean. Still, they seemed to be quite far out to sea. One thing I had not taken into consideration was the fact that it was a little harder to walk upon the mudflats than on dry land, and the children began to tire when we were little more than half way across.

By now, I also estimated that the tide had turned and was beginning to creep closer. What to do? Should we retreat back to the mainland or keep going, now that we had reached over halfway to safety on the island? I decided to keep going. Still, the waters crept closer. I could see the look of concern upon Edyth's face. She shot me glances from time to time, which told what she was thinking. We had made it so far, but would we meet our end in the briny waters of the sea?

Slowly but surely, we tramped toward the island. Slowly but surely, the waters rose and came nearer. Still, we pressed on, trying to coax the children to walk just that little bit faster. Now, the children, too, became concerned. They, too, could see the rising waters, and fear was beginning to fill their minds.

I estimated that we were about three-quarters of the way across the causeway when the first small waves began to break over it. There was no turning back now. We had to press on. Had I miscalculated this journey?

Soon, the water was lapping over our feet, and the girls began to cry. I lifted Cathryn onto my shoulders, and Edyth hoisted Aelfled into her arms. The boys ran beside us as we waded through the encroaching water. I say 'ran', but it was less than that as we battled on through the rising tide.

At length, I thought the waters were becoming shallower. We must be reaching the rising land of the shore. At last, we gained the shoreline, and we all collapsed, weary but relieved, upon the sand. The waters continued to rise, but we were safely on the island.

"How does the water rise and fall like this, John?" Edmund asked.

"I don't know," I answered him truly.

After a short while, we rose again and made our way into the centre of the island, where the old monastery stood.

We entered the small settlement, where a man was drawing water from a well. We approached the man, who glanced up, showing little interest in our arrival.

"Where might I find shelter for my family?" I asked.

"Fleeing the Normans?" he asked.

I nodded.

"The monks have constructed buildings near to where the old priory stood. They will give you sanctuary."

I thanked him and moved on. On a slight rise in the land stood what was left of the old monastery — now just a few timbers pointing to the sky. Around them were huts of differing sizes. A monk stood at the wooden gate, watching our arrival.

"Good day to you," I said, "I seek refuge for my family from the invaders, who are laying waste to the countryside."

The monk nodded.

"I am Brother Paul," he said, "You are welcome here."

He was a tall man, as I remember, with a long, perhaps mournful face. Nevertheless, he smiled down upon the children and, for the first time in a goodly while, they smiled properly and looked relieved to be in a place of safety at last.

"Firstly, we must find somewhere for you to rest."

At the rear of the old monastery site, the monks had built some small huts for their own shelter, and also to house the other refugees who had arrived upon the island. Brother Paul led us to one of the huts and ushered us inside. It was, as I have said, small, but it would do to shelter us from the weather that blew in from the sea. I was sure that we could make ourselves comfortable there for now.

"Thank you," I said to the monk, "We are grateful to you for this lodging. Edyth and I are happy to work to earn a living, and the children are of an age where they can help out in the fields or otherwise."

Brother Paul nodded and smiled.

"I think we can find a meal from somewhere," he said, looking down into the faces of the children.

Their eyes brightened, and Aelfled drew close to the monk and wrapped her arms around his long legs. At first, he looked a little surprised by the show of affection and gratitude from one so young, but he laid his hands upon her head.

"Bless you, my child," he said and then disappeared through the door.

"Come and find me in a short while," he called back, "And I will find you a meal."

We arranged our meagre possessions around the hut and decided where each should sleep. I would find a bed near the door for protection from what, I knew not. A few minutes later, we made our way to the larger hall that had been built, and entered. There, in the middle of the floor, were a number of cooking fires. Bending over one was Brother Paul. The smell of cooking invaded our nostrils, and my mouth watered at the thought of a good meal.

Brother Paul beckoned to us, and we sat ourselves around the fire. Upon a rough griddle were fish cooking above the flames. On platters were small hunks of bread. A jug of ale and wooden cups stood away from the flames. Oh, but it was a wonderful meal. As one set of fish cooked, Brother Paul would add more until we were stuffed and could eat not another morsel.

Brother Paul sat with us.

"Tell me your story, John," he said.

And so I did. I told him of all of the happenings that we had witnessed and those that we had been told of. His face was sad as he listened to my sombre tale.

That night, we settled ourselves into the hut that was to become home. I slept peacefully, more secure in what I felt was finally a place of sanctuary for my family.

Chapter 26

The Holy Island

We awoke the following morning to clear blue skies again. One of the fathers brought us some food and drink, which we greatly enjoyed. Once we were fed and had washed, after a fashion, in a bowl, we wandered down to the shoreline.

This, I explained to the children, was the very edge of England where the land and oceans meet. We gazed out over the tidal mudflats, saltmarshes and sand dunes, which merge together to form a place which is home to many strange plants and form a food supply that attracts birds and other animals to their groaning table. All in all, I thought it was a wonderful place to be.

Out on the water was a handful of small fishing boats, some manned by the local men and others by monks. Along the shore, another local drove a horse carrying a number of wicker baskets upon its back. I had never seen the like of these before, but I guessed, rightly, that they were traps to catch fish.

The children ventured further down to the shoreline.

“Take care!” Edyth called after them.

Truly, she was like an older sister to them. They flitted from one rock pool to another, inspecting each one for signs of the life which lived upon the shore.

Edmund, looking into one such pool with Arthur, suddenly let out a cry.

“John, what is this creature?” I wandered over, stepping from stone to stone and trying to keep my feet dry —which the children seemed not to care about— until I reached them. Sure enough, there was a strange animal lurking in the shallow water of the pool. It seemed to have at least eight legs and two enormous pincers thrust out from what I imagined was the creature’s head. It appeared to have a thick shell upon its back.

“I am not sure what it might be,” I said to the children, “There are so many strange creatures here. I am sure we will learn about them in time.”

We spent the rest of that day wandering around that wonderful island, taking in all the scenery and marvelling at the new life we had discovered. There were huge sandy dunes to explore and beaches, where the waves broke over sand and stones. There was a large lake festooned with reeds and rushes, where waterfowl dabbled and dived for nourishment.

Looking back at the land, we could see the hall of Bamburgh, standing upon its own mound above the waterline. Its name, I later learned, was originally Bebbanburgh. Once, it was home to the kings of ancient Northumbria. It is believed by the local people, that it had been occupied from the very first century after Christ. Up until 547AD, it was called Din Guardi, and was a British fortress and the capital of King Morgan Buic of the Bryneich kingdom. However, in that year came some forty ships, bringing with each of them twelve warriors of the Anglo-Saxons. Things in Northumbria changed forever.

From 634AD, Bamburgh was the capital of Oswald, the King of Northumbria. He had spent a good while in exile, but finally brought together the kingdoms of Bernicia and Deira under a single ruler. It was Oswald who helped spread Christianity in Northumbria. The Venerable Bede said that Oswald was a saintly king. Sadly, after ruling for eight years, Oswald was killed at the Battle of Maserfield.

Further out to sea, we could see the Farne Islands. These two groups of islands are home to uncountable seabirds and also the seals that live around the coast. (The children, in particular, would soon come to love the seals).

In the evening, we went, again, to the large hall, where Brother Paul had said we might eat again. We entered, and he looked up and smiled.

"Come and eat," he said.

Again, the monk sat with us.

“I have some news,” he said.

I stopped in my chewing and listened.

“I have spoken to Brother Adam. He is responsible for the fishing we do around the island. He says that he can take you and teach you to fish. That way, you can work for the monastery until you decide what your future might be.”

“Thank you, Brother Paul,” I said, grateful for something to do to earn my living.

“And Edyth can help around the monastery, such as it is,” he added, “I am sure we can find plenty of chores to keep her busy,” he chuckled.

“I will be delighted to help where I can,” Edyth replied.

Again, we enjoyed the meal provided for us by the monks. I was pleased that, from the following day, I would be working to support my family and not simply taking charity.

When we had finished eating, Brother Paul poured me a small cup of clear amber liquid from an Earthen jug. I tasted it. It was sweet and strong. I turned to the brother.

“What is this, Brother?” I asked, “It is good.” Edyth warily tried a cup and, with raised eyebrows and a wide smile, agreed.

"It is mead," Brother Paul replied, "We make it on the island. It is vatted with fermented grape juice, herbs and honey. The water comes from the well."

I must say that I greatly enjoyed the evening with the mead jug!

"Tell us about the monastery," I asked Brother Paul.

"Well, the monastery here was founded by Saint Aidan. He was an Irish monk. He was sent from the Island of Iona in the Western Isles to serve King Oswald and help convert the people to Christianity. Other monks from Iona soon settled here. Later, St. Cuthbert came here and became the Prior and Bishop of Lindisfarne. When he died, his remains were buried on the island but were moved to Durham after the Vikings raided and the priory was deserted."

"But Cuthbert has now returned to the island," I said.

Brother Paul nodded.

"Yes, we were forced to flee from Durham in the face of the Norman attacks. We had no way of knowing what they would do. We brought the body of the saint with us."

He stopped a while as if lost in thought.

"It was strange," he said, "When we arrived at the causeway, the tide was coming in and almost up to the mainland shore. But, as we stood there, resting the coffin and recognising that we would need to wait for a change in the waters, the tide suddenly began to recede. The local people said that they had never seen the like before. It allowed us to continue on our journey and to reach the island. We believe it was a miracle of the saint."

"Is it true that the saint's body has not decayed despite him dying so many years ago?" Edyth asked.

"I understand so, though I have never seen it myself," the monk replied.

"How can that be?" pressed Edyth.

"I don't know, my child," Brother Paul admitted.

"And what of the ancient gospels?" I asked him.

"The Lindisfarne Gospels were written here, on this island, in the early 700s. We think the artist who decorated them was probably Eadfrith, who later became Bishop of Lindisfarne. I have heard that they once had a fine metal case made by a hermit called Billfrith."

"You have seen them?" I asked.

"I have seen them. They are very beautiful."

"Why was the priory burned down?" asked Arthur.

"So many questions!" said Brother Paul, "But it is good for young people to ask questions. How else will they ever learn? Well, it happened in around

793AD. In that year, terrible omens spread across Northumbria. Dreadful storms, lightning, whirlwinds, and, some say, fiery dragons swept across the sky. These awful signs were followed by famine, until, in January of that year, ravaging Viking heathens descended upon Lindisfarne and destroyed everything they could find. Never before had such terror struck on this land. The Vikings poured out the sacred blood of the saints upon the altar and trampled upon the bodies of the saints and monks alike in the priory, like dung in the streets. It was these terrible raids that eventually led to the monks leaving the island and taking the remains of Cuthbert with them."

"Terrible times," I said, "Not unlike the times we live in today."

Brother Paul nodded.

"One of the things that the monks did was to set up the first school in this area, on the island. They taught reading and writing. They trained boys to become missionaries, and many went out into the world to preach the Gospels. We intend to rebuild a school here. Would the children like to attend?"

"Indeed they would," I put in, before the children could decline the offer.

"It would be a wonderful thing for them to continue with the little education they received by the monks in our local monastery."

"What about the girls?" Edyth asked.

"The girls would be welcome to attend," said Brother Paul, "The first school taught only boys, but St. Aidan was also keen that girls should learn, though not amongst the boys."

"It will be a great opportunity," I pronounced, and the children nodded their heads in agreement.

"Have you ever thought of becoming a nun, Edyth?" the brother asked.

Edyth shook her head.

"No Brother," she replied, "I think my destiny lies elsewhere."

She looked at me and smiled.

Brother Paul scanned both of our faces and smiled.

"I think you are probably right," he said.

On the following day, I began my new life as a fisherman. Edyth helped to clean the monastery and to gut fish, and the children were free to play, for now, until the school was ready.

Chapter 27

Shipwreck!

For many weeks, I went out to sea with Brother Adam, some of the monks and the locals, where they taught me to sail a boat and to fish for my living. It was not easy —there is much to learn about life upon the ocean.

Gradually, I became competent at the work and enjoyed it immensely. It was good to be out in the fresh air that blusters in from the sea and brings with it that particular smell that can only be experienced at the coast.

I learned to make and mend nets. I learned to handle the sails and oars of the small fishing boats that plied their trade from Lindisfarne and Bamburgh.

I learned to fish the rivers with the hand nests we threw from the riverbanks to haul out the freshwater fish and those who entered the rivers from the sea each year.

I decided that I loved the sea and could not imagine going back to my former life upon the land. But that brought with it the feeling of guilt that I had not returned to Brockford to till the land of my ancestors. What to do?

Whenever we had visitors to the island, we were keen to speak with them and to find out what was happening. On a particularly wild and windy afternoon, when fishing was not an option for us, a merchant took his life in his hands and crossed the causeway to the island, bringing goods for sale and hoping to take away some of the smoked fish that we produced. We were all at work in the smoke huts when he arrived. I must say that the smell from the huts is probably the one I most enjoy —the oak woodchips smouldering and the mouth-watering smell of the smoked fish cannot be described to those who have never smelled it for themselves.

Upon hearing of the arrival, we emerged from the huts, our faces grey with the smoke. The merchant was a small man, but with a girth the size of an elderly oak. His long, greasy hair hung down behind him, cascading from an old brown hat that perched on the top of his head. His shabby green coat was patched and sewn in a number of places to prolong its usefulness. Two lean donkeys trailed before him, panniers full to the brim with a number of goods.

The women and children had already gathered in a crowd around him, peering to see what was on offer. Brother Paul and a number of other monks, who were responsible for the day-to-day running of the priory, had also made their way down the rough path to greet the trader.

The man's name was Chapman, and he was well known to the people of the island. The children pestered him for stories, but we also wanted stories —we needed to know what was happening in the wider world.

"Come, sit with us and have a jug of ale to revive you," said Brother Paul, "We would know what is happening in this unhappy country of ours."

The old man sat upon a mound and gratefully pulled at the ale.

"Ah," he said, "That is very reviving for an old man who has travelled many a hard mile."

Two young monks took the panniers from the donkeys and took the scrawny animals away to give them some badly needed care. A feast of hay would, no doubt, do much to revive them.

We were becoming eager to hear the news and were frustrated when Chapman resumed his gulping from the jug. After a short while, the merchant put down the jug and looked around at us, obviously warming to his task of relating the news to us and enjoying our eagerness.

"It is not good," he began, which was no news to us.

"There is a terrible famine across these northern lands. I have traded a little on my way here from York. The land is waste, and there are few people in the countryside to buy my goods. I have had little food for some time, only what I can scavenge."

He said this with a glance at Brother Paul, who nodded his head.

"We will provide you with food and drink, Chapman," he said.

This brightened the man's lined face, and he continued with his tale.

"Men are eating the flesh of their own kind," he announced to gasps and groans.

I knew this to be true from my own experience, and the people of the island knew it in their own hearts and minds, but it still raised a groan and requests for God's favour for those who were the victims of this vile necessity.

"Many are eating cats and dogs and horses," he continued, "Others have sold themselves into slavery so that they might, at least, be able to continue their miserable lives. It is hideous indeed to gaze into houses and villages and see the remains of human corpses decaying into putrid filth. There were none left to bury the poor souls, for all were gone, fled or cut down by the Normans or hunger. I have heard that the terror has claimed the lives of more than

100,000 Christian folk —both men and women, young and old alike."

Now, we all gasped. None of us could conceive that great number of people, and to think they were all dead now was more than we could grasp.

"Surely, this is too great a number, given the time in which it has occurred," said Brother Paul, more in hope than conviction.

"Who knows the truth? It will probably never be known for certain how many have perished, but it is many," the old merchant replied, "Only the wolves and scavengers have benefitted from this slaughter."

Chapman stopped and resumed his slurping from the jug of ale. After a brief moment, he turned it upside down, sadly noting it was empty. Brother Paul smiled and nodded to a young monk, who went to fetch another.

Chapman continued, "The land is uncultivated and produces nothing because of the devastation that William has loosed upon us, and remains bare to this present day. The fields that were once abundant in crops and pasture, and watered by the rivers and streams, are empty.

Should you see them now, any man would lament over our once glorious cities. Surely, their magnificent towers threatened heaven itself with their stature. And now they are the hiding places of robbers and brigands."

"The country is in ruins," Brother Adam breathed.

We left the merchant and went about our tasks with heavy hearts whilst the old man dealt with the women and the monks. He sat awhile later and told the children stories, which they lapped up with great delight. Chapman knew he would have food, drink and shelter for the night at the monastery.

***

A few days later, the weather worsened, and we were all confined to the land again. No fishing was possible as the towering waves crashed upon the shore, spluttering foam far up onto the rocks and beaches. We were resigned to the fact that many of our fish traps would have been lost in this tremendous gale. We had set a number of pots for the crabs and lobsters to be found in the shallows. They, too, would be smashed beyond repair.

We sat within our hut, huddled around the fire, and I mended nets whilst Edyth sewed and mended our clothing.

A short while after dawn, one morning, I was alerted by a cry from without. I leapt up and pulled on my outer coat. I strapped on my sword and seax in preparation for trouble. I pulled open the door and strode out into the wind. The rain still poured and lashed against my face in squalls. One of the local men was calling from the edge of the village. He waved at us to come to him. Some of the other men and monks were making their way to see what the commotion was about, too.

The man had been up on the lookout point, which was a small stone hut perched upon the mount at the end of the island. He was breathless from running back to the priory. At first, he could only gasp and point out to sea in a south-easterly direction, but soon could breathe easily enough to explain what he had seen.

"A ship is aground upon the Goldstone Rock!" he cried, "I saw her hit ground. She has listed to the side, and there are men in the water."

"They will never survive in this," said Brother Adam, and a number of the local fishermen nodded their agreement.

"Some might make it onto the rock," one man said.

"What can we do?" another asked.

"Why, we must put to sea and save these souls," replied Brother Adam.

"In this?"

"They are God's children, and it is our duty to rescue whom we can."

The men looked at each other.

"The monks will launch as soon as we are able," Brother Adam said, "You must do as you see fit."

And with that, he turned and hurried back to the priory to rouse more help.

Soon, there were a number of small craft launching from the beach. One was manned by monks, and the others by the fishermen. I was on one of the fishing boats. Still, the wind raged in from the sea. Still, the waves lashed the beach. Still, the rain poured to soak us to the skin. Once you are truly soaked, you stop even trying to keep warm. You simply bear it. We set sail with difficulty through the pounding surf, taking a long route that kept us to the lee side of the rock, a distance of around two miles.

We could not put up sail, as the boat would simply have been driven onto the rocks or turned over in the waves. We rowed with all our might against the wind and tide. Upon the rock, we could see half of the ship, the other half having slipped below the waves.

As we pulled upon the oars, our muscles began to ache with the strain, and our breath came only in short gasps. I could feel my heart pounding against my chest as if hammering to be let out. The rain and the seawater spray ran down my back and chilled me to the bone.

After what seemed an eternity, we drew close to the rock. As we neared it, a couple of us fought to hold her steady in the water whilst other men reached out to help the four surviving men and a woman into the boat. We knew that if we got too close to the rocks, our boat would be smashed to firewood, and we, too, might be lost to the sea.

The men clambered aboard as the boat lurched and rocked, but the woman seemed reluctant to wade to the boat and climb in. I supposed that she was terrified of slipping into the boiling ocean. But soon, we had loaded up the survivors that we could see on this side of the rock, and pushed off again toward Lindisfarne.

Now, we must be even more careful, for the wind and seas were pushing us forward, and disaster could still result if we hit shore too quickly. I noticed that some other boats seemed to have picked up passengers, too. Those we had rescued were from the bow section of the vessel, which had been held by the rocks for some time before sinking to join the stern end.

It was only when we landed upon the beach and helped the survivors off and up onto the grass that we discovered whom we had rescued. For the people on the ship were Normans.

We stood there, unsure what to do, but Brother Adam was insistent.

"Help these people back to the priory," he said, noting our reluctance.

"They are still God's creatures," he added.

Somewhat unwillingly, we did as he asked.

Once inside the wooden hall of the priory, we stood around in groups, shivering and muttering about the 'cargo' we had just saved from a watery grave.

"Had I known, I would never have put my life at risk on such a day. T'would be better that they died," one man, called Jacob, observed.

Others nodded their agreement.

It was at this point that we discovered why the woman was reluctant to leave the Goldstone Rock. It seemed that she had two children with her on the voyage and they were now nowhere to be seen. Although she was a Norman, I am sure that we could all understand her grief and torment at that time. We had all lost people we loved, and for a mother to lose her children is beyond cruel.

We made our way home that day with mixed emotions. We had saved lives, but they were Norman lives.

On the following morning, the wind had died down to a gentle breeze, and the sun shone from a blue sky, over which scudded a few fluffy clouds. I walked down to the beach to join a group of men standing there, deep in discussion. They looked up as I approached, and some of them nodded to me.

"We are discussing what to do about the accursed Normans," Jacob said.

"What is there to do?" I asked, "We brought them to shore when we could have left them to the waves."

"Aye, right enough, but that was before we knew they were Normans. If I had known that before, I wouldn't have even wet my boots for them."

There were more mutterings until we spotted a boat coming into what passed for a harbour on Lindisfarne; in reality, it was little more than a sheltered beach.

Slowly, the little vessel glided up to the beach, guided by Brother Adam and a handful of his fishing monks. As the boat grounded, two of the monks leapt out onto the sand and shingle, and reached up to be given the bodies of two children and a priest.

"See what the ocean has spat out," muttered Jacob.

"The Norman children and a priest," Brother Adam said, though we all knew who they must be.

"We could find no other survivors or corpses."

"Gone to the fishes," Jacob growled.

"There is a good deal of wreckage floating out there," another monk remarked, "Nothing of great value," he added, obviously aware that the men might put to sea in search of any booty that might be scavenged.

"It will be on the seabed," Jacob mumbled, "But it might wash up in time," he added quietly.

The two pathetic little bodies, along with that of the priest —an old man with short grey hair and a small beard— were carried gently back to the priory.

We followed the unhappy party back to the priory hall, but stood outside whilst the monks entered. Moments later, a terrible wail could be heard from within. A mother's torment at the loss of her children is terrible to behold.

In the evening of that day, just as the sun began to wane, a group of the local men strode by, seemingly on their way to the priory. I noted that they were all armed. I fell into line, though without my sword or seax, and followed the band to see what was afoot.

Jacob was at the head, along with a man called Abraham. I had never really liked Abraham. He was a small, slightly-built man, with a weasel face scattered with a few flimsy hairs that passed for a beard. He always seemed to have something to grumble about, and his face was constantly twisted into a scowl. He never seemed to have anything pleasant to say about anything.

The crowd arrived at the priory hall and pushed open the doors. As we entered, the monks and the survivors of the wreck looked up. A look of concern flashed across their faces.

“Do you want something?” Brother Paul asked.

“Them!” Abraham replied, “We want the Norman dogs!”

“These people belong to God and are in the care and sanctuary of the priory,” Brother Paul said, rising to his full height and glaring at us from under his shaggy brows.

“These are Normans, not people,” Jacob growled.

The brother glared at him.

“I am sad to see you here. I thought better of you.”

“We will take them,” Abraham said, and a number of the men pulled weapons from their clothes.

The brothers were unarmed, and a look of horror spread across their faces and those of the Normans, as the angry crowd advanced upon them.

I made my way to the front of the group.

“Hold!” I said, “I have killed Normans with the best of men and like them no more than anyone here, but this is a sacred building, and these people have sanctuary here."

Some of the men looked at me and then from one to another, unsure what to do. They knew that I was right, but their hatred of the Normans and their fear of being spurned by their fellows was too much to turn their hands from the deed.

Brother Paul and the monks now formed up in a line in front of their guests, who cowered upon the rushes strewn across the floor.

"We cannot do this!" I cried, "It is wrong. These people do not threaten us."

"They are Normans. That is enough threat for me," snarled Abraham, and two men pushed me to the ground. My head hit the leg of a table, and a bright light flashed in front of my eyes, after which I knew no more.

When I awoke, my head pounded, and I could feel sticky blood in my hair. I peered around me, my eyes still unsteady in their gaze. The monks sat around the hall, a look of great sorrow upon their faces, along with a number of cuts and bruises. Brother Paul sat there, crushed like a beetle under a cartwheel. He shook his head in disbelief.

"They were in sanctuary," he whispered.

The ground was slippery with blood, and Norman bodies lay where they had been slaughtered, the two men who had seemed to lead the group without their heads.

As I sat there staring at the gruesome scene, one man stirred and seemed still alive, and he gasped, his lungs filling with his own blood. I went to him, and he looked up at me through clouded eyes. I knew that nothing could save him, but I cradled his head in my lap until, with one last long breath, he died, and his eyes became sightless.

I rose from the ground and turned to Brother Paul.

"We must give these people a burial," I said.

"The men said that they would not allow them to be buried upon the island. We shall have to take them to the mainland," another brother replied.

And so it was that we carried out the bodies and loaded them onto a donkey cart. We set off for the causeway as the tide was out, and we could cross in safety. When we reached the mainland end of the causeway, a grisly sight awaited. There, on poles, were the heads of the two Norman men. I leapt down from the cart, ripped the heads from their ghastly mountings and returned them to the bodies in the cart.

"Are the men mad?" I cried, "What do they think would happen if a Norman patrol should find these? Do they think they would just ride on by? This could bring death and destruction to everyone on the island!"

The Normans were duly buried in the best graves we could dig within a little woodland, where they were likely to be undisturbed, and we returned to Lindisfarne. Upon our return, I found Jacob and Abraham walking through the village. To my shame, I used some choice of words that I would not normally utter in remonstrating with them about their foolish and sickening deeds. Jacob, at least, seemed sheepish and made little reply. Abraham was his usual offensive self. I left them standing and strode home.

Chapter 28

St. Cuthbert's Ducks

It was upon a bright and breezy morning when the sun shone at the same time as splashes of rain spattered down from quickly drifting clouds. They scudded across the sky as I sat upon the shoreline with Brother Adam. We busied ourselves with mending fish traps whilst we gazed out to the seas —our workplace. I had, that morning, scavenged the rock pools and managed to find one large crab. That would make a tasty meal, I thought, boiled and mixed with mussels, cockles and other seafood that Edyth and the children had collected.

Various kinds of seabirds swooped and dived and floated upon the waves, scraping a living from the ocean. An 'ah-ooo' call arose from the lapping water, and I looked up to scan the birds before me. A bird called again —a bulky bird, which seemed much bigger than the others around it.

"That bird over there, the pretty one with white upon its back and black below, is a fine fellow," I said, "He would make a tasty meal, roast and stuffed with herbs."

Brother Adam looked up at me from his work.

"We never catch those ducks," he said, "Nor the brown bird that follows him —his wife. These are eider ducks, though we call them St. Cuthbert's ducks."

"Why?"

"Well, Cuthbert lived for a goodly while upon Inner Farne. People rarely wandered there except to ask for his help or advice. So he lived among the animals. Now Cuthbert was a great lover of animals, and, it is said, the eider duck was his great favourite."

"I can understand that," I said, "They are truly beautiful birds."

"The drakes are," Brother Adam agreed, "Though the ducks are much more drab brown. It must be so to protect the nest. In the spring, when the weather turns, they will come ashore to build their nests. They nest on the ground, of course. The female will pluck down feathers from her own breast to line the nest snuggly. When the clutch of green eggs is laid, she will not leave the nest, even if danger approaches. You could walk up to her and stroke her, and she will not move, though we should not —she is still a wild bird, and what people think of as tameness is nought but the courage of a mother guarding her children."

"I have seen the brown ducks with their ducklings," I said, "And they appear good mothers."

"Oh, they are," Brother Adam affirmed, "As soon as possible, after the ducklings hatch, the mother will line them up and take them to sea."

"Is that not dangerous?"

"There are things on land that are more dangerous," Brother Adam observed, "The duck will often take her offspring to strange places that we would think unsuitable, such as cliffs, and there she will throw herself off. The ducklings, having no fear as we would, launch themselves after their mother."

"Are they not killed?" I asked, incredulous.

"Some are, but most are not. The ducklings are light and just seem to float down as a single feather would before landing on the waves below."

"It is a shame that some must die," I said, "Surely, it would be better if she made better plans so that all of her children survived."

Brother Adam looked at me and smiled.

"Truly, you have a wonderful gentle side, John, despite your exploits as a warrior. But in observing nature, we must accept that some creatures will meet their doom at a very early age. Indeed, it is common. If it were not so, then many other animals would go hungry, and others would overpopulate and seize the very world."

I pondered his words a while as I mended the fish traps before me.

“I fear that our own species will do that,” I said, “We seem to take what we want from this world rather than share it fairly.”

Brother Adam nodded gravely.

“I fear that you are right, John,” he said, “Wherever man goes over this world, he dominates and takes advantage of its resources like no other.”

“Is that not God’s will, that we should rule over the animals and use them to our own advantage?” I asked.

“Indeed, that is what God has told us —that we have dominium over the wild creatures and His world. But I do worry that we abuse his privilege, and that we don’t care for his world in the way that he had planned when he created us.”

“Are we wrong to take his animals and plants and kill them and eat them?” I asked, a little troubled by his words.

“No, John. We are all creatures of this world, and we must live like the rest of His creatures, devouring other living things as he has planned. The eider duck itself preys upon the shellfish from the ocean floor. That is the way it must be. It is our over-indulgence and waste that makes me uneasy about the way we use His world. All animals have enemies and predators, though few would tackle a full-grown eider, but no enemy is more dangerous than man. What animal kills for pleasure other than man?"

We sat awhile without speaking. At length, Brother Adam smiled again.

"One good thing we may take from the eider is its down, plucked from the female's breast. It makes a soft and warm lining that has long been harvested by folk of the sea for filling pillows and quilts." *

"And is that the lining in the bedding that the monastery has provided for our family?" I asked.

The monk nodded.

"It is certainly soft and warm on a cold night," I said.

"We never take it from the nest until the birds have left so that no harm comes to them."

I nodded in approval of this.

After our labours on the shore, I wandered back to our simple home with much to ponder in the evening. I resolved that I would always feed my family, for that is the nature of things, but I would protect God's creatures from abuse and cruelty from my fellow man to the best of my ability. For, surely, this is the way that the world was planned, and the way to ensure that our world would survive until the day of judgement.

*It is illegal to collect eider down in Modern Britain.

Chapter 29

Hereward

It was some time in 1070, as I recall, that another story reached our shores. A merchant sailing boat anchored off our island, and the men crewing it came ashore for food and water. The monks and the locals were only too pleased to supply passing vessels with a few coins that they could use to buy goods from passing traders.

Of course, we were all ears to the tales of anyone who passed by, and we congregated in the priory to hear what the sailors had to tell us.

"What news do you bring us?" asked Brother Paul, as the men sat around upon the rushes to eat a meal of pottage, which they seemed to shovel into their mouths as if they'd never eaten before.

A large man with a long grey beard, who seemed to be the captain of the ship, rammed some more pottage into his mouth, the liquid running down from the corners of his mouth and mingling with his whiskers, spoke for the group.

"I have nothing good to say about the condition of the North Country," he said, spraying chewed pottage over his already filthy clothing.

In the confines of the building, it was already becoming clear that the sailors were not too particular about washing, and a stale aroma was beginning to pervade the air.

The man spoke again, this time with his mouth reasonably empty so he could better pronounce his words.

"In the south, men say a rebellion is brewing in the eastern fens. A man called Hereward has returned from exile."

"Hereward?" Brother Paul said, "I have heard the name. Wasn't he exiled by the Confessor?"

"He was that," the captain replied, and gave a loud belch that seemed to indicate that he was enjoying his meal.

"Young Hereward was exiled when he was eighteen. He had been disobedient to his father and had caused a good deal of trouble near his home. It is said that he killed a man, though none could say whether or not it was self-defence. Anyway, he was declared an outlaw by Edward. It is also said that he had many adventures during his exile."

The captain looked around at our absorbed faces and gave a little smile. He was obviously pleased that we were paying him such close attention.

With a swig of ale, he continued, "I heard a tale that he was once in the forest, hunting for his supper, when he came face to face with a huge bear. They say it was the largest bear ever seen on this island of ours. It stood eight, nine, no ten feet tall and was as wide as a church door!"

Gasps came from the attentive audience. This looked likely to be a wonderful tale.

"Well," the captain continued, "The great beast caught a sniff of Hereward and turned in his direction."

Our eyes opened wide.

"The beast turned and plodded toward Hereward, who just stood there, as if in defiance. When it got close, it rose to its full twelve feet."

"I thought you'd said it was ten feet tall," Brother Paul said.

The captain looked flustered for a moment.

"Ah, yes," he said, "But that was without its great head, which was two feet itself."

Brother Paul smiled and nodded his head as if in understanding.

"Now, where was I?" asked the captain, "Oh, yes. The great bear came toward him, but Hereward stood his ground. It drew nearer so that Hereward could smell its foul breath, and then it swiped with a huge paw, bigger than a platter. Its great claws were bigger than roof nails, and they still dripped blood from a deer it had just killed."

Further gasps went up from the assembled crowd, which was growing by the minute. (I noted that the dead deer seemed to be a new aspect of the story).

"Now Hereward ducked beneath the great paw and, with his seax, he stabbed the bear in its huge chest. Well, a great howl went up from the wounded beast, and it tried to grab Hereward in its terrible embrace. But Hereward was too quick for that, and he danced around the animal and pushed it from behind. The beast toppled over, and Hereward lost no time in jumping onto its back. He wrapped his arms around the bear's neck and hung on, trying to slit its throat. But the bear was not finished; oh no! It rose onto its four paws and then to its two back feet and tried to shake Hereward off. Hereward hung on, but his seax slipped from his grasp. Now, he was disarmed. How he hung on, we shall never know. Oh, how the beast raged.

It twisted and turned and shook its great head, but still, it could not break the grip of Hereward. At length, the animal lost its wind and flopped down upon the ground. Hereward leapt from its back and grabbed for his seax. He turned upon the beast and flashed the blade before its eyes. But the animal just lay there, looking up at him, totally defeated. Now, the great man stood back and gazed into its eyes. He just couldn't do the beast more harm, and so he just turned his steps and left it there to recover from its wound and exhaustion."

Now calls of "Yes!" and "Wonderful" went up from the crowd.

"Tell us more of this man," I begged, warming to the captain, though I had no doubt that his tales were somewhat dressed up and dramatised.

Another of the sailors joined in the storytelling now.

"They say that, down in Cornwall, he met a Cornish princess who was betrothed to a man she didn't love. The poor princess was locked away by her father until the day of the wedding. But Hereward would have none of it. Late at night, when the sun had gone and there was no Moon to cast light, Hereward broke into the hall where she was held and rescued her. They say he galloped away with her until they were safe, and then left her in the care and protection of a good family he knew."

Well, this was getting better and better.

"What else happened?" Jacob demanded.

The captain regained the storyteller's role.

"Oh, he fled to Flanders for his own safety, and joined in an expedition for the Count of Flanders, Baldwin V, against Scaldamarialand. They say that, while in exile, he married a woman from a wealthy family, called Turfida. Men say that she fell in love with him even before she had met him, having heard of his heroic exploits."

"And yet he is now back in England?" asked Brother Paul.

"He is," the captain confirmed, "But it was not a happy homecoming. He is the son of Edith, a descendent of Oslac of York, and Leofric of Bourne, nephew of Ralph the Staller. When he arrived at the family home, he found that his family had been killed by the new Norman lord who had taken the land as his own, and Hereward's brother was slain and beheaded, his head set above the door on a spike."

"Oh!" went up the cry.

We had all seen terrible things, and you would have thought that we would have become hardened to horror by now, but it still shocked us, even now. Brother Paul shook his head, and the other brothers gathered there, closed their eyes and whispered prayers for the departed souls.

"And so he fled into the fens?" I asked.

"God bless you, no, my lad," the captain replied, "That was just the start. Hereward had a group of good men around him whom he trusted with his life. All were great warriors, and they were now hunting for Normans. Well, Hereward and his men questioned the locals, and they pointed him in the direction of a hall where the Normans were holding a drunken feast.

When they arrived, they dismounted in a wood and crept quietly to the hall. They entered through a hole they cut in the wattle. Not one of the Normans noticed their arrival. Why should they? They were confident that the people held no threat to them. What could the stupid English do to them? Were they not a defeated people?"

A growl went up from the hall as we listened.

The captain continued his tale, "Hereward and his men crept forward, behind a curtain, until they could survey the scene. Sure enough, the Normans were filled with English food and drunk on English ale. In the middle of the floor was a local man. He knelt upon the rush-strewn floor, beaten and bruised. His head hung low, and blood dripped from the end of his nose.

'What use are these weakling Englishmen?' one of the Normans laughed. 'If they are all like this one, we will have no problem ruling here. They are no more dangerous than an old horse.' But they didn't know that just a few feet behind them, was a force of warriors such as they had never seen before."

"Yes!" we all cried, "Hereward must kill them all!"

"Well, that is exactly what happened," the captain continued, "His men had spread out around the hall, still unseen and unheard by the stupid Norman guards, who thought they were safe.

A whistle went up from Hereward's lips, and his men leapt out and began to butcher the Normans. Most of them were drunk, and those who weren't were too slow. Hereward and his men hardly stopped for breath as heads were parted from shoulders by blows from the great swords of the Englishmen, and other drunken men died, gurgling on their own blood upon the floor. The English servants cowered, not knowing who these terrible fighters were. Hereward called to them not to be afraid, and that they were safe. At this, some of their numbers leapt up and, picking up knives from the table, they began to join in the slaughter of the men who had just been ridiculing them."

"It took only a few minutes until the ground was strewn with their bodies. Men say Hereward himself killed fifteen of them alone. We heard that he had then gathered his followers and, with the cheers of the local people ringing in their ears, they set out for Hereward's home. When they reached the family hall, Hereward emptied a sack upon the ground, revealing its grisly cargo. The warrior then nailed the Norman heads above the door. From there, he went to Medeshamstede (Peterborough) Abbey, where he was knighted by his uncle, Abbot Brand."

"And where is he now?" I asked, breathless.

"Well, he has fled to the Fens, where it will be difficult for the Normans to find him."

I should explain to you that the Fens are an area or wetland in the south-east of the country. Some parts are thickly forested, and others are open marshlands.

Hereward and his men had made their way to the sanctuary of the Fens, where they were given food and shelter by Abbot Thurstan of Ely.

As the day died and the stories began to slow, a group of us spoke earnestly as we began to drift back to our homes to consider what we had heard.

On the following morning, I sat uneasily, breaking my fast on some bread, smoked herring and a little cheese. I told Edyth what had been said by the sailors the previous evening, and she listened intently whilst busying herself around, tidying and putting things in place that belonged to the children, who had already gone to the little school that the monks had set up for them in the priory.

It always appeared that Edyth was not really paying attention to what I was telling her, at these times, but she could always give me a good answer if I quizzed her upon it. I have never understood how women can seem to be paying no attention and yet listening intently at the same time.

I stopped in the telling of the tale.

"Edyth," I said, "I had thought to go down to Ely and fight alongside Hereward to try to win back at least some of our land from the Normans."

She stopped in her tracks and stared at me. Her face was a mask of horror.

"John Aelricson, don't you dare leave me here, and our family too! We have need of you here to help us keep body and soul together. What would become of us?"

Our family? Was that how Edyth saw it now? If so, I was delighted, though it now made my task all the harder.

"The brothers would care for you," I said weakly, not knowing what else to say.

"No, John!"

I sat for some time, fiddling with a fish trap I was mending.

"Edyth, I must. I have already made plans with Jacob and some of the other men. We have decided on our plan of action. We will go south and fight under Hereward in one last attempt to save our land."

Now Edyth stopped and slumped to the floor. She sat there before the fire, and I could see the tears welling in her eyes in the flickering light. She stared into the flames as if something there would comfort her. She knew that I had made up my mind.

At length, she looked up at me, and I could see the stains running down her cheeks.

“I cannot lose you, John,” she whispered.

There was a brief pause.

“Do you not know that I love you with all my heart, and that I could not bear it if…anything should happen to you. We are a family,” she said.

I stared at her. She had never actually said those words to me before, though I always hoped that that was how she felt.

“And you must know that you and the children are the most precious things in the world to me,” I said, a well of emotion surging up within me.

“But if there is a chance —a small chance…”

“You know there is no chance,” she said sadly.

“We are occupied. We are but the vassals in this land now. It is no longer our world. It is a Norman world, and we must accept it.”

“I cannot accept it,” I muttered, “I must try. If I don’t, then I would always wonder —could I have done more? Was I too afraid? Am I a coward?”

“You are no coward, John Aelricson!” she cried, “You are one of the bravest and best men I have ever known, and you must not throw away your life and the life we will have together for a lost cause.”

I looked down at the ground.

“We leave in the morning,” I told her.

Chapter 30

To Ely

It was upon a grey morn, but with a weak sun beginning to break through brooding clouds, that we all arose and made ready for our leaving. Edyth had said not more than a handful of words to me since breakfast, and I could see the worry behind her eyes. The children, too, sat quietly, finishing the last few mouthfuls of bread and honey. I busied myself with checking my equipment and testing the sharpness of the sword and seax I had belted on.

Once my travelling equipment was ready, I carried it outside and slung it over the old horse I was to take with me. He snickered and bared his huge yellow teeth in complaint, but then, he complained about everything he was asked to do.

When all was ready, and all of my travelling companions had assembled by the priory gate, I turned to the downcast family I was leaving again. My heart wept as I scanned the miserable faces before me. How could I do this to them again? And yet, it had to be done. I approached them and wrapped my arms as far around them as I could.

“Take good care of each other. Listen to Edyth and do as she says. If you are in need, go to the brothers, who will surely take care of you in my absence.”

I could feel the sobs that wracked them, and the tears ran freely down all of our faces.

“I shall return soon,” I told them, though I was far from sure that that would be the case.

“Take care, John Aelricson, and come back to me safely,” Edyth said, trying hard to hold her emotions in check.

“I will, I swear it,” I said.

And so, off we plodded across the causeway before the waves, which would soon enough engulf the sands around our island and seal it safely from those on the mainland who didn’t have recourse to a boat. I looked back on a number of occasions and saw my family standing there, watching me leave them. I blinked tears from my eyes and tried to focus on the journey before us.

As we made our way south, we kept the sea on our left, and the hills rose toward the heavens on our right. After some time, around noon, we stopped awhile to eat some of our fare of dried fish and bread, washed down with skins of ale from the priory’s brew-house. I gazed out to sea and marvelled at the glittering waters, now shining in the clear sunlight that had burnt back the clouds. I pondered on the waves, as first they rushed toward the land and retreated again. I stared at the great curved line that seemed to be where the ocean stopped.

"Why can we not see further over the sea?" I asked no one in particular.

Brother Luke looked up from his fish.

"Why, that is as far as any man can see," he replied.

"But why does it seem to stop suddenly? Why doesn't it just fade away?"

He looked perplexed by my question, and he, too, stared out over the gently heaving ocean.

"I don't know," he said honestly.

"That is as far as I can see over the sea, and yet, at night, I can see the Moon and the stars, and they seem so much further away," I mused, "The Earth is flat —that much is obvious to anyone who has ever walked this land. But why do the ships that approach us appear a little at a time —first the masts and sails, then the hull, as if over a hill? Why don't they appear all at once, as a man met upon the road does?"

Brother Luke stared at me.

"I don't know," he said and then went back to his meal, though I knew from his expression that he was deep in thought.

"Why do the tides run in twice every day?" I pondered aloud.

"Why does the water wash up onto the beach and force its way around our island and up our rivers, only to slip back again, as if it has just become too tired to keep trying?"

"What questions you ask, John," he said.

In truth, I had often pondered these things as I sat in the evening and gazed out to sea.

"I suppose it is just as God wills it," he added and bit a lump from the hunk of bread in his fist.

But why would God will these things? I thought. To what purpose?

We finished our meagre meal and sat awhile longer. At length, we rose to continue our journey. I looked at the brooding hills to the west. I remembered our stay upon Yeavering Bell —that great heap of land from whose windy summit we could see for many miles around us.

"Why does the land rise up into great hills and mountains?" I said.

"Who knows what purpose God had in His wondrous works," Brother Luke said, his voice beginning to show the irritation of my constant questions.

"Perhaps it is because God made many animals that like to live in different places —the mountain hare and grouse high up in the hills, and the gulls and gannets by the seas," he said.

That made sense to me. Each animal would live in its natural home, so those homes would need to be specially created. Of course! That had to be the answer.

But, as we tramped onward toward the River Tyne, I still didn't know why ships appeared a little at a time, nor why the waters rose to float our fishing boats only to leave them high and dry upon the mud flats a while later. I looked up again and scanned around me, the thoughts whirling around in my mind.

"Why…?" I said.

Brother Luke snapped his head around and the look upon his face was unmistakeable.

"Oh, never mind," I said.

***

Unknown to us, further south, a small but well-armed and drilled Danish army was making its way across the very seas that we gazed out upon every day. They ploughed the ocean under the orders of King Sweyn Estrithson of Denmark. His aim, we were told, was to establish a camp, a headland, upon the Isle of Ely. And there it was that Hereward joined them.

Over a meal of venison and ale, Hereward sat with Sweyn's men and discussed what they could do to rid the land of the hated Normans.

"I say that we storm Medeshamstede (Peterborough) Abbey," said Hereward.

The Danish leaders looked up in surprise. Osbern, a huge man with a great bushy red beard, looked carefully at the Saxon.

"You would storm one of your own abbeys?" he asked.

"I would," replied Hereward.

"For what reason and to what ends?" the Dane asked.

"I…*we* must save the great treasures and relics from the covetous Normans, who are led by Thorold, a Norman Abbot, who succeeded the late Saxon Abbot, my own blood kin —my uncle. I hear that being but a Norman stranger to this land, Thorold neither loves his monastery nor his convent. They say he has given sixty-two hides of church land to certain stipendiary knights so that they might defend him."

"But the treasures?" questioned Osbern, now more interested.

"There are many wonderful things in the abbey. More beautiful than any man can dream," said Hereward.

The Danes leaned forward to hear more.

And so it was that, a few short days later, on a misty morning, ideal for the purpose of approaching without being seen, a body of men, armed and enthused by the thoughts of righting a wrong or looting treasure, depending upon whether you were Saxon or Dane, approached Peterborough up the River Nene, in the Danish longboats.

Once close enough, the boats crunched upon the gravel of the shallows, and the men disembarked as quietly as possible. They climbed a small hillock under the cover of trees and looked across at the abbey of Peterborough and its settlement, surrounded as it was by a massive stone wall. (Indeed, its name of Peterborough meant the fortified place of St. Peter).

The early-morning mist was just beginning to lift from the abbey fields as the warriors emerged and made their way toward their target.

Hereward had planned his attack carefully. His men and the Danish warriors divided themselves into small groups, and each group stealthily approached different gates in the great walls. Here they waited until the cock crowed as that was when the huge doors would be opened to allow the people of the burh to go about their business.

Peterborough was, by now, a thriving market town, and merchants and pedlars would soon enter through the great gates to tender their wares. Men would leave by the same gates to tend to the fields around the town, wherein the people of the town could be fed.

It was not long before the gates creaked open, and bleary-eyed guards stretched themselves before their day's duties began. Soon, men began to approach the gates, in twos and threes. They nodded to the guards as they passed into the town. Some carried bundles that appeared to be goods to sell. Many chatted and whistled merry tunes as if they had not a care in the world. However, as more and more strangers arrived, some of the guards became uneasy and began to question those who entered as to what their purpose was.

"Why, I come to buy a good cockerel," said one man.

"We are here to offer our services as labourers," others announced.

None of it was true.

Soon, it became obvious to the sleepiest guard that something was afoot.

"Call out the master of the guard," one man said to his comrade in arms, "I am troubled by the number of strange men approaching and entering the town."

And so it was that a number of Hereward's men, along with the Danish warriors dressed as Saxons, entered Peterborough, whilst many awaited their turn in the surrounding countryside.

Hereward and a few of his men whistled as they made their way through a gate and tried to disappear into the local population. A guard looked them over and held out his spear to stop them.

"What is your business in the town?" he said.

Hereward looked at him.

"To right a wrong and to rescue English treasures from the grasp of greedy Normans, who have no love of it but only see it as a resource to plunder."

And with that, he drew his sword from beneath his cloak and ran it through the guard's belly, gutting him like a fish.

"To arms, men," he cried, "The deception is over. We must fight for what we want."

Hereward's men now drew out their disguised weapons, and the bloodshed began.

Many of the local people fled in terror at what was unfolding before them. Some drew arms or anything they could find as a weapon and joined the battle against Hereward and his men. Some entered the fray on the side of the Saxon attackers. Soon, monks appeared, armed and ready for combat — monks were not always peaceful men of God.

The battle raged for some time. More monks and locals appeared, and more attackers, both Saxon and

Dane, emerged from the countryside to fight their way into the town. Many men and boys died that day. Many streets and alleyways ran red with blood that day, and the dust beneath men's feet became sticky with gore.

It soon became apparent to the leaders of the attack that the monks and locals were putting up a stern resistance to the assault, and that little progress was being made. Hereward, weighing up the situation as any good leader would, called to his men.

"Light fires! Burn down the houses so we might force our way into the town and find Thorold —I would have his head!"

And so it was that burning brands and tinder were taken from the local homes, and fires were started in the houses near the gates. At first, the locals tried to draw water from the wells to douse the flames, but it was impossible in the teeth of such a battle. Even in quiet times, the timber and straw-thatched houses would have been difficult to extinguish. Soon, the flames were licking at other buildings in the strengthening breeze blowing into the town from the west. It was but a short time before most of Peterborough was engulfed in flames.

Now, locals, monks and attackers alike ceased their fight and stared around them.

"Out, men, out!" cried Hereward, and the men he still had standing retreated to the gateways and out of the town, leaving the locals to do the best they could to save their homes and possessions.

It was not long before the people of Peterborough fled their burning town and, herding children and animals before them, stood transfixed at the terrible sight before them. Tears flowed, and women wailed. Children cried and screamed in terror. Men stood, disbelieving, tears also streaming down their faces and heads buried in their hands.

Hereward and his men retreated to the edge of the woodland and watched the carnage they had created.

"It was not meant to be like this," Hereward sighed.

The town burned for most of the day. As the flames burned themselves out, the local Saxons began to filter back in to see the destruction of the place they had called home just a few hours before. Monks filed sadly into the town to see what damage had been done to the conventual buildings and the treasures of the abbey. But it was to no avail, for their buildings were completely destroyed.

Indeed, all of the town stood in smoking ruins, save for one house and the abbey church. Prior Athelwold and some of the older monks searched through the remains of their abbey and the abbey church in a desperate attempt to rescue the riches and relics contained there.

After a while, the Danish warriors assembled with a still-stunned Hereward and his men. Osbern spoke for all.

"Hereward, it has been decided that we should return to the fray and salvage what we can from the ruins. Why leave here empty-handed after such a battle?"

Hereward looked at him.

"What have I done?" he asked.

"You have done what you came to do. You have sacked the town, and now you must complete the task and take the riches of the abbey from the Normans."

"And what of the Norman Abbot?" asked Arnulf, another Dane, "It was your wish to rid the town of this man?"

"What you say is true, and we must now return to the town if only to complete the task. But it is with a heavy heart that I do it. What disaster I have brought to the Saxons of Peterborough," Hereward returned.

And with that, the forces of the attackers rose, drew swords and spears, and made their way back into the smouldering ruins of the town. There was no resistance this time. The townspeople simply stared at their attackers and shook their heads in despair.

"It is William the Bastard who brings this upon your town, not I," said Hereward, though he knew, and they knew that was only partly true.

The force of warriors now made their way to the abbey church, where they hoped to find Abbot Thorold and any treasures that might have been spared in the inferno. Upon entering the church, they discovered the Prior and a handful of monks who had survived collecting together what they could.

"Ah, what have we here?" asked Osbern, "The men of Christ have begun the job for us. Have they not gathered together the treasure that we shall take with us when we depart? I thank you, gentlemen."

"The relics shall be saved for the Saxon people," Hereward told him, "You may take some of the money and treasure for yourselves."

"And what fate should we inflict upon our men of the cloth? Perhaps they will enjoy reposing in the arms of their Lord tonight."

"No man will be harmed!" warned Hereward, "We have done enough damage already. These men will return to Ely with us under my protection."

Hereward turned to Prior Athelwold.

"Where is Thorold?" he asked.

"Thorold is absent at Stamford," the elderly monk replied.

"Then I have not yet rid this place of the Norman," Hereward mused.

And so, with the relics and treasure packed in sacks and tied firmly to the backs of the monks, the procession of warriors left the devastated town behind and made their way back to Ely, where safety lay…for now.

Chapter 31

St Cuthbert and the Vikings

As we travelled on, I had many conversations with Brother Luke about so many things. We crossed the River Tyne upon a small ferry raft and found ourselves in my own land, between the Tyne and the Tees.

"Brother Luke," I said, "Tell me what you know of St. Cuthbert. He lived on Lindisfarne, didn't he?"

"Oh, indeed he did," the monk replied, and proceeded to tell me the story of the saint.

"Well now, Cuthbert, they say, was born around 635, in the borderlands. Some say that he was just an ordinary man —perhaps a shepherd. Others say that he was of noble birth. Sadly, he was orphaned at the age of eight."

"How terrible," I said, "At such a young age. What happened to him?"

"Ah, well, God looked after him. They do say that, once, he had injured his knee and could barely walk. But a miracle happened, and an angel on horseback cured the injured knee."

"Is that true?" I asked.

"It is what men say," Brother Luke replied.

He was silent for a while.

"Did I ever tell you about how he controlled the wind?"

"No," I said, "Tell me about it."

"Once, some fishing boats were being blown out to sea on a powerful off-shore wind. They were in grave danger of being swamped and blown over, and, almost certainly, every man would have been lost."

"I know how that feels," I declared, "It is not easy to tack in on an offshore wind. I often wished that I could control the wind!"

"It seems," the monk continued, "That St. Cuthbert prayed, and the wind changed direction, and the boats were blown back in again, and all were saved."

"Wonderful!" I exclaimed.

"On another occasion, a blaze began and was threatening to burn to the ground a woman's home. Again, the saint prayed, and the wind changed direction and blew out the fire."

We were silent again, for a while, whilst we both pondered the stories that Brother Luke had told me. Could all of this be true?

I looked at the monk walking beside me.

“Have you any more stories about St. Cuthbert?” I asked.

“Indeed,” he replied, “I have heard that, in 651, I think the Prior said that St. Cuthbert was on the hills above Melrose by night. He saw, with his own eyes, a soul being transported to heaven by a host of angels. He wondered all night whether he had really seen it. On the following morning, a messenger brought news that St. Aidan, the very founder of Lindisfarne Priory, and the man who had brought Christianity to our part of the world and who was protected by none other than King Oswald, had died.”

“No!” I exclaimed, “That is astonishing!”

“That was what inspired Cuthbert to join the monastery of Melrose under the care of Prior Boisil and Abbot Eata. Some even say that he was buried with some of Eata’s bones in his coffin.”

I had heard stories about St. Cuthbert in the past, but nothing like this.

“Please, Brother Luke, tell me more,” I begged.

My curiosity was roused, and I was hungry to hear more about the saint’s life. Was he not the saint of the North Country?

Brother Luke laughed.

“Your thirst for knowledge is insatiable, John, but it does you credit. No matter what a man knows, he should never stop learning. After a while, Cuthbert was given the job of 'guest master' at the monastery in Ripon. It was a very responsible role. But it was at a time of great unrest within the church. We had divided into two sides. On the one hand, was the Celtic tradition, to which Cuthbert belonged, and, on the other, the Roman tradition.

Old King Osiwu was falling under the influence of the Roman church. In the early 660s, they say, Cuthbert was banished from Ripon because of his Celtic beliefs and returned to Melrose. But all was not well for him there, for they say he caught the plague and was very ill."

I shuddered at the thought of the plague.

"Now Old King Osiwu was becoming annoyed at the rift in the church, and so he called a great Synod at Whitby. It was at the Synod of Whitby, in 664, when it was decided that all should follow the Roman tradition. There was much bad feeling on the side of the Celtic monks, and many left this land. But Cuthbert was a man who could bring people together and said he was prepared to accept the will of the church and the changes. When he was around 30 years old, he became Prior of Lindisfarne."

"So that is how he comes to be linked to our little island home," I said.

Brother Luke nodded.

"He became famous for his teaching, and large crowds would often gather to hear him. They say that great eagles would fly over and drop fish at his feet, and that the meat from sea creatures would be washed up on the beach to feed him. Some say that warm loaves of bread would suddenly appear."

Now, I was truly astonished.

"Is this really true, Brother Luke?"

"It is what I have heard," he replied.

"Now, Cuthbert began to need time alone, and he began to retreat to some of the uninhabited islands of the Farnes. They say that he rowed out to a small island inhabited only by terns, and built himself a small shelter. I also heard that he was able to move huge boulders until he could see nothing of the outside world except the sky so that he could speak with God."

"I should not like to live on such an island," I said, "It would be lonely and terrifying when there was a storm. And I think I should miss my family too much."

"No," Brother Luke replied, "It would not suit every man."

"Later, there was more strife within the church, and King Ecgfrith asked Cuthbert to return from his island and become Bishop of Lindisfarne. He did great work amongst the people, moving between them and nursing them through the plague. But, eventually, as must happen to every man, he became ill and died in 687."

"The people demanded that Cuthbert should become a saint, and it was done. Now, as I understand it, in 698, some 11 years after he had died, his coffin was opened, and what do you think they found?"

"Oh, I know this," I said, "They found that his body was just as it was when he was buried. There was no sign of decay."

"Quite right, young John."

The monk continued to tell me his tale.

"The reason why they raised his coffin was to 'elevate' his remains. It was at this time when the most beautiful book was written —The Lindisfarne Gospels. They were meant to be used in the 'elevation' ceremony, which was to be a day of celebration for his life."

"He was reburied on Lindisfarne, but it was not to last for long. Later, Cuthbert was dug up for a second time after the raid by Viking pirates. The monks of the island were unprepared for such an event —it was unimagined— and many of them died or were taken prisoner. Many of the treasures of the priory were stolen. The monastery was burned to the ground, and many remaining monks moved to the mainland. I think the monastery was finally abandoned in 875 if my memory serves me well."

"I have heard tales of the movement of St. Cuthbert," I said, "Will you tell me what you know?"

"The story has it that St. Cuthbert's coffin and a number of treasures from the priory, including the Lindisfarne Gospels, were taken to the mainland, where the monks wandered for many years. The pagan Vikings attacked like hornets and, like packs of wolves, they robbed, tore and slaughtered. They spread across the north country like a pestilence. The monks were driven westward to lands where wild beasts roamed and ruled the land. Then, they decided they should leave this land and go back to Ireland."

"But, as they set off from the west coast, a huge storm blew up. The waves swamped the boat, and the sacred gospels were washed overboard. The monks were devastated! They believed that St. Cuthbert was giving a message that he didn't want to go to Ireland, so they swung the boat around and returned to England."

"Once back on land, they cried out in sorrow, and tears ran down their cheeks. Bishop Eardulf led a frantic search for the Gospels, combing the beaches and strandlines for any sign of the book. It was not to be found until St. Cuthbert appeared in a dream to one of the monks. The saint directed them to Whithorn, and there, by a miracle, the precious

Gospel was found, none the worse for wear for its time in the ocean."

"Incredible!" I cried, "What happened next?"

"It is said that the monks travelled to a place called Crayke in the autumn of 882. It was a wild and dangerous time, for the Vikings now ruled these northern parts, though they were not popular rulers at that time. In fact, they say that Halfdene, their king, had to leave the area for his own safety."

I had not heard the tale of Crayke.

"Did they not return to our own north-east?"

"They settled in the old Roman settlement of Chester-le-Street for around 100 years, but there was great fear of further attacks, and the monks decided to take the body to Ripon, but, I understand, they didn't stay there for very long. Later, they decided to move back north. It was on this journey that a wonderful thing happened."

"It was then that he was finally laid to rest, isn't it?" I asked.

"True, John," he replied, "I shall tell it to you as I heard it. As I understand the tale, on their further journey to find a permanent home, they arrived at Wrdelau, a hillock in the east of the country, not too far from the sea. It was here that the wagon they were using became stuck in the mud. The monks tried as best they could to free it, but it was no good. They fasted and prayed for three days and nights until St. Cuthbert himself appeared to them in a dream. He told them to go to 'Dunholme'. The problem was, they had no idea where 'Dunholme' was."

"Just as they were beginning to think they would never solve the riddle, along came two milkmaids. One exclaimed that she had lost her dun (brown) cow. The other maid said she had seen the beast at the 'dun holme'. In better spirits, the two maids set off to find it. Now, the monks decided to follow behind, and, in another miracle, the cart moved easily out of the mud."

"Dunholme, of course, as we all now know, was the great rocky outcrop, almost surrounded by the waters of the River Wear. Here, they settled and built a new shrine for the saint. It was known as the 'White Church'. It became the permanent home of the relics. And we should take cheer, John, for the path we tread now is none other than St. Cuthbert's own journey, from Chester-le-Street, south to Durham."

I smiled at the thought.

"Is it true that St. Cuthbert was buried with King Oswald's head?" I asked.

"It is true, John," the monk said.

"And he will lie there forever?"

"I hope so, John," he replied, "I hope so."

Chapter 32

Ely

The monks of Peterborough had certainly put up a brave defence of their town and monastery, but many had perished or were taken hostage by the Danes. Hereward looked at the dejected rabble of monks, their faces long and haggard and tear stains still marking their faces through the dust and grime of battle and fire. He would have preferred to leave the men to rebuild what they could, but he knew his Danish allies would never agree. To the Danes, the monks were just as much treasure as the gold they had plundered. Could they not sell these men on the slave markets of the continent?

Hereward wandered over to Osbern, who was standing with his foot upon a chest of treasures and scanning the dishevelled huddle of men before him. Some old men, others little more than boys, who had just begun their lives in the service of God. And now their dreams lay shattered before them.

"Osbern, I know that you look upon the monks you have taken with some scorn, but I would ask that they be treated more kindly. They are men of God, who wish none harm."

Osbern turned, his good eye scanning Hereward. The other eye had a great scar across it that had not knitted together well, and it gave the eye a diagonal squint. It was the result of a sword flash across the Dane's face.

"They wished my men harm when they wielded swords against them at Peterborough."

This much Hereward knew was true. The monks had fought hard to defend their monastery.

"Would you now value them as highly as slaves, had they knelt before you in surrender?" Hereward asked.

"No," Osbern mused, "I would not. And that does make them all the more valuable."

He was quiet for a moment.

"I will instruct my men that they are to be treated better…I wouldn't like to see their value fall," he added with a grin.

***

At length, Thorold returned to his monastery to find that little remained but the church. He sat upon his grey mare and assessed the damage. It was almost complete. A few of the monks who had escaped capture or death shuffled forward to greet him.

“My lord,” said one grizzled old monk, whose teeth had long since departed from his jaw, save from two yellow old pegs in the front, “Our abbey is razed, and most of its wealth has been looted. We did all we could to defend it but were overwhelmed by a terrible force of Saxons and Danes.”

Thorold glared down at him and the other pathetic human beings before him.

“Then you did not fight hard enough!” he bawled, “You seem to have survived the carnage. Why is that? Did you run from the attack like young maidens?”

The old man’s head dropped, but another younger monk spoke up.

“We fought as best we could, my lord, but we were no match for warriors such as these. We had neither the manpower nor the arms.”

“Pathetic!”

Thorold turned in his saddle to address the growing crowd of townspeople.

“I will have the heads of the leaders of this raid and any others who helped them in this destruction. Dane or Saxon, I care little which. There will be a wailing and a gnashing of teeth before I am done with this. Now get you gone and clear up this devastation for rebuilding.”

And with that, he spurred his horse toward what was left of the church.

***

It was a weary column that would wend its way into Ely that night. As they entered the encampment, boys ran out to take the horses. The monks, footsore and bleeding and with only a few pathetic remains of sandals on their feet to protect them, were hustled to a low hut. The door was flung open, and the monks were encouraged to enter by the points of Danish swords.

Hereward looked down upon the sorry sight. He dismounted his horse and shoved the reins into the hands of a lad, mumbling something about rubbing it down and feeding the beast. He strode over to where a couple of Danes were prodding their swords into the backs of the monks. Hereward grabbed a sword in his gloved hand and glared down at the man wielding it.

"Harm these men again, and I will personally gut you like an eel!" he snarled.

He looked at the other Dane and spat out, "Got that?!"

The two men nodded and skulked away.

Hereward beckoned to two of his Saxon followers.

“Take in some water to bathe their feet. And find them some food and drink. Set a guard on the hut — as much to keep the Danes out as keep the monks in.”

The two men nodded their understanding, and Hereward tramped off to the main hall.

As Hereward and his senior warriors entered, Osbern and Arnulf looked up. The Danes knew that the huge Saxon was unhappy at the treatment of his kinsmen, though, of course, they didn’t share his concern for the monks of a different religion. What were they to the Danes but a commercial opportunity? But, to keep the peace between them, they nodded and smiled as Hereward approached.

“How are your monks?” asked Osbern.

“They are as well as might be expected after such a gruelling march under difficult conditions,” Herewald snapped.

The Danes nodded as if in sympathy. Arnulf broke the silence that had descended, “I have given orders to the Danish warriors that your monks should be treated with a little respect. They will be safe from further abuse at the hands of our men.”

Hereward looked at the Dane. He was sure that he could discern a smirk across his face. He often had this feeling about the man, and it niggled him.

Hereward nodded.

"Every man deserves some respect," he said, "Unless his name is Thorold," he added, with a wide grin.

As the night wore on, food was brought to the hall, and copious amounts of ale were drunk by both Saxon and Dane alike. A huge roast hog was brought to the top table, and there it was carved —high on the hog for the leaders, of course. From there, it descended the tables according to the rank of the diners.

There was much carousing, and coarse jokes flew back and forth between the tables, and men laughed until their ribs ached. Games were played in the centre, between the tables, and Dane tried to best Saxon and Saxon to best Dane. Mostly, the two sides took victory and defeat lightly, and slapped one another's backs in good sport. That was until a huge Danish warrior entered to wrestle a Saxon youth, much smaller and leaner than he. Hereward looked with concern at the incongruous pair.

The two circled one another, the Dane grinning. Fat and ale ran down the long beard of the Danish warrior, and his braids danced around his shoulders. Suddenly, the huge man rushed at the Saxon, his arms outstretched to grab him in a bear hug. But the Saxon was more nimble and, with a quick step, he leapt to the side, sending his adversary crashing into a table. Oaths were cast from the men whose ale had been spilt and whose food was now on the rushes, being hungrily devoured by the dogs.

The Dane righted himself and turned again. This time, he approached more cautiously until he felt he was within grasping range. One arm flew out and grasped the young Saxon by his shirt front. Now he had him! But again, the Saxon youth foiled his efforts. His foot came swiftly out and caught the Dane by his knees, and the man lurched forward and fell flat upon his face on the Earth floor.

Slowly, the man arose, a look of sheer fury upon his face as the assembled company laughed at his tumble. A murderous look came into his eyes as he surveyed his opponent. His hand flashed to his belt, and a knife appeared in his hand. There were gasps from the audience and a look of fear spread upon the young Saxon's face.

It was at that moment that a knife leapt into the hand of Hereward and flew across the room to catch the Dane in the huge arm muscle that was about to bring an end to the young man's life or certainly scar him for life.

The Dane screamed as the metal blade embedded itself in his bicep and drew blood in spurts to spray across the floor. He grabbed at the handle and drew the knife from his arm, dropping it to the rushes. His free hand grabbed the wound and held it tightly, and he turned to face the top table, from whence he knew the blade had come. Hereward was now on his feet.

The Dane's face was purple, and he cursed the Saxon leader.

"I should kill you for that!"

"You could try," Hereward answered, "But you would need to pray hard to Odin to protect you."

"You could have killed me!" the man yelled.

"Had I wanted to kill you, you would be dead in the rushes by now," Hereward returned, "Learn to fight fairly in contests, and treat victory and defeat the same…though I am happy for you to fight in any way that promotes victory in a real battle."

A chuckle ran around the hall, and the man knew that the time had come to back down. With a grunt and a glare at the young Saxon, he shuffled off to have his wound dressed.

In the hall, after the entertainment, men became more and more merry on the ale being liberally served. As always, the warriors around the hall began to sing their songs of war and ships and women. The voices would fall and rise in great crescendos, and then collapse again in raucous laughter.

***

The monks sat miserably in their hut, listening to the uproar from the hall and wishing that they were anywhere else in the world. They all knew that

Hereward's guards were outside and that any attempt at escape would be futile. Athelwold, the captured Prior, however, was more deeply in thought about the relics that had been looted from the monastery. It was unthinkable that they should be taken by the heathen Danes and probably destroyed if they could find no buyer for them.

He began to probe at the foot of the wattle walls. Around the hut, he went, watched by his puzzled brothers. After a while of prodding and poking, Athelwold found a section of wall that was not as firm as the rest. Slowly, he worked the panel of wattle, making the daub flake and break off. He worked as silently as he could, but he could not stop the hazel boughs from squeaking and squealing against one another as he worked them back and forth.

All at once, the door opened, and a guard stood in the doorway.

"What's all the squeaking about?" he asked.

"Rats," said Athelwold, thinking quickly.

The guard looked him over and glanced around the room to see nothing but the huddled bodies of his prisoners, prostrate on a few thin straw mattresses upon the damp Earthen floor. He grunted and shut the door again, dropping a bar across it from the outside.

Now, Athelwold went back to work. The monks now realised exactly what he was about. They began to cough and wheeze as Athelwold worked upon the hazel wattle. At length, the section of the wall gave way far enough to allow a man to crawl through.

"Are we to escape?" a young monk asked, now beginning to see some hope in their predicament.

"No, my son," the old monk replied, "We would not get far, and many would be dead by sunrise. I have an 'errand' to perform. Luke, you will assist me," he said to a lithe young monk.

The man nodded.

The two monks slid noiselessly through the hole in the wattle. They lay still, holding their breath, praying that the guards had not heard them. It would not do to be discovered. As their hearts began to calm, the two men snaked across the damp grass and bare soil until they rounded the hall and were unlikely to be seen.

"Luke, we must find a way to enter the hall, but without those inside knowing of our presence," the Prior whispered.

"I cannot see how it will be possible, Prior," the young monk replied.

"God will provide the way through alcohol," the Prior grinned, "We must be patient."

After a while, though the carousing continued, it was noticeably lighter and more slurred. Now, the two men crawled upon their knees to the entrance. No guard had been set —what man in his right mind would attack a hall full of Danish and Saxon warriors, no matter how drunk they might be? And Ely was a safe haven.

The Prior and the monk slipped quietly in through the doors. A dog looked up as they entered, but lay his head upon his paws again and closed his eyes to slumber. The two slipped behind a curtain that hung from the wall and made their way to the rear. Athelwold knew what he was seeking would be at the rear of the hall, where it was safest.

Slowly, slowly, they made their way, stopping on occasion to listen. The only noise was of a few drunken men singing and arguing. All else was still.

At length, the Prior had found exactly what he wanted —the relics that had been stolen from his abbey. He and Luke began to stow the most precious relics in their habits, including one which Athelwold would not leave behind —the arm of St. Oswald.

It had been many years ago now, in a conflict with the pagan Mercians, led by their formidable king, Penda, that Oswald had lost his life. He was killed at the Battle of Maserfield, near Oswestry, in 642AD. Defeated and broken, he had ended his life in prayer for the souls of his men. His body had been brutally dismembered, and his head and limbs had been displayed on stakes for all to see. Now, Athelwold was determined that they would not fall into the hands of the pagan Danes, who would not respect them as they should.

After taking what they could, the monks made their way back just as cautiously as on their outward journey. This time, of course, they were carrying a precious load. Slowly, they crawled to the small entrance to the hut they had made and passed the relics to the others, waiting there. The two men wriggled back to their prison, and Athelwold lost no time in hiding their precious load within the straw mattresses.

***

A few short days later, Hereward was joined in the hall by Osbern and Arnulf. (The Danes had not discovered that the relics were missing, not imagining that it was possible for anyone to take them).

"Ah, Hereward, we have news," said Osbern, looking up and turning his good eye as the Saxon leader entered.

"You are leaving," said Hereward.

The two Danes looked startled.

"How did you know?" asked Arnulf.

"I know that Sweyn has changed his mind about the invasion. He has made a pact with William the Bastard, and is pulling you back to your own land. We, too, have spies," said Hereward, with a grim smile.

"You are correct. Your spies serve you well. We leave on the morrow. We will take what booty we have and some of the more valuable monks to sell in the slave market. You may do what you will with the rest."

Was that a badly-hidden smirk on Arnulf's face? Hereward would swear that it was.

And so it was. The Danes sailed on the morning's high tide, taking with them what they could. It was later said that many precious relics were lost at sea, but who knows. Hereward watched as the dragon ships navigated eastward across the sea. What now?

Chapter 33

Revenge and Witchcraft

One steel-cold morning, deep in the fens at Ely, Hereward and some of his men were surveying a new causeway that the Normans had managed to build almost equidistant between the stronghold and the Norman camp, when a scout returned to the temporary scouting camp of the Saxon leader and his followers.

He was dirt-caked and bone-weary and strode straight to his leader's rough hide tent and entered, unopposed by the spear-wielding guards at the entrance. They knew who he was and that he would have important news for Hereward. Each man gazed at his face to determine whether his news would be good or bad. But the scout's face was a blank sheet of parchment.

As the scout entered, William and a handful of his followers looked up.

"Joseph," Hereward said, "Come, sit and eat with us. Pour him ale; he looks as if he needs it."

The man threw his cloak back and seated himself upon the ground. He first lifted the skin given to him and quenched his thirst with a long draught.

“My lord,” he said, “I have news. You will remember Frederick —brother-in-law of William de Warenne?”

“I knew him well,” Hereward chuckled, “Until the day I killed him, in fact. I heard that he wanted to kill me himself. He tried to trick me and cause my downfall, but he had not reckoned with cunning, for he was not cunning enough.”

The men around the table laughed heartily.

“It now seems,” Joseph, the scout, continued, “That William de Warenne has vowed to avenge the killing and bring you to your doom.”

“Has he indeed?” the Saxon mused, “Well, we shall have to find a way to thwart him in his plan. I should not like to meet my doom.”

More laughter rang around the hall.

“But we must take William de Warenne seriously. He is no idiot.”

“What do we know of him?” asked Peter, one of Hereward’s trusted men.

“Oh, William de Warenne was one of the prominent Norman barons whom William the Bastard summoned to the council when he decided to oppose Harold. He was at the Battle of Hastings, of course. Fought well, as I heard it, and was richly rewarded by our illustrious Norman king with a number of holdings here. They do say that his lands stretched over thirteen counties, from Northumbria to Essex. And now, it seems, he has a special longing to hunt me down and send me to my Maker. What of Norman patrols?"

"My lord, I have encountered a number of patrols very near here. The Normans are searching the fens hard for the secret path."

Hereward pondered the situation.

"And they have managed to build this causeway up to this spot. If they continue, then it is only a matter of time before they reach Ely."

Suddenly, a cry went up from outside the tent, "Warriors approach!"

Hereward and his followers exchanged glances and rose as one. From behind a smudge of cloud and the grey tendrils of mist, men were appearing, walking, loaded with weapons. Bosses on the shields they carried shone like wolves' eyes in the faint light of the sun as it broke through the scudding cloud.

One man led the procession of soldiers. He was tall, with eyes brown as a hunting fox. He smiled at Hereward, showing his white teeth within the bearded face. His boots were soaked, and clods of mud slid off onto the slightly drier ground around the camp.

"Morcar!" said Hereward, "It is good to see you again. Welcome to my humble abode. Come to my tent and shed your boots. Dry your feet before my fire."

Morcar smiled and bowed his head to his host.

"I will do so," he said, "The soles of my feet are raw with walking, though I have felt the soul of this country through them on this march from Northumbria."

Morcar was, of course, our former Saxon Earl of Northumbria who had been ousted by William.

I was with Morcar and Aethelwine, Bishop of Durham, in the fens that morning. A local guide had brought us this far along a secret path from the south. My own feet were also wet and sore, and I, too, was glad to shed my boots and rub them with a hank of sack-cloth.

As they walked to the tent, Hereward slapped Morcar on the back.

"So what happens in the rest of the country?"

"A good deal of killing," Morcar replied.

"William de Warenne has vowed to kill me himself, I hear," said Hereward.

Morcar glanced at him.

"I didn't know that," he said, "I have heard that our conqueror is growing tired of the Saxon resistance, and will continue to send men against us.

I gather Belsar is one of William's knights will who will lead the attack."

"Belsar and William de Warenne," Hereward said, "We are honoured by such illustrious company."

***

It was some little while later that scouting reports began to filter in that a force of Normans was approaching our camp —engineers and soldiers. No doubt they would be coming to continue their work on the causeway. We had no time to retreat to the safety of the stronghold at Ely, to make a stand there, but were trapped here in our hidden world, humming with the life of birds, frogs and insects.

The force continued to approach the new causeway, which provided a dry route through the ever-wet marshes and fens. Rumours flew about our camp of the terrors that lay ahead for us. Their soldiers were all giants of men, armed to the teeth and with blood lust in their eyes. They had webbed feet and could swim through the fens to surround us and other such nonsense.

But slowly and surely, the enemy did approach our haven. Their forward party spotted our camp and called their force to a halt. For a good while, their leaders stood and peered at us. It was a stand-off. Upon a dry bank at the end of the section of causeway, they set up a camp and seemed to be preparing for an assault upon us. Nothing further happened that day. We had no doubt that the party had sent the news back and was awaiting reinforcements. If we left now, under cover of darkness, we would get back to Ely but would lead our enemies there, too. We must remain.

And then, the following morning, just as the sun squeezed above the horizon and the last grey tendrils of fog curled against a pink sky, the Normans made their move.

In a column, they formed up and made their way along the new causeway. Every man was dressed in mail and some degree of armour. Each carried a spear, a shield and a great sword. Each man meant business that morning. The horses they had brought along the causeway were also dressed for battle and flared their nostrils at the unfamiliar scents of the marshes, and perhaps in anticipation of what they knew was to come.

Slowly, the column made its way, cautiously, along the causeway. Men looked nervously from side to side, where the sucking mud of the marsh might spell doom for any man who might step unwisely. Slowly, slowly, they progressed until the leaders reached almost the end of the causeway.

Now, we prepared ourselves for an attack but watched even more keenly as something strange began to happen. For it seemed to us that the causeway had moved —was moving— beneath the troops. Now, Norman eyes began to swivel, looking uneasily from side to side to understand what was happening.

As we watched, we knew exactly what was happening. The causeway itself had begun to sink under the weight of men, armour and horses. The beasts threw their heads back and reared as the very ground under their feet seemed to buckle. Their panicked cry filled the air, along with the yelled commands of the officers and the anxious shouts of enlisted men.

Men and horses fell from the causeway into the water and mud beneath them. Desperately, they fought to return to their camp through reeds and draws of deeper open water, where the roots' rushes could not penetrate the mud. What a sight of chaos and terror played out before us. Man and beast, drowning before our eyes. We stood there, open-mouthed at the carnage before us. No man speaking.

At length, the Normans who were able to escape had done so, leaving only a few men to try to rescue and salvage what they could from the disaster. I imagine that the camp upon the dry bank was a sorry sight that night. Horses shivering. Men drenched and shattered by their ordeal, staring into the flames of the campfires, each lost in his own thoughts, perhaps for absent friends who had not returned from the marsh that day. The smell of fear in the air. The usual light-hearted banter of soldiers…absent.

***

Two days after the calamity on the causeway, we remained in our camp in an attempt to guard the rest of the path back to Ely, when a strange thing happened. A call rang out from a guard. We all pricked up our ears.

A voice called again, "Come. See this."

We all sprang to our feet, wondering what sights we would be treated to today. Would it be a further mishap for the Norman enemy, or would it be another, more credible, threat to us?

We climbed to the top of the stockade to see a strange sight indeed. Across the wreckage of the marsh causeway, now repaired to an extent by the Norman troops, was being carried a tower of wood. Was this some sort of assault tower? Surely, Belsar would not even think of such an assault?

The tower finally came to a halt, a little way from the Norman camp. A figure could be seen, mounting a ladder within, climbing to the top. Imagine our surprise when an old woman emerged at the summit. She was bent with age and wore a long cloak of wool with a shawl around her scrawny shoulders. A cloth covered her head. In one hand, she held a stick, and with the other, what looked like a bag of some sort.

And there she stood, gazing out from her perch across the damp ground to where we stood, gazing at her. The Norman soldiers who had manoeuvred the tower into position now made their way back across the causeway.

She raised an arm and began to curse in the strange fenland accent of the area.

"Give up your arms! I curse you! You will live forever in damnation! Hell awaits the man who does not bend his knee to the masters! I curse you with magical charms!"

And with this, she plunged her hand into the bag and brought out the wings of a dead crow. This she waved before her face and then thrust towards us, all the time chanting some magical rhyme.

Some of the men began to shrink with fear.

"We are cursed! We cannot fight against the magic of a witch! What must we do?"

"You will do nothing," yelled Hereward, striding towards where we stood upon the edge of the outlier camp.

He stood there, solid as a boulder, and called out across the space between us and the tower.

"Get you gone, old woman. We have no fear of your mad incantations. You have no power over any man who follows the Lord and his conscience. Get you gone!"

The old woman peered across to where our leader was standing, with an evil, weasely look. Her hand delved again into the bag she carried. This time, she drew out a skull. It was like a man's skull but smaller —like that of a child.

"I curse you and your leader with the sacred skull. You have no power that can overcome this magic."

"We'll need to see about that," Hereward muttered.

He turned his back and clambered down from the camp's guard post. He strode off to his tent and disappeared inside.

We stood there, still, watching the old witch. Now she did a strange, loping dance around the tower top. Then she would dip into her bag and bring out bones, animal parts and what looked like stones. At one point, she took out the body of a black rat and hurled it towards us. But she was old and not as strong as she had been in her youth, and the rat fell just a few short yards from the tower. We stood fascinated by the performance.

Some men still shied away and descended the walls to hide away from the witchcraft, but others, myself among them, stood fascinated and yelled insults at the woman. Many of us were beginning to enjoy the show.

At one point of the performance, I saw the blur of a figure moving through the reeds, away from the fortress and toward the tower. I was quite certain that I saw it again, around the foot of the tower. Yes, there it was again.

As we watched, a faint wisp of smoke began to curl itself around the base of the tower. The old woman didn't seem to notice it until a yellow glow lit up the tower from below. Now, she stopped in her curses and gazed down over the flimsy wooden parapet. Frantically, she moved from side to side of her rough wooden turret, assessing the danger that beset her. A thin cry went up.

"Save me! I am but an old woman."

Now, she tried to clamber down to safety, but the flames grew larger and flickered up the supporting timbers. There was no escape other than leaping from the tower, though that meant almost certain death.

As the flames grew in ferocity, she wailed a mournful note. Men began to approach again from along the causeway where they had retreated, presumably to steer clear of any magical curses the witch might throw from her lofty perch. But it was too late. All at once, the tower began to lean to one side. Then, the opposite side seemed to crumble, and the whole edifice collapsed into the flames. The last we saw of the witch was when she fell into the flames. We could still hear her screams and cries for a short while longer, until they stopped abruptly.

As the fire died down, watched helplessly by the Norman soldiers, we descended the guard post again into the safety of the camp. A figure suddenly appeared through the main gate. It was a tall, well-built man, covered with a long brown cloak and hood. The man stopped and threw back the hood. It was Hereward.

"I trust she is a little warmer now," he said, and disappeared into his tent. We stood, dumbfounded.

Chapter 34

The Potter

Rain seethed around us upon a dank and dreary morning. A small group of us had been ordered to leave the safety of the stockade and travel a little way into the marsh, as the food was beginning to run low, and we needed to restock the larder. This particular larder was stored deep in the ponds and streams. We approached a large mere and looked for the tell-tale sign of brightly coloured fabric tied in a low bush. On a frond of the bush was a hidden line leading into the water.

One of our numbers began to wade into the water, following the line beneath the surface of the light-reflecting water. At length, he dragged up the carcase of a deer. Deer are often stored at the bottom of ponds and streams as a way to keep the meat cool, and to stop it from spoiling.

When the deer was killed, its stomach would be opened, and the intestines pulled out. These would be emptied of food and filled with sand and stones to act as anchors. Filled to a couple of feet, they were then tied off, and the animal sunk in the mire.

Sometimes, however, it happened that carcasses would bloat and rise to the surface.

The best part of the deer was the brains. They were a delicacy. The brains were heavy in fats and were very nutritious. Once back at our refuge, we set to work cutting off the mouldy bits to get to the good meat below. We would feast well tonight…but it could not last forever. We were now almost cut off from any escape route.

***

Sometime later, in the fortress of Ely, we sat around, talking the talk of warriors and scraping the deer hide to make into ropes. Some told fantastical tales of bravery and battles, large and small. Others moaned about the rations we were allowed, as soldiers always do.

But all gossip stopped as a tall man emerged from the hall. His breeches were torn and ragged. His tunic was filthy with grey clay marks. His cloak had certainly seen better days and hung from him like a cobweb to a wall. His boots were shoddy and holed. When he looked at us with his filthy face and shaggy hair beneath a battered hat, we all gasped, for there was no doubt in the minds of those who knew him that the man was no less than Hereward himself.

"My lord, what is the meaning of your rough dress?" one man called out.

Hereward strolled over to where we sat.

"I fancy that I should pay the Normans a visit in their camp."

We all gasped at the prospect of our leader putting himself in such a dangerous position, but it was typical of the man who was a leader of men.

"I was riding in the fen today, surveying our causeways, when I chanced upon a potter coming towards me through the fen. I chatted to him for some time, and he agreed to change clothes with me so that I might more easily slip into the Norman camp."

"My lord, think of the danger. You could be recognised. What would we do then?"

"I doubt it. None of the men in the Norman camp has seen me close enough to recognise me. In addition, the potter says that some of the Norman guards saw him enter the fen but paid him little attention. They obviously didn't see him as a threat. Therefore, they will not be surprised to see him leave again. I can spin a merry yarn about being turned back from Ely by warriors of the dastardly Hereward."

He chuckled at the thought.

A short while later, the fortress gate was opened, and Hereward, now complete with a bony donkey and pottery wares, left along the secret track through the fens. After a while, he made his way out of the fen and toward the Norman camp.

“Halt!” a sentry’s voice rang out as the jangling of the donkey’s harness brought him up short from the daydream he’d been enjoying —a daydream of Normandy and his family, perhaps.

Hereward pulled the donkey to a halt before the man.

“Will you allow an old potter to enter your camp? I have wares that would be useful to men who must cook for themselves over a campfire.”

The guard approached the ‘potter’ and looked him up and down, grimacing at the ragged and filthy dress of the man before him. Hereward dragged a filthy sleeve across his nose to clear off the drops of liquid snot forming there. The guard grimaced again. He looked over the donkey, a thin and badly kept animal that had seen better days some years ago. He scanned the pots hanging from the beast’s pack.

“I suppose it can do no harm,” he said, “Enter the camp with your wares, though I don’t know whether the soldiers will be interested in your poor wares.”

“There is nought wrong with my pots,” the ‘potter’ said indignantly.

The guard just grunted and trudged back to his guard point. Hereward urged the donkey on and entered the camp —a typical soldiers’ camp— filthy, noisy, and full of confusion. Eyes turned toward him as he cried his wares. A few soldiers came forward and looked over his pots, but most just glared at him or turned away indifferently.

After selling a few pots to the men, Hereward made his way to the great tent that he knew would be the headquarters of the Normans. He ground-tied the donkey and pulled a pack from its back. Seating himself with his back against the hide tent, he opened a ragged piece of cloth to reveal a meagre meal. A piece of boiled hare, a lump of cheese, a few oatcakes and a jug of ale were all the fare he had.

Leaning back against the tent, he contentedly munched on his meal and listened to the conversations inside.

"William insists that we build him a third causeway and proceed to send the soldiers along it to attack Ely," a voice from inside the tent said.

"But we have built two already, and Hereward's men have destroyed them," another voice protested.

"The causeways at Stuntney and Little Thetford failed. Why should another at Aldreth fare any better?"

"What choice do we have? The king is adamant that we try again. He says that this time, Hereward will fail, and we will reach his stronghold. Imagine, if you could capture Hereward, you could avenge the death of your brother-in-law, Frederick, last year."

"I am sworn to kill Hereward for that," the second voice said.

Hm, no less than William de Warenne after my blood, Hereward thought. He had indeed killed Frederick the year before.

"What do you think you are doing?" a voice growled.

Hereward looked up to see a Norman captain glaring down at him.

"My lord, I have stopped to eat and sup after selling to some of your troops my fine pots. I will be on my way soon."

"You won't! Stay there! Don't you realise that this is the headquarters tent?"

"Oh, I didn't know, my lord, but I have done no damage to it. My donkey has nibbled a bit of grass, but that is all. I am a simple man and meant no harm."

At that, the tent flap opened, and William de Warenne emerged.

"What is the noise? We are holding a meeting here!"

"This potter, my lord. Eating his meal against your tent."

"I meant no harm, my lord. I am but a poor potter. Perhaps I could show you some of my fine pots," Hereward simpered.

"And what would I want with your rough pots? Don't you know who I am?"

"No, my lord. I have never seen you before. Are you the king?"

"Of course not!" William snapped.

The guard tried to hide a smile.

"I am William de Warenne. Now tell me, what have you overheard here today?"

"Why nought, my lord," said Hereward, "I was not listening, and I am sure I would not understand your fine words if I had heard them. I am, as I say, a simple man."

"What shall I do with him, my lord?" the guard asked.

William mused.

"Keep him here for now. We will let him go when the next part of the plan is complete. We can't be sure that he will not let slip anything he heard."

The guard nodded.

"Come on, you! I'll find somewhere for you to sit for now."

Hereward wrapped the remains of the meal and rose to follow the guard. At length, he found himself sitting beneath a wagon beside the guard tent, his donkey tethered to a wheel beside him.

"Keep an eye on him. Don't let him leave," the guard said to his companions sitting around the tent.

"Ought we to put him in chains?" a guard asked.

"No, I don't think he'll go far, and he wouldn't be hard to catch with that old donkey trailing after him."

Hereward stretched out beneath the wagon a short time later and pretended to be asleep. The donkey just stood, with its head almost to the ground.

"You couldn't get one good meal from that animal," one of the guards commented.

"No, but his master seems to feed quite well," another replied, "He is a big man for a poor potter."

"Hm, we must watch him carefully," the first guard said.

After a short time, Hereward pretended to wake. He stretched himself and yawned widely. He crawled out from under the wagon and scratched himself. After another stretch and yawn, he spat upon the ground and began to wander off toward some bushes.

"And where would you be going?" a guard asked.

"I must relieve myself, sir. You would not like it if I should do it here, beside your tent. I have not had good food for some days and..."

The guard thought a moment.

"Don't be too long," he said, "And don't stray too far."

"I will be back before you know it," Hereward said and bowed to the guard, who just glared at the 'potter' and turned to go into the guard tent.

It was sometime later that it occurred to the guard that the 'potter' had been gone a long time. He bustled over in the direction the old man had taken, but there was no sign of him. He called but received no reply. He turned on his heel and ran back to the tent. The donkey still stood there, asleep on its feet.

"Has anyone seen the potter?" he asked.

The other guards shook their heads.

"I fear we are all in trouble," the guard said.

A little later that evening, a rather damp and dishevelled Hereward approached the gates of the fortress.

"Will you allow an old potter to enter?" he called.

The guards on the gate chuckled and drew back the great log that held the gate out from its fixings, and the gate swung open.

"It is good to see you safely returned, my lord," said one guard.

"Have you learned anything of the Normans' plans," asked another.

Hereward winked.

"Indeed I have," he smiled.

***

On the following morning, after a breakfast of cold venison and ale, Hereward drew all of his captains to him. He told them of the plans he had overheard, and they discussed at length how they should meet the enemy. When the meeting was over, men bustled about the fortress, making the equipment that Hereward would need to defeat the Normans again.

Two weeks later, when all was prepared, a large force left the stronghold, guided by a local man. Their destination: Aldreth. It was not an easy journey, along ancient paths and through meres and marshes. Without the local guide, it would have been a deadly dangerous journey. There were so many deep pools and sucking marshes that a stranger could blunder into.

After quite a struggle, the force arrived at the newly constructed causeway near Aldreth. The scouts had been out here for some time, watching the progress of the Norman engineers. How hard they worked —dragging timbers into the marsh, sinking posts in the sodden ground, and safely fastening it all together so that it was strong enough to bear the weight of the Norman soldiers as they crossed it.

Hereward and his men settled themselves into a 'cold camp' on a raised knoll. The knoll was covered with alder trees, and silver birch had begun to colonise the relatively drier piece of land. There could be no fires lit for fear that the Norman guards would see the smoke, so the men ate cold rations. The camp was as quiet as the grave; only whispered conversations were allowed.

At night, when the marshes became as black as pitch unless a little moonlight illuminated them, groups of men set out for the causeway. They peered into the darkness and watched silently, still as a kestrel's shadow, as the Norman guards wandered up and down in the gloom. They barely seemed to look toward the marsh; there seemed little point, as they could see for only a yard or so ahead of them. With them, Hereward's men carried bundles of dry kindling. When the guards wandered away, they carefully placed them beneath the boardwalk.

The men were always up before the sun to be sure they would be ready for what was to come. Before one misty dawn, a large number of men were already hidden in the undergrowth beside the causeway. It was not long before Norman scouts appeared. They scanned the marshes ahead of them and then moved on. A short while later, the tramp of Norman feet could be heard, coming towards the hidden Saxons. Soon, from out of the haze, the troops appeared. As they approached the warriors, a Saxon scout crept close and signalled that the Norman force was all on the causeway.

Hereward gave a hand signal. His men leapt into action. Burning brands were put to the kindling, and the reeds, covered in animal fat beside the causeway, were also lit. The Saxons now retreated to a safe distance and watched as the smoke wreathed up around the Normans. There were soon yells in Norman French as flames licked around the timber track. Shrieks of pain could be heard as the Normans were engulfed in the flames. Both the causeway and the surrounding vegetation were now well alight. Men turned and tried to return to camp, only to find the causeway behind them in flames. They began to leap into the marsh, where many were sucked down and drowned in the cloying mud.

Now, Hereward's men arose from their safe hiding positions and immediately began to pour arrows onto the panicking troops. Slingers began to rain down heavy stones upon the men, and many fell, wounded, into the water. After a couple of hours of slaughter, when blood flowed, warm and sticky, across the surface of the marsh, Hereward and his men left the scene of devastation.

Norman bodies still lay, floating in the water and hanging over the reeds. Their injuries were terrible. Men were badly burned, and the smell of charring flesh hung above the marsh. Many lay with arrows protruding from their bodies, many through the neck, where Hereward's arches had aimed them. The Saxon thirst for blood had been satisfied that day.

Hereward surveyed the scene. His hard eyes showed no emotion. Today, they must clear the camp and return to the stronghold. The Saxon leader knew that his deadly enemy, William, would be in a furious rage at the way the outlaw troops had massacred his troops again. His thirst for revenge would be more powerful than ever.

Chapter 35

Betrayal

A few days later, in the Norman camp, Belsar paced like a caged animal. His instinct was to hunt, to stalk, to destroy the enemy, and yet his attempts had been foiled…for now. Now, he had another plan in mind.

"When did you tell Abbot Thurstan's monk to arrive?" he asked of his compatriot, William de Warenne, his face angular, mouth wide and cruel.

"The monks of Ely grow tired of the siege. Thurstan has promised that the monk can show us the secret way to Ely, has he not?"

"He should be here by now. If he does not appear in the next few minutes, I will send out the captain of the guard to bring him to me, but he will regret it."

"I think we have found Hereward's Achilles Heel with Thurstan and his monks," said Belsar, "We have told our good Abbot that the land surrounding Ely is currently owned by the monastery and will be divided up for the Normans. They have sought to protect their land and have agreed to help us. Hereward and his men have been sold out."

At that point, the tent flap was opened by a guard, and a tall, thin monk entered, his hands hidden in the sleeves of his habit.

"Hands!" William de Warenne snapped.

The monk slowly withdrew his hands to reveal that they carried no weapons. The man had not an ounce of fat upon his wiry body, and as his cowl fell to his shoulders, it was apparent that he was as bald as an egg.

The monk nodded to both Normans.

"You asked for me?" he said quietly, a faint smile turning up the corners of his thin mouth.

Not a face to meet on a dark night thought Belsar.

"We did, Brother Adam," replied Belsar, "We have been advised that you might be able to 'help us'."

The monk peered at the two Norman knights with eyes that were red and had slits.

"In what way?" the monk asked, though he knew very well what he had been sent by Thurstan to do.

"We understand that you support the efforts of the king to…bring the country to peace," Belsar told him.

"Peace should be the aim of all good men," the monk replied, but his words were hard as steel and as cold as ice.

"We need access to the safe haven where Hereward and his men are holed up," said de Warren.

Brother Adam grinned mirthlessly.

"I did hear that the last assault had not ended well."

The Normans glanced at one another. Both men had summed up their visitor, and their impression was not favourable. It was obvious that the man was a toad who would sell his own mother if it brought him favour.

"You can guide us to a secret causeway?" Belsar asked, becoming a little impatient with the monk's attitude.

"I can," was the curt reply.

Belsar reached into a chest by the rough campaign table. He took out a small leather bag. He shook it, and a jingle could be heard within it.

"I trust this will 'encourage' you to show us the way?"

The monk nodded, and he permitted himself another slight smile.

"When do you wish to pay Hereward a visit?"

"The day after tomorrow, in the morning," Belsar replied, "Be here well before dawn so we are not delayed in our mission."

"You can count on me," Brother Adam said and turned and left the tent.

"We'd better be able to count upon him," Belsar growled, "Or he will find himself without the eyes to see a track through the marsh."

***

In the stockade of the fortress, two days later, we sat cleaning and sharpening our weapons. It was a fine day, with a fair breeze blowing across the fens. The air was filled with the sound of metal on stone, and the whisper of soft, green leaves swished like velvet in the breeze. There was also the chatter of men and the drone of insects. As the early morning wore on, the breeze picked up a little and whirled the dust upon the floor of the fortress.

Around mid-morning, when the sun was almost halfway to its highest point in the sky, a scout returned to the fort. He was admitted to the stockade and hurried across toward the hall. As he passed, he took a moment to shout to us.

"The Normans are coming. They have found the secret track!"

We looked from one to another, incredulous at this news. Our only way of coming and going safely was now known to the enemy. Nothing worse could be imagined.

The fortress became a hive of activity as men dashed to and fro, gathering weapons and chain armour that they knew would be needed soon. I was one of Morcar's men and busied myself with my own affairs.

I began to think of Edyth and the children. What were they doing? Were they safe? Would I ever see them again? Was I wise to come south to support Morcar and Hereward? These are hard questions for a warrior to ask himself before a battle. They were words that could destroy a man's will to fight or harden it. And here I was, drawn back to the conflict like a dog to its vomit.

We were well drilled and had prepared for this eventuality, and so the fortress was ready within an hour or two. Now, the stockade and its surroundings seemed to have gone still. The breeze had dropped again, and the leaves seemed to hang motionless upon the branches. Men stood like statues, peering into the marsh to the south, waiting for a first glimpse of the enemy.

I pondered on how Hereward must feel. He was a Saxon leader, but to the world outside, dominated by Norman law, he was a felon, a wolf's head that anyone may cut down. Our leader stood upon the parapet, muscles cording his back, and gazed with lake-blue eyes at the path he knew the enemy must come. They had set off at dawn, creeping through the marshes and woodland that surrounded us.

It was only a matter of time before the first sounds came to us upon the air. The tramp of feet. The whinny of horses. The clang of metal weapons. Soon, we began to see the advance guard of Normans approaching like a stream of ants upon the forest floor. Now, the only thing that protected us was our fortress. I felt almost naked and vulnerable. My stomach churned. I had been in battle before, I told myself, but I think every warrior feels the same before another clash, and the man who says otherwise is a liar.

The Norman troops approached to a safe distance —approaching us close now would be a suicidal step, heavily armed and protected as we were. The soldiers threw off their kit packs and settled down to prepare. Sections of troops moved around the fortress to cut off any thoughts of escape. It seemed an impenetrable screen was encircling us.

There was no sleep that night. We stood there, peering into the gloom lit only by the campfires of the Normans. We threw burning kindling over the stockade walls from time to time to throw light upon our surroundings and make it more difficult for the Normans to surprise us with a night attack.

On the following morning, in the half-gloom of dawn, we saw activity in the Norman camp. Slowly, ballistas, which had been constructed during the gloom of night, were dragged forward. Now, the Normans began a barrage of our stockade. Arbalestiers began to draw back the cords of their crossbows and send flurries of bolts skyward to wreak havoc amongst the men upon the stockade walls.

Men screamed as they were hit and then fell like autumn leaves to the floor, either dead or terribly injured. We fought back as well as we could behind our protecting walls, sending arrows, like swarming bees, toward our enemies, and with some success. Our slingers, too, leapt into action, hurling their stones from the piles we had built up in the fortress.

But the Normans had another weapon —fire. Their archers drew back their bows and rained fire upon us, and soon, the fortress was bathed in red by the flames of burning Saxon buildings. Men and women rushed around, throwing water from the well upon the blazing timber and thatch. Some tried to beat it out with brooms and cloth. Some were saved, but other buildings were not.

After a morning of battering, the Norman infantry began to prepare for an assault. The fortress had taken a good deal of damage, and some of the walls were almost in ruins. Men stood at the gaps, ready to repel the enemy. We looked from one to another, weighing up the danger. The sweat of fear ran down my back in rivulets.

And then they came. They burst across the land between us with wild cries. The scene was madness. We poured more fire onto our advancing enemies, and they, in turn, raised their wooden shields before them to protect themselves as the arrows thumped into them.

A Norman knight now rode forward, and, with a wave of a pennant, he urged their infantry on. In short order, the enemy was at the very walls and gateways of the stockade. They probed the holes in the walls to find the weakest spots. Some were killed as they ventured into the gaps, but their compatriots simply trod upon the bodies, and slowly, they forced their way inside.

Now, the fighting was hand to hand in the muddy lanes of the fortress. The Normans swarmed upon us, and the hard-trodden Earth was soon strewn with bloody bodies. Some people seemed drawn to the smell of blood, and the Normans became ever more crazed as they fought their way through us.

Behind the first line of attack were horsemen, watching the whole scenario. One man rose in his stirrups and gazed at the top of the palisade, where Hereward himself stood. He took a bow from an archer beside him and accepted the proffered arrow. He notched the arrow to the bowstring and aimed.

The arrow flew toward Hereward, who had seen it fired. He ducked behind the fence, and the arrow flew harmlessly by, embedding itself into the timber frame of a building.

Now, Hereward himself raised a bow and let loose an arrow in return. It flew true to its mark, and William de Warenne tumbled from his saddle.

"Oh, William, I thought you were going to avenge Frederick," Hereward said with a chuckle.

As the battle raged on, I recall looking around me and seeing Hereward battling with two soldiers a few paces away. Like the bellow of a stag at the rut, Hereward used every curse he knew, and some of them many times over! He, like the rest of us, was covered in the blood-spray of fallen men.

For myself, I was being slowly backed into a corner below the fortress's palisade fence platform. A huge Norman was slowly prowling toward me, a look of grim enjoyment upon his face as he relished finishing off the boy before him. No quarter would be given; that much I knew. What to do? I could not get past him to safety. Could I fight my way out? I doubted it, considering our difference in size and his advantage of weaponry. Was this it? Is this how it ended?

Out of the corner of my eye, I became aware of some movement in the fence. It appeared to wobble, and then I was certain that it was moving. The

Norman didn't appear to notice it until it was too late. At the last moment, he glanced upward and tried to cover his face from the falling debris. In a heartbeat, we were both buried under the fallen defences. I knew no more.

When I awoke, the Norman was still lying before me but unmoving. I tried to rise but found that I couldn't. I was pinned there under a large rail that had once supported the fence posts. What to do? Should I cry out for help? What if there were none of my fellows still alive? What if the Normans were still here? I could expect little mercy. I lay still again, listening. I could hear a babble of voices in what I thought was Norman French. I could also hear screams and wails, but they seemed to come from a good distance away. I decided that I had to escape from my wooden prison or face certain death.

Slowly, I wriggled my body until, finally, one leg came free; then, more easily than I had thought, another came loose. It took time and not a little effort before I was completely liberated from the ruins of the fence. I could now crawl. My heart pounded in my chest, and blood thumped in my ears as I slowly began to worm my way out.

I stopped a short while at the body of the Norman who'd tried to kill me. His neck was broken. His eyes were sightless, and blood had congealed around his mouth. I knew that the Normans would, eventually, come and clear away their dead, so I must make an attempt to escape soon. I could not risk capture. I did take a rather fine knife he had strapped to his waist. He wouldn't be needing it where he had gone to.

After a while, I found myself lying under the very edge of the fallen timber. I poked my head out to behold a terrible sight. Many men lay dead in the dust with terrible injuries. The very Earth was brown with dried blood. The air was still a fine mix of dust and smoke, which made me choke. I decided that my only course of action was to crawl out and try to make my escape through a hole I could see a little way down the fortress fenceline.

As I exited the wooden debris, it creaked, and part of it fell away with a bang. A murmuration of starlings rose from where they were perching and flew off, calling. I crouched stock still. Nothing happened. No one seemed to notice. Breathing again, I made my way to the gap. I peered around the fence to witness a dreadful occurrence. I had known that William was a cruel man, but this?

As I watched, Saxon warriors were tied down to the ground, and terrible tortures were enacted upon them. One man screamed a terrible scream as a great Norman soldier knelt down beside him, and his eyes were gouged out as he lay there. Hands were sliced from arms as I watched, and grown men wept and begged for a swift end.

I heard one man cry out defiantly, "It is better to fall into the hands of God than into those of the Norman tyrant!"

God is certainly *not* listening today, I thought.

Slipping around the wall, I darted into the safety of a large rock a few feet away, peered out again over its bulk, and then, bending from the waist, sprinted as best I could across the open ground to the fen forest beyond. Gasping for breath and retching from sheer terror, I threw myself beneath a blackberry bush. And there I lay until the sun began to dip behind the trees. Now I knew that I had to move. I could not stay there. I would certainly be found eventually and would then suffer the tortures of my companions.

As I quietly moved off, deeper into the forest, I wondered if anyone else had escaped. Was I alone? That was a thought that churned my stomach. Where was I? How would I find my way out of here? The safe path was no longer safe, and I had no guide.

Slowly, I travelled on under the cover of darkness, testing every footfall for the softness of the marsh. I decided that I would move away from the fortress far enough so that I would not be discovered, but then lie up and travel by daylight, when I would be safer from a watery death.

After a while, I stopped and lay down upon a tussock of grass to rest my weary body —though I found it harder to rest my weary mind.

I eventually slipped into a troubled sleep and awoke with green sunlight on the leaves above my head. I raised myself. My body ached more than I can ever recall before. I had nothing to eat but quenched my thirst from the marsh. What to do? What choices did I have? I could remain here and almost certainly die, or move on and perhaps live, I told myself. And so, I stirred myself and walked on. Travel was slow, but I made gradual progress. I was unsure whether I was moving further into the forest now, or toward the edge.

It must have been around noon when I settled myself against a tree to rest awhile. A vixen trotted by towards a dense bush, seemingly oblivious to my presence. What a beautiful animal, I thought, in her pelt of red and white. I wondered if she was denning near here.

I was jolted from my reverie by a sound, a sharp crack from somewhere behind me. A deer? The fox looked up and made a sudden dash for cover. Not a deer! I sat there, hardly daring to breathe and trying to shape myself into the trunk of the tree to blend with my surroundings. (My clothing was brown and green, the colours of the Earth, and so I hoped and hoped).

Yes, these were footsteps of men quietly making their way through the forest. Was it a Norman patrol in pursuit of me? Had they followed my tracks upon the soft Earth and at the edges of rivers and streams?

Presently, I heard voices clearly enough to recognise the language. It was Saxon. Slowly, I arose from my seat and peered around the trunk of the great tree. Making their way toward me through the undergrowth was a group of men I knew. I stepped out before them, and they stared at me, uncertainty etched across their faces.

From the rear came a tall man. He looked at me.

"John, John Aelricson," he said, his smile as warm as sunlight.

I was taken aback that Hereward knew my name. I was a no-body —a mere boy. The men came forward now and greeted me. Hereward clapped me on the back.

"How did you manage to escape?" he asked, "Never mind. Tell me over a meal later. It is frugal, but it is food."

And so we moved off together. I was never more relieved. Now, I was with men I could trust and who could release me from the grip of this forest.

Chapter 36

Defeat and Acceptance?

On that evening, as we sat in a woodland glade, gathered around a fire over which were roasting squirrels the men had captured, I told my story of escape and heard those of the others of Hereward's men.

"Morcar was taken," Hereward informed me, regret etched upon his features.

"He was a good man," he continued, "But I know nothing of his fate."

The men had listened, appalled by the story I had to tell of the fate of our warrior captives.

"And what must we do now?" I asked, "Is our resistance to the Normans over? Should I return north and try to rebuild my life there?"

"You must do what you feel right, John," Hereward answered, "We intend to move through this forest and mount an attack on Stamford. It will be a small token of our resistance, but I am sure that men will hear of it and return to the fray with us."

And so it was that a short while later, when we felt we were strong and prepared enough, we set off, determined to mount a quick attack upon Stamford. We hoped this would be the spark that might re-light the resistance to William.

The part I shall now tell you really happened, despite people today condemning it as the fantasy of an old man. Yes, I am an old man now, but I am sure that my memory does not fail me in this. I am sure that it really happened. I sometimes dream about it, even now. You must make up your own mind.

We had decided, by using the sun's rising and falling, the direction of travel we thought we must take to Stamford. Through the density of the great forest, we trudged, cutting back the undergrowth with our swords. My arms and legs became scratched and torn by branches and briars. Small animals fled at our approach, and the birds gave forth their alarm calls.

As we travelled on, I became aware, as did we all, that we seemed to be making little headway, and that some parts of the forest we passed through, we had passed before. Here were the tell-tale signs of our passing —limbs lopped from bushes, footprints in the soft Earth, large trees whose unusual shapes we remembered all told the tale. We were lost. We were lost within the vastness of Rockingham Forest.

At length, we entered a small glade, where a large tree had fallen, perhaps in a gale, and created a pool of light on the forest floor that was being exploited by the plants of the understory. Wildflowers bloomed, and small saplings raced toward the light to plug the hole before another could. Here, we stopped and slumped to the floor. We were tired, hungry and thirsty; rations were low. Our spirits, I felt, were even lower.

Hereward stood there, gazing around him, looking up at the sun as it moved upon its path across the sky. In truth, he was as confused as the rest of us about our position, though he would never admit it.

"I think —no, I am sure that we must move off in that direction once we are rested," he said, pointing back into the depths of the forest.

We were not as convinced.

Hereward sat and ate what little food he had left in his pack, as we all did. As we sat there, dispirited and worn, a strange thing happened. From the glade's edge, a large wolf appeared. His pelt was almost completely black, and his eyes seemed to glow yellow from its sooty fur. He opened his mouth to pant as he stared at us, revealing terrible canine teeth that could rip the throat from a man who tried to harm him. We all sat there, motionless, watching him. Men sat with a morsel of food poised before their mouths, entranced by our visitor.

As we watched, the wolf, who seemed to have no fear of us, lay down upon a grassy knoll and watched us intently. Some of us looked around a little nervously —where there was one wolf, there may be more.

At length, we were rested and fed, though frugally, and it was decided that we should move off toward where we thought our salvation would be. As we arose, so did the wolf. It looked at us and gave a gruff bark. Then, it turned and began to walk in the opposite direction. As we watched, it turned again, returned a short way and gave another bark. We looked at one another. What did it mean? Did it mean anything? The wolf barked again and turned toward the forest track.

"It is almost as if it wants us to follow it," one warrior whispered.

We stood and looked at one another again.

"What shall we do?"

Still the wolf watched.

"I think we should follow it and see where it leads us," declared Hereward, "It is a sign."

And so, we set off after the wolf. It made its way through the twisted undergrowth, moving on, then stopping and watching our progress. It was certainly leading us. There could be no doubt.

We travelled on for what seemed like hours until the forest began to dim as the sun dipped toward the hidden horizon. Now, we began to struggle to see, though the wolf, with his yellow eyes, seemed not to be troubled by the gloom. And then something happened that I would not have believed had I not been there, and which I am sure you will struggle to accept as true.

As we struggled on, staring into the gloom, lighted candles appeared on every tree. The gloom was lifted. And then, to the surprise of all who were there, a candle appeared upon the shield of every man who carried one. There was no flicker in the breeze. Indeed, the flame burned steadily, no matter how the wind blew. We marvelled at it.

By dawn of the following day, we could see the woodland edge that marked the end of the great forest. As we approached the open land, the wolf turned one last time and gave an unearthly howl. Then it turned and headed back into the thick undergrowth. We never saw it again.

We rested there in the sunshine. Hereward looked thoughtful.

"It is a sign," he said, "There can be no doubt. The wolf is an animal of St. Peter. He sent it to show us the way. It is a token of the apostle's gratitude for saving what we could of the treasures of the Saint's Abbey of Peterborough. We must return everything we can, whenever we can."

I can see that you are uncertain as to the truth of this story, but I have told it to you as an old man remembers it.

***

For some time, we lived at the forest edge, foraging for food and gathering together a new following. We camped in a glade beneath the canopy of a huge oak tree.

Plans were drawn for the forthcoming action against the Normans. But it was one sunny morning, with the birds singing their little hearts out in the trees and the hum of bees upon the air, that a Norman arrived in camp. We immediately grabbed for weapons, but the man raised his cloak to reveal that no sword hung at his side. When the man reached the centre of our camp, he dismounted from his horse — a large grey mare— and looked around at our suspicious faces. Hereward strode forward. He looked the man in the eye.

"What is your business here?"

"My lord, I come in peace. You can see that I am not armed."

One of Hereward's men approached the Norman and searched his body. He nodded at Hereward.

"State your business," Hereward said.

"My lord, the king would speak to you of terms. He is eager to form a truce between his men and yours. He wishes all of the bloodshed to cease and that all of the people of the kingdom should live together in peace and harmony."

"Does he, indeed?" mused Hereward, "And where would he meet with me?"

At this, some of the followers cried out in indignation, "No! We cannot make peace with the tyrant!"

Hereward waved his arms until the assembled throng became quiet.

"I am intrigued," he said, "Tell the king I will meet with him, provided we are all assured of safe passage if no truce is reached."

"My lord, the king has said that you will be given that assurance. An escort will arrive at dawn tomorrow to lead you to the king's camp."

Hereward nodded, and the man re-mounted his horse and turned its head homeward.

Once the man was out of earshot, there was a much-heated discussion concerning the situation. Arguments went on for some time, swaying first this way and then that, until all cases were heard. It was clear that no matter what we said, Hereward had made up his mind. He looked around at our faces, the concern etched upon them.

"I must go," he said, "I must know what the king is thinking. I, too, would like to see an end to this carnage."

He looked around us again.

"And none of us knows how much longer we can hold out against his forces."

Faces fell, but we all knew the truth of it. Hereward was right.

"One thing does occur to me, though. We must move camp to a more secure location, which no Norman messenger can simply ride into if tomorrow's talks fail!"

Chapter 37

In William's Lair

On the following morning, we arose from the new camp we had set up during the night. It had taken us quite some time to disassemble all that we had constructed and move it further into the forest, where we felt that we would be safer from the Normans.

Before dawn, we ate a meal of fish from the marsh and set off toward the old camp, and here we settled to wait for the escort. Being naturally suspicious of William's intent, we planted look-outs at strategic points to see what was approaching and give us time to retreat if we felt that a trick was afoot.

In due course, a small troop of Norman soldiers appeared from behind a small copse where we had a man hidden. He had not raised the alarm, so we knew that there were no more troops behind the escort. As the Norman messenger and his small band entered the clearing, the messenger looked about him, obviously taking in the fact that we had de-camped since he last visited us. He smiled as he must have realised that we had no great trust in his king.

Hereward approached him.

“I am ready to leave this place to meet the king. I, too, will bring a small troop of my men…just to even up the odds a little.”

The messenger smiled again.

“The king has personally assured you safety from harm, but your men will also be welcome and protected from any hurt at our camp.”

After giving out some last orders to his leading men, Hereward picked up his sword and shield and mounted a horse that the Normans had brought for him. The guard troop, however, would have to walk.

“You will not require weapons, my lord,” the messenger said.

“I’ll keep them just the same, as will my men,” Hereward answered, and the man nodded.

As the chosen men lined up to go with Hereward to the meeting, I lined up with them. Hereward looked at me.

“John,” he said, “This is no quest for a young lad like you. These men are all warriors.”

I looked him in the eye.

“My lord, I fought at Stamford Bridge, Hastings and here at Ely. I, too, am a warrior. I would come with you to see the Norman who says he is now our king.”

Hereward gazed at me for a while, his mind working behind those lake-blue eyes.

"John, you are the bravest lad I have ever fought with. You *are* a warrior. Fall in with my men, John Aelricson. You shall come with me to meet William the Bastard."

The Normans glared at him for the insult to their king. For myself, I grabbed my sword and shield, and joined the warrior bodyguard of Hereward, whom men called 'the Wake'.

***

Hereward and we men, followed the Normans out from the forest edge and then turned north after a while. We walked until mid-day when we paused to rest our legs and to partake of a meagre meal. We looked on in jealousy at the somewhat more substantial rations of the Norman soldiers. It had been a while since I had eaten well, and my mind wandered back to the meals my mother used to cook for us, so long ago now and yet so recent.

I thought of my family —the family I would never see again, and the family I hoped to see again soon. I had a duty to my little family, and yet here I was, fighting for what looked more and more like a lost cause, though I would never have voiced such an opinion to anyone else. I knew, though, that it was in the backs of the minds of other men in our group.

After a short break, we began the march again, and it was not until late afternoon, with the sun falling from the sky to allow night's cloak of darkness to cover us, that we arrived in the Norman camp. We scanned all around us, trying to judge the number of troops we saw, sharpening weapons and sitting around chatting and playing dice. As we passed by, they stopped what they were doing to gaze at us. After a short while, I lost count of the Normans and decided that there were, simply, many men.

Soon after our arrival, and after a few of us had relieved ourselves in the pit the Norman soldiers had dug, we were escorted to a large leather tent. Guards stood to each side of the door, spears in hands. As our messenger approached, the two soldiers moved aside and allowed him to open a flap. We were quickly ushered inside.

The tent was empty. We glanced nervously around the interior. In the corner was a campaign bed with furs strewn upon it. In the centre stood a small table with scrolls and folded maps laid upon the surface. Behind it was a chair, padded in bulls' hide. I remembered seeing a similar one in the priory, near my home village. My home village —what was left of it now, I wondered? It had always seemed such a safe and homely place, but now…

We sat ourselves upon the reed-strewn floor and waited to see what would happen next. The men fingered their weapons. After a while, the tent flap opened again, and half a dozen Norman commanders entered, followed by a man whose clothes and coronet revealed him to be no other than William, the man who had all but conquered my nation. He was a large and stockily-built man with the Norman hairstyle —with the back portion shaved.

We rose, as was the required good manners in such a circumstance. The king looked us over, glancing at the swords we still had strung to our belts. It would have been good manners to leave them outside, but we didn't offer, and no one asked us to give them up. I think they knew that we would not.

William spoke first.

"I imagine you are Hereward," he said, approaching our leader.

"I am," Hereward confirmed.

"Then I am pleased that you have come here today, a free man and a guest at my table. We will speak of the situation and how we might prevent any further unnecessary bloodshed."

Hereward just regarded him and made no comment.

Another chair was brought and placed before Hereward, who took his seat at the other side of the table to William. We stood around and behind our leader in a sort of curtain of protection. This was not lost on the Norman commanders also present, and they glanced at one another.

The two principals spoke of the situation in the country and explored avenues for compromise. (I think Hereward was wise enough to know that driving out the Norman invaders from our land was simply a dream, and one that could not now come true). The late afternoon and evening wore on with discussions until William interrupted the proceedings with a call to eat.

We were led from the king's tent to another, larger tent in the middle of the camp. Here, we assembled around a long trestle table and were served with venison, bread and cheese. Ale and wine were brought to the table, and I have to say, we enjoyed a hearty meal. Sweet honey cakes finished the repast, and we all sat, enjoying the feeling of a full belly.

In one corner of the room, four men had appeared and began to make music to entertain us. I think, finally, we all began to relax. Hereward and William continued their conversation, and all appeared well. Would this be the turning point when peace descended upon our beleaguered nation?

The Norman commanders at the meal sat upon an adjoining table and conversed in their own tongue, which we struggled to understand.

As the evening wore on, it was obvious that some men were becoming a little the worse for wear from the ale and wine that flowed. The musicians abruptly ended their playing and shuffled quickly from the tent. At the Norman table, one of the commanders rose from his seat and raised his cup.

"My lords, I would ask you to drink a toast to the new masters of these isles and the new king, William."

The Normans all raised their cups and drained them. The Saxons did not. It was noticeable that a new tension had descended upon the occasion, and Saxon hands strayed nearer to the swords that we had been allowed to keep by us.

Another Norman rose from his seat.

"The Saxons have learned, I am sure, that they are no match for a Norman army. They are a crushed people and will bend to the will of their new masters."

Another Norman called out, "Well said, Ogger."

William just looked on. Why did he not stop this? It was obvious that we were being provoked, and yet he did nothing.

At this moment, Hereward arose. He lifted his cup.

"I would ask you to drink a toast to the native people of this land, who have fought hard to preserve their dignity and their way of life."

"But what sort of life would you preserve?" said Ogger, "It is a primitive existence, which can only improve under Norman rule. You should be grateful to us, not continuing this ridiculous resistance."

Now Hereward rose again, and we all moved our hands to the pommels of our swords.

"Without the protection of your men around you, you would not dare to utter those words."

"Not only would I dare, but I repeat them again," said Ogger, and he drew his sword from its scabbard.

We all stood, and the rasping sound of swords being drawn filled the silence that had fallen. Now, Ogger came from behind his table and strutted into the centre of the room. He raised his sword above his head.

"Now, Saxon, place your sword at your feet and bow your head to your king!"

Hereward leapt across the table, his sword in his hand and faced the Norman, as the Norman commanders formed a protective ring around their king. It was now the sound of metal on metal that filled the air as Saxon and Norman exchanged blows. Still, William did nothing.

We had all drawn our swords, as had our Norman opponents and a stand-off now occurred. Each side eyed the other warily, watching for the slightest sign of attack. Norman soldiers now appeared outside the tent, and we all knew we were trapped. Only the contest between Hereward and Ogger continued. Blows were exchanged for blows, and the contest seemed even until Ogger became over-confident and lazy and failed to bring up his sword far enough to parry a blow. He was caught off balance, and a blow from the flat of Hereward's sword hammered into the side of his head so that he sank to the floor, unconscious, blood pouring from his head above his left ear.

"Seize him!" William bawled, and four Norman commanders leapt into action.

The others just stood with their sword points aimed at our chests. We knew we had allowed ourselves to walk into a well-planned trap, and we cursed ourselves for it. Even if we could fight our way out of the tent, there were scores of Norman soldiers to apprehend us and bring a swift end to our lives. We stood helpless, whilst the Normans dragged Hereward away. Our leader was captured and imprisoned.

William now rose from his seat, a grim smile across his face.

"Go, Saxons, and tell the rest of Hereward's deluded followers what happened here this evening. You cannot defy me and my right to rule this country. Saxon rule is dead."

The following day, it was a dispirited group of men who tramped back into the Saxon camp without their leader.

Chapter 38

The Beginning of the End

Hereward was now William's prisoner and expected no mercy from the Norman. He sat alone in a dark, airless cell in one of the wooden castles that William had built across the land. His wrists and ankles were chained to the wall. His head hung down, and he was deeply dispirited.

The sound of leather boots upon the floor and the chink of chainmail made him look up. The beam across the door scraped open, and it opened with a creak. The gaoler, with a torch in his hand, backed by four Norman men-at-arms, entered. Is this it, Hereward wondered? Will I see another dawn?

"Get up!" a guard bellowed, "We're moving you on."

The guards roughly hauled Hereward to his feet and hustled him from his dank and dreary cell. He blinked as the first beams of sunlight entered his eyes. They marched off to where a small troop of soldiers sat waiting on their horses. Hereward was led to a covered cart and bundled inside. When the small wooden door of the cart was locked and bolted against escape, the driver cracked a whip to urge the horses into action.

Slowly, the little cavalcade left the confines of the fortress toward yet another wooden castle where, we supposed, the Normans thought their prisoner would be more safely confined.

An old beggar sat beside the track leading from the fort and held out his moth-eaten old hat.

“Spare a coin, sirs?” he rasped.

The Normans looked down upon him with disdain as they passed, and as one trooper rode by, he spat upon the old man. The old beggar wiped his forehead where the spittle had landed. He stared after the procession and, when they were finally lost to his vision, he rose and disappeared into a nearby coppice.

For a couple of hours, the troop and cart trundled slowly along the pitted track until Hereward felt as if his insides had been stirred with a spoon. Upon reaching a spot where the forest lay back from the track, the column halted, and the Normans dismounted their horses. From their saddle packs, they took their rations and sat around on the ground to eat. Hereward looked through the barred opening to the cart.

“Will you let me out?” he asked, “I need to pee.”

“Pee in the cart,” one of the troopers said, “It won’t make you smell any worse.”

His companions laughed merrily. Hereward glared at the man, who quickly turned away.

As the Normans enjoyed their meal of dried meat, cheese, bread and ale, two pedlars appeared upon the road. They rode mules and had piles of rough cloth upon a third thin mule. As they approached, the Normans looked up briefly and then fell back to their chatter and the business of eating.

From the other direction, around a sharp bend in the track, two men on foot appeared. Each carried a large bag across his shoulder and had a quarter-staff in his hand. The Normans appeared hardly to notice these two new travellers.

As each party approached, the Normans glanced up again and watched their approach.

One of the cloth traders called out, “Cloth, sirs? Fine cloth. Wool. Very warm.”

“We want no cloth,” the troop leader replied, “Be on your way.”

But the two men stopped anyway.

“But sirs, you have not seen the fine goods we carry,” the pedlar cried.

“And what would you be carrying that would interest us?” the commander asked.

The two pedlars put their hands into bags upon their saddles and pulled out two swords.

"You might like to see these at close quarters."

The Normans looked up in surprise. They had taken off their weapons as they sat to eat to make themselves more comfortable. Now, they scrabbled about to retrieve them. It was at this point that they noticed the two men who had been walking toward them from the other direction. These two men ditched their bags and threw back their cloaks to reveal chain armour and swords. They dragged shields from the bags and came at the Normans from the other side. At the same time, men began to appear from the surrounding woodland —every man armed and ready for combat.

The soldiers leapt to their feet, hastily buckling on their leather belts, and drew their swords to defend themselves. They took up a formation where every angle was defended by a man so that the Saxons could not take them from behind. Hereward's men moved gradually forward until they were within a sword's reach of their enemies. They stood there for a heartbeat and then lunged forward and engaged the Normans in battle.

More men poured from the woodland until the Normans were surrounded three or four deep by Saxon warriors. Swords flashed, and a Norman head flew from its shoulders. Blood spurted from the neck until the body crumpled to the ground, where it leaked into the dirt. The sickly stench of blood was everywhere as further Normans fell.

One trooper had been unable to reach his helmet, and a sword blow split his head in two like a log for the fire, spilling grey matter. It was but a few minutes before all resistance was over, and a pile of Norman corpses lay upon the ground, in the middle of the track. They were quickly stripped of weapons and armour. No Saxon warrior was even grazed.

The men quickly released Hereward, their leader, from the cart.

"You should have released me sooner," he said with a grin, "I would have enjoyed that little skirmish."

The Norman horses were soon rounded up, and the Saxons prepared to leave.

"Should we bury them to allow their spirits to rise to heaven?" one man asked Hereward.

"No, leave them. The Normans will find them soon. Then William's spirits will fall," Hereward replied.

***

Within the wooden fortress, the Norman king of England had flown into a terrible rage as news of Hereward's escape was received. His senior officers had assembled in the king's chamber and were receiving the lashing of their leader's tongue.

"Where is the troop commander? Have him brought to me!"

"I fear it is too late, my lord. His head is split in two to his neck, and he is in Heaven, making his own peace with The Lord."

"The whole troop? I have lost a whole troop to a bunch of Saxon savages? How can this be?"

The Norman king paced the rough, rush-strewn floor of his fortress, his face purple with anger.

"It seems the troop fell foul of a large band of men, my lord. There are signs of many feet upon the turf."

"This is complete incompetance!" William screamed, "How are we to return him to imprisonment now? He will never agree to another truce now that we have shown him how duplicitous we have been!"

At the rear of the room, taking in all that was happening, was the captain of the jailers who had guarded the Saxon during his incarceration at the fortress. The man slowly stepped forward and cleared his throat. William turned to him.

"What? You had something to say?"

"My lord," the man bowed low to his king.

"It is my belief that the Saxon can be persuaded to parley again. I have conversed with him at length during the time we held him. He is, perhaps, more keen to reach a settlement than he would show to the world. I believe he would listen to reason and return to negotiations."

The king mused.

"And how should we go about approaching him again? How would we persuade him that he would not be harmed or imprisoned this time after what happened the last time he moved amongst us?"

"It might take a little persuasion, my lord, but I think I could talk him around to try for another peace."

William sat down at the head of the table and stared into the middle distance. Could it be done? Could he free himself from this Saxon irritant? Should he offer new terms or play a waiting game until the Saxons were demoralised and would finally beg for forgiveness for their resistance? How many more of his good men would die during the waiting game?

For what seemed an eternity to the Norman commanders around him, William sat, still as a statue, staring at the wall. At length, he awoke from his trance and looked up at the captain of his jailers.

"Go to him. Tell him that I regret what has happened and that I will pardon what he has done and ensure his safety."

"I will set off at once, my lord," the jailer said.

He bowed low to his monarch and swept from the room to begin his task.

William turned to his commanders.

"Will this be an end to it? Have I done the right thing?"

The commanders were too shrewd to disagree with their king. Most simply nodded, though the glances between them betrayed their inner thoughts. The Saxon should be finished, or he would be an eternal thorn in their flesh.

***

It was upon a warm, sunny day, whilst Hereward and his men lay within a glade, enjoying the warmth, that a messenger arrived in camp. He quickly dismounted from his horse and rushed over to Hereward, a look of concern etched upon his face. Hereward sat up and gave the man his attention.

"My lord, a delegation of Normans is upon the road. One captain and a troop of six men-at-arms. We have detained them. Their leader says that he has a message from William."

Hereward pondered.

"Do you think it is a trap?" he asked.

"No, my lord. Our scouts have not found any other Normans upon the road."

"Hereward, do not go. How can you ever trust William? We must continue our struggle. Only the defeat of the Normans will free our land," I said to him.

Hereward looked at me.

"John, you are a brave lad. I know that you would fight forever against the conqueror, but I fear that we will never defeat him, and that a truce and peace for the people of this country is the best that any of us can hope for."

He smiled, but I just stared at him in disbelief. Could our leader be ready to bend his knee to the Norman? Could our resistance really be over? Could all of this have been in vain? I felt sick to the pit of my stomach.

"I will meet the Norman captain and will speak to him. Take me to him."

And with that, Hereward rose and strode to where a horse was already being prepared for him. With the messenger and a handful of warriors, he left the camp. The rest of us just sat in the afternoon sun, contemplating the future. Many faces looked blank. Some looked to others in an attempt to see what each man was thinking.

I rose and wandered over to the tree line, where I sat upon a stump and contemplated my future. Was I to return home to my family defeated in my task? Was everything for nought? Would we never be free to rule our own lives, or were we to live under the Norman yoke *forever*?

Chapter 39

Bitter Defeat!

Hereward and his small band of warriors, followed by the Norman troops, again trotted through the gate of William's wooden fortress. Soldiers looked up and watched as the little party passed by on their way to William's makeshift keep. Was Hereward a brave leader who understood the situation he found himself in, or was he just a fool to ever trust the Norman invaders again?

The huge Saxon and his men were quickly escorted to the presence of the Conqueror. The Norman commanders did not ask them to give up their weapons, as was the custom, as it would probably have been insensitive, given the history between the two adversaries. It was, however, noticeable that they, too, retained their arms and formed a protective curtain around their leader.

"Hereward, it is good to see you again. I can only express my regret at the way in which my men have treated you. I have dealt with the miscreants."

Hereward just stood there and stared with icy eyes at William, and the Norman's discomfort was obvious.

"I can assure you that such an unfortunate situation will not happen again," the king blustered.

Hereward stood before the king, solid and straight as a pine tree.

"Tell me your terms truthfully, and I'll consider my response," he replied.

"Why, all I desire is that the people of this fair land should all live in peace under the protection of myself and my troops. I only have the interest of the country and its people in my heart."

Again, Hereward stared the king in the eye.

"And why would my people need the protection of Normans? We had fewer problems before."

"And what of the Vikings?" the king asked, "This poor country has suffered much conflict during its history. What of the Celts to your west? Conflict flares regularly between Saxon and Celt."

"We have always coped. There will be challenges ahead in the future, but my people wish to face them as Saxons, as we have always done. We wish to be free."

The king pondered for a second, thinking of a reply to the Saxon's arguments. Suddenly, he rose from his seat.

“But why are we sitting here? We would be much more comfortable in my quarters. I will send for food and drink, and then we can rest and talk about the best way forward for both of us.”

The Norman and his commanders led the way and jars of wine and sweetmeats were hurriedly brought to the king’s table by servants.

The afternoon passed with the two sides in conference. There was much discussion, with William assuring Hereward that all of his deeds and those of his men in resisting the Normans were pardoned forthwith, and that the two sides should live in peace.

As night drew on, the Norman and Saxon leaders began to relax, though not so Hereward’s bodyguard of warriors. They stood stock still and glowered at the Norman’s watching William’s back. At length, with a wide yawn and draining his cup of wine, William arose from his seat.

“Hereward, I have arranged quarters for yourself and your men. It is far too late for you to travel back to your own camp now, and we shall meet again in the morning. Travelling will be much easier tomorrow.”

And so it was that Hereward left the fortress, unharmed, the following morning, and made his way back to our camp to tell us of all that William had said and the treaty for peace that they had agreed.

There were many downcast eyes that day, though for many others, I think it was a relief of sorts. If William was as good as his word, perhaps we could live a better life. No man could say for certain.

***

A few days later, we made our way, this time, to the town of Stamford, where a number of Saxon leaders were to meet to discuss the Norman's terms. Upon arrival, some of the more senior leaders made themselves as comfortable as they could in the inns of Stamford. Most of our group, myself included, were to make camp in the woodland surrounding the town. I was uneasy about the situation, still not fully trusting the Normans, and worried that Hereward and his commanders were hemmed in like animals in a trap.

Discussions began and went on during that day, and ale flowed freely amongst our number. That evening, we enjoyed a hearty meal —the best I had tasted for many a long day. Oh, I can taste it now, that meal of hare, chicken and stewed vegetables, bread and ale.

As the sun went down over the rooftops of Stamford, we all began to tire, and many had already dropped to sleep where they sat. Hereward arose and bade us all goodnight. He was to sleep in a room at the inn, the better to get his rest. His chaplain,

Almund, undertook to keep watch for him, that no man should pose a threat to his leader.

Now, Almund was a strange man whom I had never quite fathomed. He was, at the same time, a pious clergyman and, at others, a small weasel of a man whom I had little feeling for.

We lesser warriors left and slept that night on the bare Earth, on a sack, surrounded by our colleagues-at-arms, some of whom rent the night air with their snoring.

But that night, unbeknown to the warriors in the woodland, Hereward was, once again, betrayed and in grave danger. Once he had decided that Hereward was fully asleep, Almund arose from his sack by the door and pulled his cloak tightly around him. He took up a candle, lit it with a taper from the last embers of the fire, and stepped into the street, sheltering the spluttering flame from the breeze. He peered along the dark lane that ran by the entrance to the inn, and waved the candle up and down five times. Within a minute, sixteen heavily armed Normans appeared and quietly made their way to the inn.

"Almund, you are certain that he is asleep?"

"I am. He snorts like a pig. He is oblivious to all around him. He thinks I sit in front of his door, taking the first watch of the night."

“Good,” the Norman said, “Then he will give us no trouble. When his men awake and look for him in the morning, they will find him with his throat cut. You must be left with a pretty bruise on your head, Almund. Nobody will ever know the truth of how it happened.”

Almund blanched at the thought of the bruise to his head, but he knew that he would need a cover story. If it was thought that he had slept on his watch and had not been vigilant, then he would suffer at the hands of the Saxons. If any man ever knew the truth of the matter, then his life would be forfeit.

The group of Normans padded into the inn and climbed the rough, wooden stairs to the room that Almund indicated to them. Quietly, they lifted the latch of the door and crept, cat-footed, inside. At first, they took care to walk near the walls to stop the floorboards from creaking. Slowly, they surrounded the rough bed upon which the Saxon leader was resting.

The leader of the men raised his sword and struck it down upon the sleeping form. But rather than slicing into the very innards of the man, it clanged upon a shield that covered his body. Now, Hereward leapt from the bed and, with the lance he had hidden in the folds of his coverings, he stabbed at the nearest of the Norman attackers. Three fell immediately as his lance found their throats and severed their windpipes. The men fell in a gurgle of sound as they fought to take a breath, to no avail. Now, Hereward swung the lance and forced his enemies back toward the walls of the room.

He drew his famous sword, Brainbiter, from its scabbard and whirled it around his head. The Normans spread themselves around him and moved forward menacingly as one. Hereward turned slowly and surveyed his enemies, none of whom, it seemed, were too keen to make the first lunge, having seen their comrades fall.

At length, the soldier who seemed to be the leader of the men rushed forward with a snarl and thrust his sword at Hereward. He was only rewarded by Brainbiter's cold steel entering his innards and spilling his entrails upon the floor. He looked at Hereward and then at his spilt guts in disbelief and crumpled to the floor, his eyes wide in horror. The air was thick with the sickly stench of blood, and one, perhaps less experienced attacker, turned and vomited at the horrific sight before him. The Normans drew back to consider their next move.

"Move together upon my signal," said one of their number.

The men waited, watching the Saxon intently.

"Now!" the Norman cried, and the somewhat depleted group of warriors moved quickly for the kill. But Hereward was alert, and with a great swing of the sword, he saw off yet more of the group with the great Brainbiter. Two heads flew across the room and bounced upon the bare boards to roll with sightless eyes toward the walls of wattle and daub.

The incredulous Normans, still alive, looked at one another, unsure of what to do.

"We must finish it," growled a grizzled old soldier, "William will have our hides if we fail."

The soldiers knew that this was true. Any failure on their part was unthinkable, and they must continue to attack their prey.

Slowly, the remaining men circled Hereward, trying to catch that moment when he let his guard slip. It did not come. The Saxon continued to turn upon a penny, keeping his assailants at bay. Becoming more and more desperate, the soldiers began to let their own guards slip, and as they pressed in, Hereward caught them one by one. Men died terribly, and blood slathered the floor of the room. Soon, only two were left.

"Help us, Almund," one cried.

Hereward's eyes widened. So, his own chaplain had betrayed him. Upon seeing Hereward stop for a moment, distracted momentarily, one of the men closed in for the kill. Sadly for him, Hereward was still very much alert, and he caught the man with a blow to his arm that severed most of his sword hand from his body. His scream echoed around the inn, but none came to investigate the noise. Discretion, it seemed, was the better part of valour.

Finally, as Hereward dragged Brainbiter from the arm of the Norman, the last man saw his opportunity. What a hero he would be when, finally, he would report to William that he had fought against all odds to kill his mighty foe.

The man leapt up onto the bed and brought his sword down heavily. It rattled off the metal edge of Hereward's shield and rebounded, sending a shiver up the man's arm. Hereward righted himself and, with the shield boss, he rammed his whole weight into the Norman's face, smashing his nose to a pulp and thrusting his head back upon his shoulders with a crack that told Hereward that the man's neck was broken. The Norman lost all feeling within his body and slumped, dead to the floor.

Hereward leaned upon his shield and caught his breath, shaking his head to bring his heightened senses back to a state of normality. He was alerted by a whimper from outside the door. Slowly, shield before him and Brainbiter held ready, he tiptoed to the door and listened. There it was again. He gently pushed open the door, only to see Almund curled in a heap upon the stairs. The clergyman shivered as if a winter storm had caught him in the open. He sobbed and snivelled as Hereward looked down upon him.

"So, Almund, you have betrayed me. Why? Why would you betray me, who once gave you a place of security within my walls?"

Again, the monk whimpered but said not a word. He stared up at the huge form of the Saxon warrior before him, but looked away from Hereward's eyes.

Hereward moved forward until he stood above the trembling form. Almund looked up in terror, knowing what fate lay ahead of him. Hereward raised Brainbiter and thrust it through his chaplain's neck. The man gave a brief scream and then collapsed in a heap upon the stairs.

"It is a shame that I couldn't trust you, Almund," Hereward said to the unhearing ears.

"But you must see that the fate I have given you is better than that you would have suffered at the hands of my men."

***

It was but a couple of days later, in our woodland camp, that Hereward and his small party mounted their horses and pulled their heads around.

"My people," the Saxon leader began, "It is with great regret that I have decided that the only way open to me is to flee into exile. William will never stop trying to kill me, and I fear that before too many days have gone by, he will succeed. We must all accept now that the fight is over. We have been defeated by the Normans despite the fierce resistance we have shown him. I am proud of what we have done, and I am proud to have known every man here…and many who are not here.

My beloved wife, Turfida, has suffered for this cause, but has now entered a convent, where I know she will be safe, but I must leave for another place where I can live each day without looking behind me. My own lands are forfeit to Ogger the Breton, which is a cause of much sadness to me. Go back to your own homes now, with your heads held high. Always know that you were brave in the face of insurmountable odds. Always be Saxons. Goodbye, my friends and God be with you."

And with that, he turned his horse and rode out of the clearing camp, and we never saw him again.

Chapter 40

Return to the North Country

Thin shafts of light filtered through the boughs of the woodland glade as I arose from my blanket in the goat-leather tent that had sheltered me for so long. But this was it. This was my last day as a Saxon resistance fighter. Today, I would begin the long journey home to the north country, where I had been born and had grown from a boy to a warrior.

How odd that seemed. John Aelricson, campaigner for the Saxon cause against the Norman oppressor —John Aelricson, fisherman and farmer? What would I do? Where would I go? Would I return and settle on Lindisfarne with my family or what was left of them? Or should I return to Brockford, the village in which I was born? What would I find at Brockford? Would it even be possible to regain the land I once worked? Would it be workable after the ravages it had suffered at the hands of the Normans. I must see. I must go there and see it for myself. Could I bring myself to return when the time came? I didn't know.

A little later, the time for me to depart and leave my friends and comrades in arms had come. I ate a meagre meal of a few small dried fish we still had and a little corn meal baked upon the fire. It would have to do. I would need to forage on my journey home, as others were still camped in the clearing, not knowing what to do with the lives they had been dealt. I couldn't take their stores away from them. God knows they needed every morsel.

I saddled myself a horse we'd taken from a dead Norman —he was not in need of it anymore! I packed my few belongings, fastened my shield and lance to my saddle and belted on my sword. I still would not travel across my own land without my weapons —what a change had come to pass!

I said my goodbyes to the few who still inhabited the camp —fewer every day— mounted up and turned my steps toward home. It would take me many days, I knew, but at least it gave me time alone to think about my future.

The first days of the journey were peaceful. I stopped at villages and towns along the way, conversing with the local people and enjoying the hospitality of many a warm hearth. I told them the story of our resistance, and they listened avidly to the news. I drew clean, fresh water from village wells and streams to quench my thirst as I journeyed on.

As I travelled north, the stories of Hereward that had already reached the ears of the people grew more and more fantastical. Frankly, most were untrue and simply legends that always seemed to blossom in the wake of any great warrior. I tried to temper them with a little truth, but the people seemed to prefer the fanciful tales to the facts. After a while, I just allowed them to revel in their imaginings.

I was a little short of Lincoln, near the River Witham, when I rounded a bend in the road which passed through dense woodland. At the side of the road before me sat a band of grizzled men. There were five of them, as I recall. I drew back on the horse's reins a little to slow him whilst I considered the situation. The men looked up at me but remained seated upon the turf.

Slowly, I walked my horse forward until I had almost reached the group. One man, who must have been around forty, but looked much older, stepped out onto the path before me. He thoughtfully surveyed me as I approached, more slowly now. As I came near, I reined in the horse and stood.

"Good morrow," I said, "How far am I from Lincoln?"

"Too far for safety," the man replied.

As I looked at him, I noticed an iron collar around his neck. I knew the word 'condemned' would be engraved into it, and the king's seal would be upon the clasp. This man was an outlaw.

"And why am I unsafe?" I said, "I have not felt so in my journey from Stamford."

"You have come from Stamford?"

"I have."

"And what would a lad like you be doing in Stamford and making his way north alone?"

"I fought with Hereward," I said.

The men broke into raucous laughter.

"He *fought* with Hereward!" one exclaimed, and his great belly shook with laughter.

"And what did you really do for Hereward, wash his clothes in the swamp?"

"I am a warrior," I said, beginning to feel uncomfortable and not a little annoyed.

"I fought by his side until he was forced into exile."

The merriment went on for a few more moments, and then the men's faces became more solemn.

"Hereward is in exile, you say?" said the outlaw.

I nodded. The men looked from one to another. This was news to them. They had obviously hoped that Hereward and his soldiers would win the day and restore the kingdom to how it was but were not so keen that they would put their own lives on the line for it.

After a brief pause, one of the band spoke again.

"So, great warrior, what do you carry in your pack?"

"My own belongings, such as they are," I replied.

"I wonder if they would be of any use to the likes of us in our great cause —staying alive. Indeed, they might be of more use to us than to a young lad like yourself."

"Perhaps the lad would let us inspect them," chimed in another of the band.

"There is no point in you inspecting them," I said, "As I intend to keep them myself to aid me in my journey home. And besides, I am sure that stout men of this land such as you would not like to end in the pillory as common thieves…or worse."

"Well, now, it could be that common thieves are what we are," said one, "So just dismount like a good lad, and let us see for ourselves what you might be carrying. What is of no use to us, you may keep."

"I will not," I said, trying not to show the tension I felt in my voice.

"You will need to take it…if you can."

I drew my lance from its holder and pointed it at them. One of the men grinned and advanced. As he raised his hands to try to grab at me, I thrust the lance forward and caught the outlaw in the shoulder. The lance found flesh and entered, spraying blood across his rough woollen shirt. I pulled out the lance, and he grabbed at the wound, trying to stem the bleeding.

"Why, he's stabbed me!"

Another prowled forward, and I drew my sword from its scabbard and whirled it in his direction, clipping the side of his face with the edge and pointing the tip at his throat. He stopped stock-still, his eyes widening at the speed with which I had reacted.

"Move a muscle, and I'll slit your windpipe!"

"I…I do believe that the lad is truly a warrior of Hereward. There are few men with keen reactions like that, nor with the fearlessness to stand his ground with a group of miscreants such as us."

The outlaw backed away.

"Young Sir," the outlaw leader said, "I am impressed by your bravery and prowess as a fighter. You are welcome to pass upon your way, or you might sit with us a while and recount the stories of what you have seen. We are but crude brigands, whilst you have fought for this land, and for that, I salute you."

I must have looked dubious.

"I swear to you that you will not be harmed in our camp. Lawbreakers we might be, but we are not dishonourable."

Strangely, I believed him, and I followed them to their rough camp, beneath a great, spreading oak tree.

Once there, the injured outlaw bathed his wound in the stream that ran by a few yards away. I looked around and found some cobwebs. I asked one of the men to give me a little of his wheat flower, and I made a crude poultice to protect the wound — another skill I had learned in Hereward's camp.

I sat deep into the night when the sun had long tipped its gaze to the horizon, talking with the men. Their apparent respect for me convinced me that I could indeed trust them, and, at length, I settled myself by an ancient tree trunk —yellow with lichen— and fell asleep beneath the stars.

I rose again, just as the darkness of the night dissolved in the first rays of light of the new dawn. I breakfasted with my new-found friends before I mounted my horse again and headed north. Truly, the experience had been strange, though I later reflected that I had camped alongside many rough-and-ready men over the last few years. They were not bad men. Most had led hard lives and only wanted to live a little less like animals and more like God's children.

***

Some while later, after a largely uneventful journey from Lincoln, I crossed the River Tees and reached the banks of the River Wear, upon which my old home of Brockford stood. I journeyed west, up toward the hills, until I reached the old priory. It was empty and abandoned. The buildings were falling into disrepair and had obviously suffered great damage in the carnage that had befallen our land. Sadly, I sat upon my horse and stared around me. I turned my horse's head and trotted up the valley to Brockford.

I cast around me, as I rode, at the fields and woodlands I knew so well. No crops grew. No animals cropped the grass. The farmland grew only weeds. As I approached Brockford, I reined in again. There was Cerdic's hall —silent as the grave. There was our little church, which had been built by the sweat of the villagers. Weeds grew in the small cemetery and around the door, which hung upon just a single iron hinge and swayed back and forth in the light wind. There was the mill, with its great wheel, now still as a corpse. There was the village.

Devastation! I urged on my mount and entered our village. The stockade fence was leaning at a crazy angle. The animal pens and houses lay smashed and rotting upon the ground. Broken tools were scattered, rusting.

On one side of the village was my own home. It was burned to the ground. Just a few of the main timbers stood like broken teeth in an old crone's jaw. Some of the pottery that my mother had used each day lay in shards upon the bare Earth. A faded shard of cloth flapped like a flag in the breeze. This is where I was born. This is where I grew up in the bosom of my family. The bodies of my loved ones lay nearby. Some were in marked graves, but others were who-knows-where.

Scenes of happy times entered my mind and passed through in a procession. My mother, cooking. My grandfather, telling us his tales. My father, mending his tools. The warm glow of the fire. My young brothers and sisters and their games. I smiled at their memory, my eyes seeing only the good times.

After a while, my eyes focused again on the reality. I suddenly realised that bitter tears were streaming down my cheeks. This was Brockford, and yet it was not and could never be again. That much was obvious. My home had ceased to exist in any meaningful sense.

I slipped from my saddle and wandered into the centre of the house I had once called home. I don't know why I did it. I kicked at the ash, sat down upon the blackened Earth and sobbed until I had no more tears. Then, aching inside, I remounted my nag and pulled the reins to head her out of Brockford in a northerly direction to Lindisfarne.

***

I crossed the Tyne and wandered up the lanes near the coast, looking all the while at the ruination of what was once a vibrant countryside. No men toiled in the fields. No sheep ran upon the fell-sides. No women washed clothes in the rivers. No children's laughter broke the silence. Even the birds seemed quiet. Where were the larks, singing, high in the sky? Where were the blackbirds calling to declare their territory? Where was the short-eared-owl swooping over its territory?

Gradually, I made my way northward. I stopped off now in some of the small fishing villages along the coast, where I was lucky enough to be given meals of the delicious local fish that I had not tasted for some time. People, in general, are generous to a fault, I found, even though their own lives have been turned upside-down and their own survival might hang by a thread.

It was upon a bright, warm afternoon when I trotted my horse down a narrow lane that led to St. Cuthbert's path across the sands to Lindisfarne. I dismounted and coaxed my horse onto the soft sand, still wet from the receding tide. I knew from studying the position of the sea that I would have plenty of time to make the crossing safely before the sands were engulfed by the waves again. My horse was very wary of this new ground, particularly when his hooves slid down into the soft surface, but I gently coaxed him forward, following the line of wooden stakes fixed into the mud.

It was not long before we stepped ashore on the Holy Island. I mounted up again, and we trotted into what was left of the settlement —the small wooden priory and the lines of rough huts that served as people's homes. At the clip-clop of the horse's hooves, the locals looked up.

"Hey, it is John. John Aelricson. He's returned."

People in the huts around the village began to emerge.

"John, what news?"

I drew my horse up to the front of the hut that I'd lived in with my siblings and Edyth. The small dwelling seemed deserted until the small wooden door opened with a creak, and Aelfled emerged.

She stared at me for a heartbeat, obviously unable to believe her eyes, before ducking back inside, calling, "John. It is John. He has come home."

At that, the hut erupted, and the rest of my family spilt through the door. Oh, how they flocked around me, and we hugged until I thought we would squeeze each other to death.

The door swung open again, and Edyth emerged, blinking into the sunlight.

She smiled at me and said, “You have returned safely to me, John Aelricson.”

“I have,” I replied, “And I will never leave you again.”

Now, the rest of the villagers flocked around us, keen to hear what news I could give them. Some of the monks began to approach from the direction of the priory, equally keen to hear my story.

But it was at that point that I glanced down at Edyth’s belly, realising that it seemed distended and swollen.

“Your child will be here soon, John.”

It was at that point that I knew that my family would survive.

Chapter 41

Epilogue

William the Conqueror was a ruthless man. However, a writer of the time did say this about him: 'He kept good law.'

The eleventh century was a lawless age when a strong ruler who kept order was admired.

'If anyone displeased William the Conqueror, he would have their hands and feet cut off...and gouge out their eyes for good measure.'

The Norman Conquest in 1066 was not well accepted in the north to begin with. The conquest of Durham proved very difficult, and there was great bloodshed, which continued up to 1080.

William had an imperfect grip on the area and largely did not consider it part of his kingdom. In fact, the Domesday Book makes no mention of Durham or Northumberland.

"In his anger at the English barons, William commanded that all crops and herds, chattels and foods should be burned to ashes, so that the whole of the North be stripped of all means of survival. So terrible a famine fell upon the people that more than 100,000 young and old starved to death. My writings

have often praised William, but for this act, I can only condemn him." —Orderic Vitalis

The Normans built a motte and bailey castle at Durham around 1071-2, but it remained an isolated stronghold. Beyond the walls of Durham, the countryside was not fully secure. Gradually, control was established, and the lands in Durham were given to those who had accompanied William at Hastings. Guy de Baliol was awarded land in Teesdale, and his nephew, Bernard, built Barnard Castle around 1093. Bowes Castle —another Norman keep— was built on the site of an old Roman fort.

The foundation stone for Durham Cathedral was laid in 1093 near the site of the White Church, which was built as a shrine to St. Cuthbert. The major phase was built in just 40 years.

By the end of the 11th Century, the people had accepted the Norman rule. The granting of huge powers to the Bishops created an enclave where the Bishop of Durham had the powers of a prince.

William returned to his dukedom in Normandy in 1073 and, later that year, conquered the province of Maine. While he was away, Waltheof and Ralph, Earls of Norfolk, began to plot against him. Geoffrey of Coutances led the struggle against the uprising and afterwards ordered that all rebels should have their right foot cut off.

On William's return in 1076, Waltheof was executed —the only time capital punishment was inflicted on an English leader during his reign. The Earl of Norfolk managed to escape to Brittany.

CHANGES IN THE SOCIETY

After the Norman Conquest, almost all of the Saxon nobles lost their land. William seized it and gave it to his own loyal followers. They were allowed to hold their land in return for providing soldiers for the king for many days a year.

Edwin and Morcar

Edwin's lands, centred at Gilling West in his brother's Northumbrian earldom, were given to Alain Le Roux in 1071, and the district was renamed Richmondshire.

Though they were pardoned, they again turned against William in early 1071. But Edwin was soon betrayed and killed, while Morcar joined the rebellion, initiated by the Abbot of Ely and tactically organised by Hereward the Wake, against William the Conqueror at the Isle of Ely.

When the island was opened to the Normans, Morcar was captured and imprisoned. He remained in captivity until William's death in 1087 when the dying king ordered the release of all his prisoners. After a brief period at liberty, Morcar was again imprisoned by William Rufus and died in captivity.

In 1072, William the Conqueror stripped Gospatric of his Earldom of Northumbria, and replaced him with Siward's son, Waltheof, the first Earl of Northampton.

Gospatric escaped into exile in Scotland and, shortly afterwards, sailed to Flanders. When he returned to Scotland, he was granted the castle at 'Dunbar and lands adjacent to it' and in the Merse by King Malcolm Canmore. This earldom, without a name in the Scots-controlled northern part of Bernicia, would later become the Earldom of Dunbar.

Gospatric did not long survive in exile, according to Roger of Hoveden's chronicle:

"Not long after this, being reduced to extreme infirmity, he sent for Aldwin and Turgot, the monks, who at this time were living at Meilros, in poverty and contrite in spirit for the sake of Christ, and ended his life with a full confession of his sins, and great lamentations and penitence, at Ubbanford, which is also called Northam, and was buried in the porch of the church there."

The Church

William also transformed the church in England. In those days, the church was very prosperous and powerful, and the king needed its support. William replaced senior Saxon clerics with men loyal to himself. Lanfranc, an Italian, replaced Stigand, the Saxon Archbishop of Canterbury, with the agreement of the Pope. Lanfranc then ousted the Saxon Bishops and Abbots and replaced them with Normans.

"By the advice of William [fitz Osbern], Earl of Hereford, and some others, during the time of Lent [1070], King William commanded the monasteries of the whole of England to be searched, and the money which the richer English, because of his ravaging and violence, had deposited in them, to be seized and carried to his treasury." —Florence of Worcester

The People

Among the lower orders of the people, there were also many changes. In late Saxon times, the peasants were beginning to lose their freedom. This course continued under the Normans. However, slavery declined, and it died out by the middle of the 12th century.

In 1085, William decided to carry out a huge survey of his kingdom to find out how much wealth it contained. The result was the great Domesday Book of 1086.

William died in 1087, and he was succeeded by his son, also called William (he is often called William Rufus because of his rosy complexion). His brother, Robert, became Duke of Normandy.

"I persecuted the native inhabitants of England beyond all reason. Whether nobles or commons, I cruelly oppressed them; many I unjustly disinherited; innumerable multitudes, especially in the county of York, perished through me by famine and sword...I am stained with the rivers of blood that I have shed." —William I

The Hereward of Legend

It was as a resistance leader that Hereward first became famous, but soon, incredible stories were attached to his name. Within eighty years of Hereward's death, his legend was everywhere, in the Estorie des Engles of Geoffrey Gaimar from around 1140 and the Gesta Herewardii Saxonis ('Deeds of Hereward the Saxon').

The author of the Gesta, writing around fifty years after William's attack on Ely, says that he remembers seeing fishermen dragging Norman skeletons, still in their rusty armour, out of the fen, and that Hereward once slew a Cornish giant!

Many songs and poems were being repeated about Hereward in taverns a hundred years after his death, and in the thirteenth century, people still visited the ruined wooden castle in the Fens which was known as Hereward's Castle. But later, he was replaced by another *outlaw hero*, Robin Hood, as a symbol of resistance to oppression.

About the Author

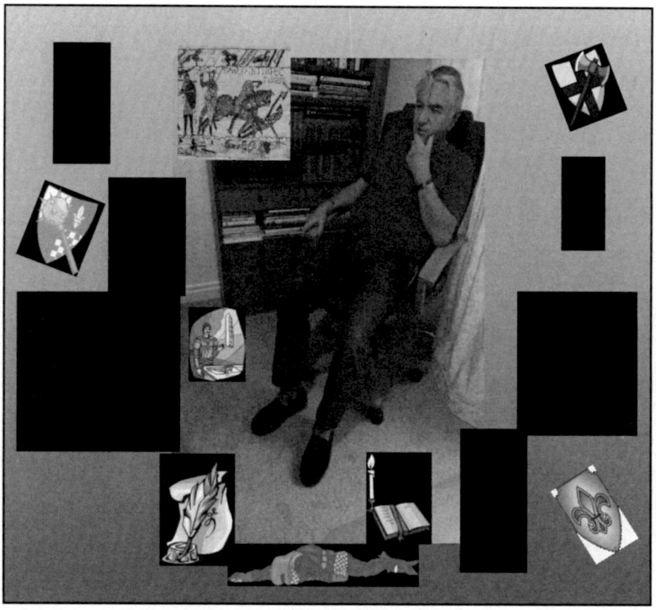

Graham Temby was born and grew up in County Durham, and now lives in the town of Bishop Auckland.

Graham spent almost forty years as a primary school teacher in Lancashire and Darlington, where he spent most of his career teaching Year 6 as well as writing books.

He spends a great deal of time in environmental schemes. For many years, he was the Education Officer for Durham County Badger Group, where he wrote an extensive Education section for the website for teachers and parents.

He was also a police support volunteer, talking to school children about badger conservation and protection, and also rewilding.

He now volunteers in a sustainable farming and rewilding education scheme in his hometown and also in Archaeology.